Mexico-U.S. Migration Management

Program in Migration and Refugee Studies

Program Advisors:
Elzbieta M. Gozdziak and Susan F. Martin, Institute for the Study of International Migration

Mexico-U.S. Migration Management

A Binational Approach

Edited by Agustín Escobar Latapí and Susan F. Martin

LEXINGTON BOOKS

A division of
ROWMAN & LITTLEFIELD PUBLISHERS, INC.
Lanham • *Boulder* • *New York* • *Toronto* • *Plymouth, UK*

LEXINGTON BOOKS

A division of Rowman & Littlefield Publishers, Inc.
A wholly owned subsidary of The Rowman & Littlefield Publishing Group, Inc.
4501 Forbes Boulevard, Suite 200
Lanham, MD 20706

Estover Road
Plymouth PL6 7PY
United Kingdom

British Library Cataloguing in Publication Information Available

Library of Congress Cataloging-in-Publication Data

Mexico-U.S. migration management : a binational approach / edited by Agustín
Escobar Latapí and Susan F. Martin.
   p. cm.
  Includes bibliographical references.
  ISBN-13: 978-0-7391-2576-2 (cloth : alk. paper)
  ISBN-10: 0-7391-2576-1 (cloth : alk. paper)
  ISBN-13: 978-0-7391-2577-9 (pbk. : alk. paper)
  ISBN-10: 0-7391-2577-X (pbk. : alk. paper)
  eISBN-13: 978-0-7391-3059-9
  eISBN-10: 0-7391-3059-5
  1. United States—Emigration and immigration—Government policy. 2. United
States—Emigration and immigration—Economic aspects. 3. Alien labor,
Mexican—United States. 4. Mexico—Emigration and immigration—Economic
aspects. 5. Mexico—Emigration and immigration—Government policy. I. Martin,
Susan Forbes. II. Title. III. Title: Mexico-US migration management. IV. Title:
Mexico-United States migration management.
  JV6483.E75 2008
  325'.2720973—dc22
                                                      2008024515

Printed in the United States of America

∞™ The paper used in this publication meets the minimum requirements of
American National Standard for Information Sciences—Permanence of Paper
for Printed Library Materials, ANSI/NISO Z39.48-1992.

Table of Contents

Acknowledgments

Our work was possible thanks to the support of the William and Flora T. Hewlett Foundation, the Mexican Secretariat of Foreign Affairs, the John D. and Catherine T. MacArthur Foundation, and each of our institutions. We are a nongovernmental group. Our views and recommendations are the sole responsibility of the group of experts. However, we believe policy-relevant work cannot be developed by academics alone. We have benefited from the input of the Mexican Secretariat of Foreign Affairs, and we have also discussed our progress with officials from each country: in the United States, the Department of Homeland Security, the U.S. Census Bureau, the State Department, and the U.S. Congress; and in Mexico, the National Institute of Migration, the National Population Council, the Mexican Social Security Institute, and the Social Development Secretariat. A particular thank you goes to Laura Pedraza for her excellent editorial assistance. We are also grateful to various academics and policy experts from both countries who have discussed our findings and made constructive suggestions. Our views, nevertheless, remain entirely our own.

Introduction

Agustín Escobar Latapí and Susan F. Martin

The need to understand Mexico-U.S. migration is greater today than at any time in its century-long history. Its volume and complexity are greater than most observers might have imagined even a decade ago; and it operates in a context charged with serious new human, political, and security challenges. Yet, there is often confusion over the most fundamental questions about the demography, economics, and political nature of the movement. What are reliable estimates of the number of migrants, their legal status, and their rate of circulation? What role do Mexican migrants play in the U.S. labor force, today and tomorrow? What is the context that drives policymaking, either unilateral or bilateral, in Mexico and the United States? And how might the migration best be managed in a balanced and bilateral manner? Too much of our understanding derives from dated analysis or the viewpoints of experts on one side of the border or the other.

There is no room for understating the practical and political complexities of the issue. Mexicans comprise the single largest national group of authorized and unauthorized immigrants in the United States, and remittances to Mexico are growing rapidly, and now comprise over 3.5 percent of Mexico's GDP. The status quo is marked by the substantial momentum of the movement, the dependence of a very large number of U.S. employers on cheap, unskilled labor, and by increasing Mexican dependence on this "safety valve" that also provides significant incomes to more than one million Mexican households. The political scene in the United States is deeply divided over immigration, and it will be difficult to formulate policies that address the issue in a comprehensive manner. New federal and state legislation, however, is already making life more difficult for unauthorized immigrants, and could create profound legal and other divisions within U.S.

society. This could lead to a permanent underclass, unless significant new actions are taken.

At the same time, Mexico has evolved into a democracy, but one which has so far proved unable to tackle the widely recognized barriers standing in the way of a better future for Mexicans. There is bitter political division, and state governments enjoy increasing power and resources, but they operate in a less coordinated fashion than previously. Transparency has evolved very unequally, and, paradoxically, some of the poorest Mexican states are among the least transparent, which bodes ill for their development. The rhetorical value of Mexican emigration has surged, but President Fox did not, when his initiative was well received in 2001, commit the political and financial resources needed to convince the U.S. Congress and political establishment that an agreement could count on substantial and effective Mexican cooperation. And early pronouncements by President Calderón on this issue did not strengthen the notion that there is a new understanding of emigration and the need to commit to a solution. This could be interpreted as a cautionary distancing from a subject that caused Fox a great deal of political harm, as Mexico uselessly, but repeatedly, tried to approach the U.S. to reopen migration talks after 9/11. The new government, however, has shown that it is highly pragmatic and open to the realities of law and policy-making. If a new opportunity arises to seriously discuss migration, in order to arrive at a legal flow that benefits both nations and the migrants, a corresponding Mexican willingness to work bilaterally seems likely. The current scene, as of this writing, is therefore difficult, but at the same time holds some promise for a change for the better.

It is in this context that this book addresses the need for a balanced, up-to-date assessment. Its analysis draws on the most recent data and knowledge from both countries. The book has been prepared by a group of experts on migration from the United States and Mexico. It includes studies undertaken by those individuals with input from the collective team, such that the findings presented here reflect a view arising from a multidisciplinary, binational perspective.

The book's purpose is twofold. First, it aims to provide an up-to-date assessment of the main characteristics, trends and factors influencing Mexico-U.S. migration. Second, it recommends unilateral and bilateral actions that should improve migration management and promote changes in the flows leading to (1) improved regulation and management, and thus a substantial reduction in undocumented flows; and (2) promotion of the positive interactions between migration and economic and social developments in both countries.

The team includes top migration experts approaching migration from various fields: demography, sociology, anthropology, economics, policy analysis, and international relations. Our purpose is not to advance migration *theory*, but to provide the most adequate and up-to-date analysis of this phenomenon as a basis for innovative and sound policy-making. We believe adequate analysis, especially when it deals with the main forces and actors at play, helps explain observed phenomena and how they may be influenced. We have not dealt with culture, identity, or with issues of local and regional development, which would warrant specialized attention.

We have decided to come together as a *binational* academic research team because recent similar initiatives proved particularly useful in developing the best possible general assessments of this largely *binational* flow and, thanks to a profound knowledge of both countries' institutional frameworks and current policy, in suggesting the best avenues for policy-making. The *Binational Study of Mexico-U.S. Migration* (1995–1997)[1] was the first bilateral and comprehensive effort to define the scope of migration, its characteristics, the factors underlying mobility, and the various approaches to it from both governments. It significantly improved upon previous diagnoses of the phenomenon. It was a large, ambitious governmental initiative, involving twenty experts from both countries, who worked in fully binational teams. It fulfilled its mission in terms of the provision of the first binational consensus on the nature and scope of migration flows at the time, as a basis for potential policy-making. Later, in 1999, the Mexican National Population Council (CONAPO) and the Foreign Affairs Secretariat (SRE) convened a similar group of experts whose task was to outline policy alternatives.[2] Although U.S. participation in this project was less than originally intended, the group did arrive at a number of suggestions which were valuable and, to some extent, later incorporated into U.S.-Mexico talks. The U.S.-Mexico Migration Panel (2001) directed by the Carnegie Endowment for International Peace and the Instituto Tecnológico Autónomo de México (ITAM) involved a significant part of the first group and some members of this project, brought other experts on board, and consulted with policy-makers.[3] It worked during eight months, and commissioned a number of policy and research pieces. In addition to an updated description of Mexico-U.S. migration, it provided an ambitious blueprint for policy change which was taken up by both governments during 2001.

This is the first study to be undertaken in this manner since 2001. We believe a new assessment of migration and migration policy is necessary because (1) migration flows and stocks have grown and changed more rapidly than expected since the late nineties, and (2) the policy environment has shifted manifestly after the terrorist attacks of 9/11, a slowdown in employment growth, and new political contexts in both countries.

Chapter 1 was written jointly by the U.S. and Mexican demographers on the team (Lowell, Pederzini and Passel). It explores recent developments in the flows and stocks of Mexico-U.S. migration (size, composition, concentration and dispersion, origins and destinations, gender, schooling) and compares the various projections of Mexico-U.S. migration to the year 2030. Its findings derive from the use of data and analysis from both countries. It lays the necessary basis for the estimation of the size, composition, and new complexity of the population that should be taken into consideration by any new policy.

The next three chapters are written from the perspective of economics. Chapter 2 by Alba focuses specifically on NAFTA and its impact on the Mexican economy and consequently on changes on emigration pressure from Mexico. His analysis supports the view that, although NAFTA has had major impacts on trade and investment, it has failed to produce social and economic convergence. The two next chapters focus on labor and employment issues, as they relate to migration. Chapter 3 by Phil Martin focuses on Mexican immigrants in the U.S. labor market. It provides a labor history of Mexican immigration; assesses the impact of various U.S. programs and policies, with an emphasis on temporary workers; outlines an approach that helps assess the impact of this immigration on the U.S. economy; and gauges future labor immigration. Finally, Meza (chapter 4) studies the variation in the propensities to migrate that correspond to various occupations in urban Mexico. Urban areas have increased their role as areas of origin of migration, and the differential propensity to migrate by occupation is increasingly relevant.

Chapters 5 through 8 deal with policy. Chapter 5 by Susan Martin opens this section. It focuses on U.S. immigration policy, with a critical review of the major proposals debated in the U.S. Congress and an analysis of the difficulties current initiatives are facing. She outlines the political groupings that oppose each other and come together in various initiatives. Finally, the chapter offers an outline of the major areas in which bilateral cooperation could provide a substantial improvement in the management of the flow. Fernández de Castro and Clariond, in chapter 6, offer a detailed discussion of migration as a fundamental aspect of Mexico-U.S. relations, including the short period during which the two countries have come closest to a migration agreement (the bilateral migration negotiations of 2001), as well as their own analysis of the major bills discussed in the U.S. Congress. The chapter's final section offers the authors' priorities and recommendations in a scenario in which any likely immigration reform is unilateral, in the sense that it comes from the U.S. Congress. In such a scenario, they believe Mexico can and should play a role that will help any reform succeed and provide significant improvements for the migrants. Chapter 7, by Escobar, deals with Mexican migration policy. It provides a detailed analysis of current Mexican social policies in general, their impact on poverty and their potential for the regulation of migration, a survey of migration-related policies, and a discussion of the ways in which Mexico–U.S. cooperation could both improve migration management and foster the well-being and development of sending regions and households in Mexico. Chapter 8 consists of a commissioned, comparative study by Verduzco. He has studied the

Mexico-Canada temporary worker program, which is considered a model of migration management. This chapter shows that the program does indeed work well, although it has problems. From this analysis, it derives lessons useful in assessing the design and efficacy of new guestworker programs that might be applied to the case of Mexico-U.S. migration. It is nevertheless critical of recent developments in that program.

The book closes with a conclusion, which brings together the major lessons learned from this collective task. The purpose of this closing chapter is to provide a coherent interpretation to the various contributions, and more specifically to outline the major lines of action that will finally include migration within a coherent framework for North American or regional integration. The authors, who also served as cochairs of the project, tried to reflect the many areas of convergence and consensus among the team members in presenting our conclusions and recommendations. Not surprisingly, however, the individual team members did not agree on every point discussed in the book. While drawing upon the earlier chapters and team discussions, the conclusion reflects the views of the cochairs on the way forward in addressing the challenges of migration from Mexico to the United States. The aim is to create a set of coordinated policies in both countries that will (1) ensure that migration takes place along legal channels, (2) improve the living and working conditions of migrants and their families, and (3) promote Mexican development and avoid undesirable impacts on the United States, thus leading to a medium-to-long-term future in which neither country is dependent on this flow, but at the same time people are freer to move legally if they wish to do so. While the recommendations largely address the issues that each of the cochairs presents in their own chapters on Mexican and U.S. policies, the concluding chapter takes on the more difficult challenges involved in crafting a binational approach that requires compromises and confidence-building measures.

NOTES

1. Mexican Ministry of Foreign Affairs and U.S. Commission for Immigration Reform, *Migration between Mexico and the United States, Binational Study*, 3 vols. (Mexico City and Washington, D.C., 1998). Also published by CONAPO in an extended version in 2000.

2. Rodolfo Tuirán, ed., *Migración México—Estados Unidos, Opciones de política* (Mexico City: CONAPO, Secretaría de Gobernación, Secretaría de Relaciones Exteriores, 2000).

3. U.S.-Mexico Migration Panel, *Mexico-U.S. Migration: A Shared Responsibility*, convened by the Carnegie Endowment for International Peace and the Instituto Tecnológico Autónomo de México, Washington, D.C., 2001 (panel member), http://www.ceip.org/files/pdf/M percent20exicoReport2001.pdf.

1

The Demography of Mexico-U.S. Migration

B. Lindsay Lowell, Georgetown University
Carla Pederzini Villareal, Universidad Iberoamericana
Jeffrey S. Passel, Pew Hispanic Center

This chapter presents a series of statistics on our current state of knowledge about the past and present numbers and characteristics of Mexican migrants. It presents available projections on the future growth of that population and the populations of Mexico and the United States. It goes on to describe new features of the migration in terms of origins/destinations, responsiveness to the economy, changes in circulation, and selectivity by education and gender. Our goal is to provide a basic picture of what we know today about the basic demography of Mexican migration using official U.S. and Mexican data sources. Some of these data are readily available in published or online sources, other data we tabulate ourselves using public use microdata, and some statistics are estimates generated by the authors using accepted methodologies.

GROWTH OF THE MEXICAN POPULATION IN THE UNITED STATES

The story of Mexican migration to the United States has been one of ebbs and flows following the U.S. acquisition in 1848 of what were previously Mexican territories. Figure 1.1 shows that there were very few Mexicans in the United States at that time, and even at the end of World War II there were only 500,000 Mexican-born residents of the United States. However, the mid-1960s marked the passage of open legal immigration policies, and the end of the Bracero temporary agricultural work program, both of which set in motion a growing volume of legal and illegal migration and changed the nature of Mexican migration to the United States beginning in the

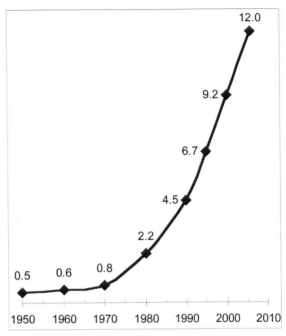

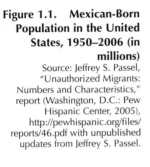

Figure 1.1. Mexican-Born Population in the United States, 1950–2006 (in millions)
Source: Jeffrey S. Passel, "Unauthorized Migrants: Numbers and Characteristics," report (Washington, D.C.: Pew Hispanic Center, 2005), http://pewhispanic.org/files/reports/46.pdf with unpublished updates from Jeffrey S. Passel.

1970s. By the year 2006, there were a total of 12.0 million Mexican-born persons in the United States.[1] So between 1970 and 2006 the Mexican-born population grew an amazing fifteen-fold, doubling every eight to nine years. As we enter the early years of the twenty-first century, there is little doubt that the flow of migrants will continue, but there are questions about the magnitude of the future migration flow and its demographic composition, its legal status, its "circularity" or transnational ties, and its choice of where to settle.

Of course, there is much concern about the growth of the unauthorized population residing in the United States. The U.S. data tend to be more reliable for this purpose, and we use here estimates based on a so-called "residual" method that subtracts an estimate of the legal foreign-born population from a total count of all immigrants, with appropriate adjustments for undercount and other sources of error.[2] The residual left after subtracting the legal from the total immigrant population suggests that, as of March 2006, there were 11.5 million total unauthorized residents, of whom 6.5 million were Mexican. Thus, as shown in Figure 1.2, unauthorized Mexicans make up 57 percent of the total unauthorized population, and that percentage has remained about the same compared with similar estimates made over the past decade. Unauthorized residents from elsewhere in Latin America, par-

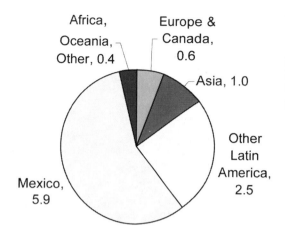

Figure 1.2. Origins of Estimated 11.5 Million Unauthorized Residents, 2006

Source: Jeffrey S. Passel, "Unauthorized Migrants: Numbers and Characteristics," report (Washington, D.C.: Pew Hispanic Center, 2005), http://pewhispanic .org/files/reports/46.pdf with unpublished updates from Jeffrey S. Passel.

ticularly from Central America, make up another 24 percent of the unauthorized population. In turn, unauthorized Mexicans are just under 55 percent of all Mexican-born residents of the United States.

There are two important features of this estimate of 11.5 million unauthorized residents that warrant special comment: (1) coverage or undercount of immigrants in the survey and (2) the legal status of U.S. immigrants included in the residual. First, one frequently heard critique of residual estimates is that U.S. surveys miss or undercount the population, especially persons who are unauthorized and that, therefore, the estimates are suspected of understating the size of the unauthorized population. However, the estimates presented here incorporate research-based allowances for undercounts of both the legal and unauthorized populations. Although the "true" number of unauthorized residents of the United States may be higher (or lower), there is no sound, empirical basis for substantially higher estimates.[3]

This estimate of 11.5 million unauthorized migrants with 6.5 million from Mexico represents the "net" number of *residents*, i.e., persons actually *living* in the United States. It does not include the bulk of Mexican migrants who circulate back to Mexico within relatively short periods, say less than a year. However, we cannot know the size of that temporary population from U.S. data alone. Finally, some portion of the residual estimate includes persons who are, in fact, "quasi-legal" because their presence has been recognized by the U.S. government without giving them permission to have come or to stay permanently. In many cases, these individuals are simply waiting for administrative clearance.[4] One U.S. Census Bureau estimate, as of the year 2000, places the total "quasi-legal" population from all countries at 19.5 percent of the residually estimated population;[5] more recent work with data from 2003 estimates a much smaller share of the residual figure in these quasi-legal categories.[6]

To this point, the discussion has focused on estimates of the resident population or the "stock"; that is the number of persons actually residing in the United States that result from the year-to-year migration of persons or the "flow" from south to north. We turn now to a discussion of the number of persons entering the United States each year, or the flow of Mexicans to the United States. We must distinguish between the gross in-flows and gross out-flows versus the net flows, where the net flow represents growth in the Mexican-born residents of the United States each year. We note that the population of Mexican-born residents of the United States has been growing precisely because the in-migration of new migrants has increased so rapidly but that the picture is somewhat different depending on data sources and definitions.

There is some agreement that during the 1980s net Mexican migration, combining both legal and not, averaged somewhere about 250,000 each year. By the early 1990s estimates based on uncorrected Census counts indicate a yearly average migration of about 300,000, while estimates based on adjusted figures suggest a larger flow of 370,000.[7] But while, by any estimate, the flow of Mexican migration picked up significantly in the late 1990s, estimates of the net flow vary dramatically between Mexican and U.S. sources.

Figure 1.3 shows that the U.S.-based estimates of net migration for the late-1990s exceed 500,000 per year on average and are about 150,000 greater than the Mexican-based estimates. It is not clear why the difference is so large, but in order to reach the U.S. population figures of the resident Mexican-born population as represented in the CPS and Census data, we must assume that the U.S.-based estimates of net migration are accurate.[8] While it may be that the true value lies in between the two levels, it seems likely that the higher U.S.-based estimates of net migration more reliably capture the new inflow to what we know is a growing resident population in the United States.[9]

There are many factors behind the rapid increase in Mexico-U.S. migration during the late 1990s. One major reason, generally agreed upon by all observers, is the legalization of some two million Mexicans by the Immigration Reform and Control Act of 1986 (IRCA). The new legal status of these formerly unauthorized persons enabled them, in turn, to spur further migration by sponsoring family members and hosting others. Another reason is that there has never been any meaningful worksite enforcement of hiring limitations (IRCA-mandated or otherwise), even while new methods of border enforcement were being implemented. Apparently, the new border regime alone failed to deter migrants who simply found new entry routes; the new regime may even have led increasing numbers of migrants

☐ Mexican & US Data Estimates

▨ US Data Estimates

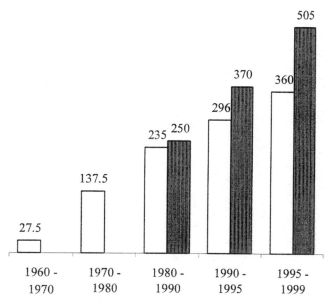

Figure 1.3. Average Annual Net Migration from Mexico to the United States, by Period (in thousands)

Source: Jeffrey S. Passel, "Unauthorized Migrants: Numbers and Characteristics," report (Washington, DC: Pew Hispanic Center, 2005), http://pew hispanic.org/files/reports/46.pdf; Elena Zúñiga and Paula Leite, "Estimaciones de CONAPO con base en INEGI, Encuesta Nacional de la Dinámica Demográfica (ENADID), 1992 y 1997 y Encuesta Nacional de Empleo (ENE) modulo sobre migración, 2002" (Mexico City: Consejo Nacional de Población, 2004).

to give up circular migration in favor of U.S. residence. Thus, migration grew because IRCA's generous legalization generated stable networks for increased migration, while IRCA's enforcement regimes failed to control the flow. Indeed, it is estimated that at least 80 percent of all Mexican migrants were unauthorized from the late 1990s and to date.[10]

The most obvious reason for the migration surge, however, was the booming U.S. economy. Both Mexican migration and the "new economy" really took off in the latter part of the 1990s as records for economic growth were surpassed through the first year of the twenty-first century. All Mexico-U.S. employment indicators took off too—plummeting unemployment rates, increasing employment ratios, and historic wage gains.[11] The age-old story of supply and demand worked exceedingly well, and IRCA's twin success (legalization) and failure (enforcement) provided the social context for an unimpeded supply of Mexican-born workers. Much of the rest of this chapter addresses several of the forces driving the migration, but the power of established migrant networks and economic demand is clearly critical.

These forces become clear if the trend in yearly flow of migration is examined. The migration figures discussed above track the "net" (immigration less emigration) growth of the population over a given interval of several years. A measure of yearly migration, in contrast, captures the flow as it changes year-to-year in response to various forces. The yearly movement measure is a much more sensitive measure of the dynamics of the migration flow, and it reflects short-term changes in the trend of the flow, which are lost in the net-migration data by period.

In fact, trends in the flow of incoming Mexican migrants correlate very well with the growth in the U.S. economy and the U.S. national rate of employment. Figure 1.4 shows that Mexican migration increased in line with surging U.S. employment growth through 2000. It then plummeted in 2001 without recovering until U.S. employment growth also bounced back in 2004. The estimates of the yearly trend in flow are derived from averaging several U.S. data sources and, as such, they are only rough indicators of the *level* of Mexico-to-U.S. migration but reliable indicators of year-to-year changes that parallel other indicators of slowing growth.[12, 13] Of course, the

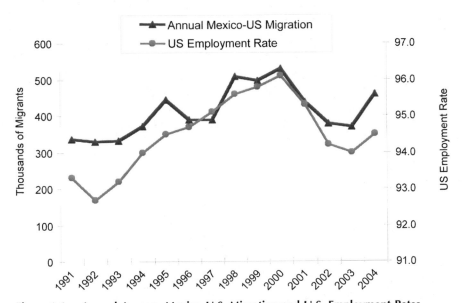

Figure 1.4. Annual Average Mexico-U.S. Migration and U.S. Employment Rates

Source: Jeffrey S. Passel and Roberto Suro, "Rise, Peak, and Decline: Trends in U.S. Immigration 1992–2004," report (Washington DC: Pew Hispanic Center, 2005), http://pewhispanic.org/files/reports/53.pdf.

flow into the U.S. is still large even since 2001 as the Mexican population in the United States has continued to grow albeit at a slower rate than in the 1990s. Indeed, it would be unwise to assume that the recent short-term downswing in yearly migration is a leading indicator of an imminent deflation of Mexican migration to the United States. Rather, we can strongly assert that the yearly in-movement tracks the boom and bust of the new economy. And so it may be that this past first-quarter 2005 up tick in U.S. job creation may soon, in turn, generate a recurrent upswing in Mexican migration yet unseen with today's data.

Naturally, the future trend of Mexican migration is of great interest to all stakeholders in Mexico and the United States. Will Mexican migration continue at high levels into the foreseeable future, or are there forces that will moderate future migration? There is a viewpoint that Mexican migration is driven by powerful social forces that have cumulated over time and will not readily dissipate; and that the medium-to-long-run likelihood is for ongoing high levels of migration.[14] However, as we have just seen, Mexican migration is responsive to economic forces, and most observers hold to the belief that future Mexican migration will, like all other historical instances of mass migration, ultimately slow down. In this scenario, Mexican population growth will continue to slow in the wake of dropping fertility rates and that economic development, at some point, would generate enough jobs to keep job seekers in Mexico.[15] Indeed, Mexico's total fertility rate (TFR) is less than one-third of what it was in 1960 as fertility has dropped from about 7 children per woman to about 2.4 or just over replacement level.[16] At the same time, the Mexican economy in the immediate years following NAFTA in 1994 grew strongly and appears to be poised to do so again.

In fact, official projections of net migration from Mexico all agree on a declining trend. We consider three sets of projections in Figure 1.5: those made by the U.S. Census Bureau; projections by CONAPO, which is Mexico's premier statistical agency; and projections by the United Nations (U.N.). CONAPO's projections are model based, i.e., they project future emigration *rates* based on known associations with forecasted demographic and economic variables. Both the U.S. and U.N. projections are based simply on an assumption of declining numbers of emigrants. But, the CONAPO and the U.N. projections start from levels of migration that are too low because the projections were made before the 2000 U.S. Census made it clear that there were more migrants than had been shown in older data. The U.S. Census Bureau projections take into account the actual higher levels of migration in the first decade of its projection compared with the other two. However, by 2010, the U.S. Census Bureau projections are for lower emigration than those of CONAPO but higher than the U.N. By 2025, the Census Bureau assumptions differ little from the

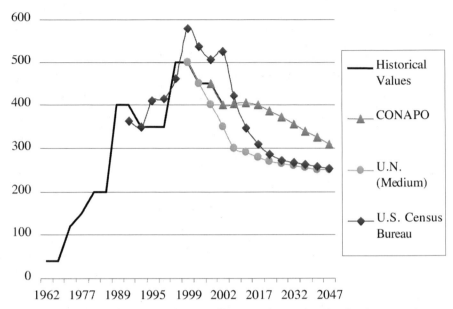

Figure 1.5. Past and Future Estimates of Net Mexican Migration by the U.S. (Census Bureau), Mexico (CONAPO), and the United Nations (in thousands)

Source: Jeffrey S. Passel, Jennifer Van Hook, and Frank D. Bean, "Estimates of Legal and Unauthorized Foreign Born Population for the United States and Selected States, Based on Census 2000," Report to the Census Bureau (Washington, DC: Urban Institute, 2004), see text.

U.N. assumptions and reflect much lower levels of migration than the CONAPO projections.

Indeed, from 2025 onward the Mexico's CONAPO projections of out migration remain higher than either the U.S. or U.N. projections, although there is not much difference between the three official projections by the time they reach 2050 (no more than 60,000 per year). However, there is a large difference between the three projections in terms of the accumulated number of emigrants between 2001 and 2050 (3.2 million for the U.N., 3.7 million for the U.S., and 4.2 million for CONAPO).[17] But, this focus on the absolute values is somewhat misplaced as each of these official projections is bound to change somewhat in the next round of periodic updates by each organization. Of greater importance, perhaps, is the fact that all three official projections explicitly assume a *declining rate of Mexican emigration* with the greatest reduction in rates forecast to occur in the second decade of the century.

While all projections are virtually certain to be wrong and the exercise is necessarily fraught with hazards, we believe that it is more likely that emigration will begin to decline in the future than to continue to stay high indefinitely or even increase.[18]

Crossing at the Border

The United States began a new strategy of border enforcement starting in 1994 with "Operation Hold the Line" in El Paso. Since then, starting next in San Diego and expanding most recently to Arizona, the strategy of deterrence has had marked effects on the nature of cross-border movement. However, as we have seen in the foregoing data, changes in border enforcement do not seem to have deterred migrants from moving to the United States. Instead, migrants have changed their major entry points away from the sites of the new deterrent efforts and are crossing over other, inland routes.

Nevertheless, data collected by both U.S. and Mexican authorities related to apprehensions of border crossers are consistent with the ACS/CPS trends reported above. There is increasing movement in the 1990s and a decline following the 2001 U.S. recession. The U.S. border apprehension data are problematic as measures of in-flow to the United States or total crossers for several important reasons: (a) they include only individuals who are caught at the border; (b) they count many of the same individuals multiple times as they are recaptured attempting multiple entries; and (c) they do not include the unknown share of migrants who escape detection altogether. So, while they are not at all reliable counts of individuals entering the United States, they are thought, nonetheless, to reflect changes in the underlying volume of the flow and are regularly analyzed to that end.

What these data in Figure 1.6 show is that apprehensions increased following the 1982 economic recession in Mexico to a peak in 1986, only then to decline in the aftermath of IRCA for three years.[19] The number of apprehensions then increased throughout the 1990s, especially in the late 1990s, and peaked in 2000. Once again, the effects of the 2001 U.S. recession appear in this data series as apprehensions fell precipitously in 2001 through 2003. Mexican data, that count individuals who are returned by U.S. agents to Mexico, show the same trend of increasing movement in the late 1990s and a sharp decline in movement after 2000.[20] Both data series reinforce the analysis of downward trends thus far with the same caveat that short-term declines do not necessarily prefigure continuing future declines. Indeed, the number of U.S. apprehensions from 2004 to 2006 are above the levels of 2002 and 2003, although the number of apprehensions has again declined from 2006 through early 2007.

Many observers of the border region point to several disturbing developments over the past decade. Of greatest concern has been the number of deaths occurring as migrants attempt to cross into the United States through routes that are in remote desert regions.[21] The most comprehensive data over the past two decades show a decline from about 350 deaths in 1988 to about 175 in 1994; thereafter the number of deaths has again

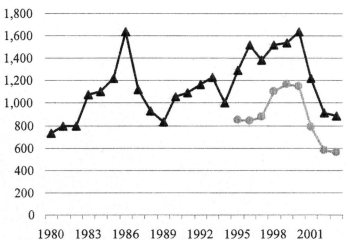

Figure 1.6.   U.S. Apprehensions of Mexican Border Crossers and Mexican Statistics on Repatriations (in thousands)

Source: U.S. Department of Homeland Security, *Yearbook of Immigration Statistics, 2002* (Washington DC: U.S. Government Printing Office, 2003).

increased to a little over 300 per year in 2002, or about the same level as prevailed in the late 1980s.[22] The U.S. General Accountability Office reports that deaths of attempted border crossers doubled from 266 in 1998 to 472 in 2005.[23] The new enforcement efforts are associated with an increased proportion of all deaths due to dehydration and exhaustion as migrants attempt to cross through arid and difficult terrain. Some analysts claim an increasing *rate* of mortality, although that is not reflected in deaths per apprehension.[24] And substantial efforts to combat deaths have been carried out by both the U.S. and Mexican governments by posting warnings, creating rescue and signal stations, and through the efforts of border agents. Indeed, the new deterrent strategies are not themselves responsible for migrant deaths *per se* as fatalities of similar magnitude are a historical fact. A different enforcement regime would probably lead to different patterns of mortality but at similar levels, so the ultimate solution lies in policies that reduce unauthorized crossings.[25] Regardless, border crossing deaths are deplorable, and all efforts made to reduce mortality at the border should be of the highest priority.[26]

Although deaths at the border do not seem to have increased significantly, research leads to different findings regarding the impact of border enforcement on smuggling and crime. Since Operation Hold the Line in El Paso, the new deterrent methods have moved unauthorized crossers away from residential areas and reduced petty crime in traditional crossing areas.[27] Thus, while the "good news" is that border enforcement has been associated with reductions in overall crime rates, the bad news is that the increased *volume* of Mexico to U.S. migration during the 1990s has been associated with increased violent crime.

Unfortunately, enforcement efforts seem to have had an ever smaller impact on reducing crime in recent years[28] as there have been suggestions that an increased incidence of smuggling, both of people and drugs, has become ever more resistant to enforcement efforts. Indeed, given the difficulty of crossing the border in the face of new enforcement efforts, it is not surprising that the share of migrants who use smugglers has increased as has the cost of smuggling.[29] Still, a statistical analysis of smuggling activities found that increased border enforcement has had a very minimal effect on the price of smuggling. Smuggling prices have increased by no more than 30 percent since the mid-1990s, during which time enforcement effort tripled. Yet, the likelihood that smugglers are intercepted has increased only marginally.[30] Enforcement's greatest impact appears to have been in moving migrants to attempt entry through new, lower-surveillance entry corridors.[31] Indeed, estimates suggest that as many as 20,000 U.S. border agents, or a little more than double the current staffing, would be necessary to have a significant deterrent effect along the entire 2,000 mile border.[32]

Settlement in the United States

The reasons for the rapid growth of the Mexican-born population in the United States over the last three decades, but especially in the 1990s are not well understood. Large numbers of Mexicans have been coming to the United States for many decades, as evidenced in part by the large numbers of apprehensions at the border, but the Mexican population in the United States did not really begin to grow until the mid-1970s. It is not clear from the available data that the numbers of people crossing the border have increased at anywhere near the same rate as the population in the United States has increased. There is some indication, in fact, that the increased enforcement efforts at the border have the unanticipated effect of *reducing* circular migration between the United States and Mexico while continuing to allow very large in-flows, leading to a build-up of Mexican migrants in the United States.

Mexican migration to the United States has historically often been temporary, especially during the period of the Bracero work program in the

1940s and into the 1970s, when most unauthorized workers were found in agriculture. These primarily male workers came for only short periods, often less than a year and/or no more than a couple of years, to earn what they could and then return home. But the increased border enforcement starting after IRCA, and especially in the early 1990s, has made border crossing more difficult and dangerous. It is reasonable that many migrants who previously may have moved back and forth choose to stay in the United States after making it across the border. So the increasing population of migrants in the late 1990s would partly reflect, not new migration, but rather more people staying. Interviews with migrants reinforce the perception that they wish to avoid crossing the border more than necessary.[33] And research finds that rates of return migration did decline, particularly following IRCA through 1994, but little since then.[34]

Nevertheless, most of the available research on the changing settlement process is incomplete. Changes in stay are followed only through the early-to-late 1990s, and inference with regard to new enforcement efforts causing changes in settlement relies on timing—specifically that changes in return migration, i.e., those occurring after 1993, reflect the new enforcement, it is argued. Little nod is given to the fact that the boom in migration seen in the late 1990s better coincides with the timing of the huge boom in U.S. labor demand of the "new economy." Further, statistical analysis of legalization or border enforcement finds, in contrast, that changes in return and migration are most highly correlated with IRCA's legalization and stabilization of family members in the United States.[35]

Indeed, Mexican data shown in Figure 1.7 demonstrate that return migration remains fairly high, as measured by return migration within a three-year period, and that return rates have actually increased in the most recent period despite stepped-up enforcement efforts. These figures are based on Mexican data taken at different points in time. The strong up-tick in return migration from the 1992–1997 to the 1997–2002 period suggests that border enforcement, which was increasing most notably precisely during this period, is not the primary driver of changes in Mexican circular migration.[36] Return is most often addressed with Mexican data because there are simply no U.S. data that capture temporary migration.[37] The Mexican census and intercensal surveys are large, random samples that regularly ask a number of questions about the length of migrants' stay outside of Mexico and their movement back from the United States. Again, if only the early to the mid-1990s is considered it does appear that migrant rates of return declined.

If one looks at the longer-term trend in rates of circulation, however, it becomes obvious that the largest drop in the return to Mexico of migrants in U.S. urban areas took place in the 1980s, especially after IRCA.[38] At the same time, the return rate to Mexico of agricultural workers in truly tempo-

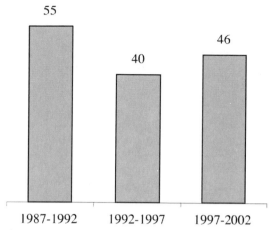

Figure 1.7. Percentage of Migrants Returning to Mexico after Three Years in the United States

Source: Elena Zúñiga and Paula Leite, "Estimaciones de CONAPO con base en INEGI, Encuesta Nacional de la Dinámica Demográfica (ENADID), 1992 y 1997 y Encuesta Nacional de Empleo (ENE) modulo sobre migración, 2002" (Mexico City: Consejo Nacional de Población, 2004).

rary or seasonal jobs has remained fairly high.[39] There are four main reasons for decreases in return migration from historical levels: (a) increases in urban employment of migrants in year-round and permanent jobs; (b) an associated long-term growth of Mexican communities in the United States; (c) IRCA's legalization program that strengthened family networks—a finding agreed upon by almost all experts; and (d) border enforcement in the last decade, but to a much smaller degree than the controversial emphasis on the phenomenon.

Patterns of Dispersion and Concentration

For the past century, most Mexican migration has originated in a few rural sending communities in central Mexico and has gone to well-known places in Texas or California or Chicago. But, both the origins and destinations of Mexican migrants have become more varied over the past one to two decades. Especially in the United States, the new patterns of dispersed settlement create challenges to often small communities facing rapid population growth and stresses on housing and schools.[40] Yet, despite the growing literature into the newer dispersed patterns of migration, Mexican migrant communities, often in cities in traditional states of settlement, are increasing and have reached historic levels.

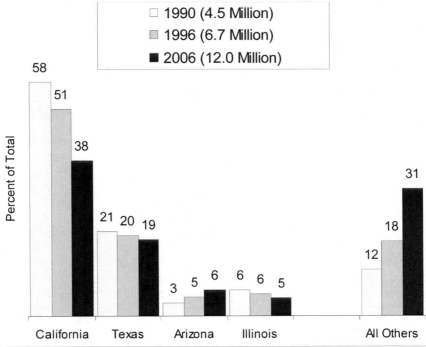

Figure 1.8. **Mexican-Born Population by U.S. State, 1990–2006 (percent of total)**

Source: Jeffrey S. Passel, Jennifer Van Hook, and Frank D. Bean, "Estimates of Legal and Unauthorized Foreign Born Population for the United States and Selected States, Based on Census 2000," Report to the Census Bureau (Washington, DC: Urban Institute, 2004), http://www.sabresys.com/i_whitepapers .asp and unpublished updates to 2006.

New Settlement in the United States

Researchers began to notice that in the later part of the 1980s a growing number of immigrants were moving to states and small localities where they had not been going before. Theorists had expected that immigrants would continue to concentrate in the central cities of a few major states and a few metropolitan areas. In the 1970s, the number of *all* immigrants in six core states (California, New York, Texas, Florida, Illinois, and New Jersey) grew 60 percent in the 1970s; further growth slowed to only 28 percent in the 1990s. In contrast, "new settlement" areas in other than traditional states grew by 45 percent in the 1980s and by an astonishing 94 percent in the 1990s.[41] This pattern of dispersal has continued into the twenty-first century as the foreign-born population in the six core states increased by 12 percent between 2000 and 2006 but by 36 percent in the "new settlement" states.

The roots of today's new settlement patterns extend back to the 1980s. In some cases, businesses actively recruited immigrants into new communities.[42] During the 1980s corporate oligopolies emerged in the processing of beef, pork, chicken, and fish. Industries began to relocate from the North Central states (especially in cities) to the South, South Central, and Plains states to be closer to the feedlots and to employ nonunion, lower-wage labor.[43] Located in small, rural communities with little local labor, processing companies in new locations recruited immigrant workers from California and Texas, as well as directly from Mexico. Over time, recruitment activities lessened to the point where, today, active recruitment is often not needed because immigrant networks draw newcomers (sometimes encouraged by hiring bonuses for friends and relatives).

Early movement encouraged at first by recruitment was later reinforced by IRCA's legalization program. Data from the newly legalized population around 1990 revealed several Mexican settlement zones with distinct demographic and employment patterns that already presaged the patterns seen in the later 1990s.[44] The job stability (if not income security) created by the new legal status permitted families to reunite and deepen the settling out process.

Outside of food processing and manufacturing, new settlement areas can also be found in the more traditional agricultural sector, particularly in specialized niches. The forces that have driven this dispersal process are complex. Growers in labor-intensive crops have cast a broader net to find workers; there has also been a heretofore unprecedented "settling out" of new immigrants in diverse places. The "Latinization" of agriculture has occurred in the apple groves of Washington State, the mushroom sheds of New England, the orange groves of southern Florida, the grape and row crops of California.[45]

The greatest shift in settlement of Mexican immigrants has been away from the traditional concentration in California. In 1990, 58 percent of Mexican migrants in the United States could be found there. In spite of growing *numbers* of Mexican immigrants living in California, only 38 percent of all Mexican residents in the United States lived there in 2006. Other traditional Mexican states of settlement, Texas, Arizona, and Illinois, have not lost much of their share of the Mexican-born population, relatively speaking. Rather, there has been extraordinarily large growth of the population residing in all other than the four traditional states of Mexican settlement, as the share in these areas increased from 12 percent in 1990 to 31 percent in 2006. In absolute terms, the growth of the Mexican-born population outside the traditional areas was even more astounding as their numbers increased tenfold from about 400,000 to 3.8 million.

The pace of population growth away from California was particularly notable in the latter half of the 1990s. Further, there is a self-perpetuating aspect to this new settlement pattern. The greater dispersion of Mexican migration means that there are more places where employers hire Mexican labor, more contacts for Mexican migration networks, and more places where Mexican families can put down roots.

Scale and Concentration in the United States

While the new dispersion has captured the limelight, there is a parallel story about the growing size of the Mexican population and its concentration in a rather few places as shown in Figure 1.9. At first blush this may sound contradictory. It is, however, a result of the fact that most of the new dispersion of Mexicans is primarily a story of small populations in rural areas and smaller U.S. cities spread over many states. So, as the total population grew during the 1990s, a growing share of Mexicans now live in new settlement areas but in rather small, individual agglomerations. Meanwhile, the size or scale of the Mexican populations, primarily in well-known cities in traditional settlement states, grew rather large. Half of all Mexican migrants lived in just twelve U.S.-consolidated metropolitan areas at the time of the 2000 U.S. Census. In contrast, it takes seventy-five metropolitan areas to account for half of the *total* U.S. population.[46]

Los Angeles alone has 1.5 million Mexican-born residents in 2000, double the number that lived there at the start of the decade, and by itself still 14 percent of all Mexicans in the United States.[47] Chicago is next in line with 580,000 Mexicans—clearly a very large number—many of whom live in just a few areas of the metropolis. Of the top twelve Mexican metros, eleven are in traditional states of settlement; the only exception is the concentration of Mexican residents in the New York City area. So it is fair to say that, even

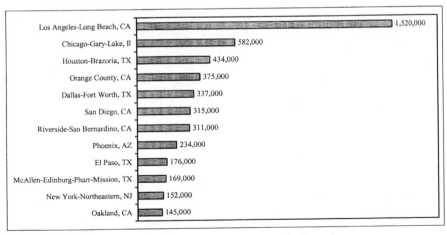

Figure 1.9. U.S. Metropolitan Areas with 50 Percent of All Mexican-Born Residents

Source: Tabulations of U.S. Census 2000 Microdata

while Mexican migrants go to more dispersed destinations, the Mexican-born population is also concentrated in a few metros where their numbers have grown to a scale reflective of the total population growth of the 1990s.

Emergent New Origins in Mexico

Coupled with the emergence of new settlement areas in the United States has been a dispersal of origins from new states within Mexico. However, the trend toward new origins in Mexico has not been as dramatic as the one seen in new destinations in the United States. Although research based on one small sample in the United States suggests somewhat dramatic shifts in origins,[48] other research using various Mexican source data going back to the 1920s finds, at least as of 1992, there was no long-term shift away from the historical concentration of emigration from Western Mexico.[49] Indeed, research that aggregates migrants using Mexican data by state of origin suggests that there has been rather little increase in the share of migrants coming from other than the traditional source states. Over half of all Mexicans reporting a migration to the United States have come from traditional states, in three different samples over time. On the other hand, while the share of Mexican migrants coming from southern and southeastern Mexican states has remained relatively small, there has been an increase over the past fifteen years (from 9 to 13 percent).

Many observers believe there is an emergent trend for Mexicans to leave from new origins—both in that they are coming from new, often southern

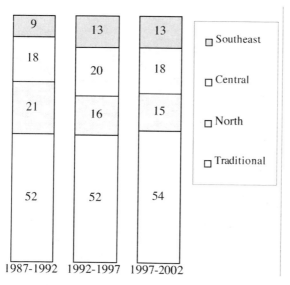

Figure 1.10. Percentage of Mexican Migrants to the United States by State of Origin

Source: Elena Zúñiga and Paula Leite, "Estimaciones de CONAPO con base en INEGI, Encuesta Nacional de la Dinámica Demográfica (ENADID), 1992 y 1997 y Encuesta Nacional de Empleo (ENE) modulo sobre migración, 2002" (Mexico City: Consejo Nacional de Población, 2004).

states, and because other evidence suggests a growing number of urban as compared with rural-origin migrants.[50] We can see new emerging states in Figure 1.10, which were not important ten years ago but started playing a role during the recent period. Veracruz is the most representative new state, followed by the state of Hidalgo. The southern states of Puebla and Oaxaca were already important in 1992 and showed a significant increase during the decade. In the northern region the case of Nuevo Leon is also remarkable. So while the regional origins of Mexican migration appear somewhat stable, there is a trend for new states to send migrants. To be sure, this appears to be a slight shift at the national level, albeit one that can have dramatic impacts at the local level of origin, and it is a trend that bears watching.

FEMALE MIGRATION

The long dominance of males among U.S. migrants from Mexico has been thought to be changing, especially among the younger generations where the duration of stay has shortened and, in some cases, couples migrate together. Females did appear to be more prevalent in the migration flow following IRCA, which made sense in light of legalization's effects on family reunification.[51] But that tendency has not played itself out in an ongoing feminization of the flow over the balance of the 1990s. Rather, there appears to have evolved a tendency, consistent with increasing rates of migrant return in the late 1990s, for relatively lower female migration but higher rates of stay.

There are many reasons for the historical male domination of migration. In rural Mexico, temporary male migration dates to the late 1800s, spurred especially by the recruitment of U.S. employers. Today, male migration often prevails because having "a wife at home is cost-efficient, conforms to gender norms, and also enables men to move back and forth without losing standing in village and kinship structures."[52] In some rural areas, so many males migrate that households where the husband is absent are the norm. The absence of males, unfortunately, is often accompanied by a lack of economic protection for women and children, and sometimes by family abandonment.[53] But legalization may have changed that pattern. In addition, young, single women especially from urban areas might create new trends as they may choose to migrate to search for more freedom, to seek a wider marriage market, to escape from monotonous housework, or to have more independence from their parents.[54]

How many females show up in migration statistics depends on whether one looks at U.S. or Mexican data sources. Statistics from U.S. households show that the number of Mexican-born women living in the United States is not too far away from the number of males. According to the 2000 U.S.

Census, the female population represented 45 percent of the Mexican-born adult population. However, males are between 70 and 80 percent of migrants in Mexican data.[55] Several factors explain the differences between the Mexican and U.S. sources. Because Mexican data sources capture only the migration information of households still in Mexico, males who dominate circular migration flows are most likely to be counted. Once women leave they are more likely to stay in the United States, and when women leave Mexico often the whole household is gone, so women completely "disappear" from the Mexican surveys. In short, Mexican women are more likely to be found in the U.S. data that best captures migrants who intend long-term residence.

As Figure 1.11 shows, the U.S. and Mexican data taken together suggest a trend toward increased female residency in the United States and, *relative to males*, decreased participation in migration over the course of the 1990s.[56] The U.S. data show an increase of females from 46 to 50 percent of all migrants arriving in five-year periods between 1990 and 2002.[57] At the same time, various Mexican data sources show a decrease of females from 30 to 19 percent of migrants in the same five-year periods.

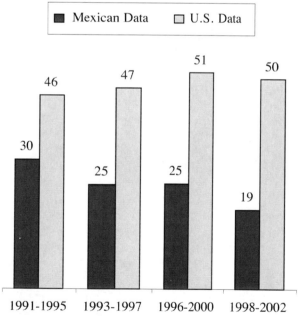

Figure 1.11. Percentage of Female Mexican Migrants to the United States

Source: Authors' tabulations of various U.S. current population surveys and Mexican data sources (Conteo 1995, ENADID 1997, CENSO 2000, and ENE 2002).

While females have been relatively less likely to migrate from Mexico, females who do migrate to the United States have a greater tendency to remain. This pattern is at least consistent with the findings discussed above that, as the Mexican data indicate, circular or return migration has increased since 1997. Males being more mobile than women are most likely driving the increased rates of return. Indeed, Mexican data readily substantiate the common-place observation that women are more likely than males to stay resident abroad in the United States. As of 2002, surveyed Mexican households reported that 66 percent of women migrants compared with 52 percent of males had *not* returned to Mexico after 1.5 years.[58] That would mean that women have been likely *a declining share of the Mexican flow*, as the Mexican data on the sex of migrants show; and women *are an increasing share in the United States*, as the U.S. data on the sex of migrants shows.

Indeed, Mexican women have several characteristics that are systematically different from men: they tend to be younger, less mobile, and more dependent on social networks and family ties than males. Around 50 percent of migrant women are in the age group from 15 to 24, compared to only 40 percent of male migrants.[59] And no more than 20 percent of female migrants, a clear minority, fit the profile of a potentially independent migrant, i.e., moved on their own, married with no spouse present, or moved either before or without their parents or husbands.[60] Only about just 7 percent of female migrants are the heads of their households compared with 29 percent of male migrants. Further, 51 percent of females report that they migrated to the United States to seek a job as compared with almost all, 92 percent, of male migrants. Mexican data also indicate that 61 percent of females but 76 percent of male migrants are unauthorized which, in turn, is consistent with differences in mobility and job seeking.

EDUCATION OF MIGRANTS

On average, those Mexicans who choose to immigrate are better educated than those who choose not to leave home. Immigrants to the United States have characteristics that help them take on the challenges and costs of international mobility. For example, they tend to be risk takers and they tend to be younger, and better off than non-migrants. Education too fits into this profile of migrants to the United States with, however, notable differences that tend to favor a relatively higher rate of emigration among highly educated Mexican women. And while the greatest *number* of Mexican migrants in the United States has little education, if we look at the combined populations of Mexicans in Mexico and the United States, the groups with the greatest share in the United States are the better-educated groups of Mexicans.

Mexican data show that the majority of Mexican residents have completed no more than a primary or six years of education and only about 5 percent have completed a college education.[61] Although substantial improvement has occurred over the past two to three decades in Mexico, women are less educated than men in Mexico.[62] Nearly two thirds (63 percent) of women in Mexico have completed no more than a primary education compared with a lesser 58 percent of men. At the upper extreme, just 3 percent of Mexican women have completed a college degree, or just half the 6 percent of men who have done so. These data show that Mexican women living in Mexico are less educated on average than are males residing in Mexico.

The U.S. data on Mexican migrants in the United States reflect the overall levels of education in Mexico. In particular, they reflect the well-known fact that migrants are considerably less educated than U.S. natives. Just under half of both male and female Mexican migrants in the United States have completed no more than a primary school education. And only about 13 percent of Mexican adults in the United States ever complete a high school education. In contrast, 85 percent of U.S. native adults complete high school.[63] In the U.S. data, however, female Mexican migrants are better educated than are male migrants.[64] At the upper extreme, 5 percent of Mexican women migrants have completed a college education compared with 4 percent of Mexican male migrants in the United States and 27 percent of U.S. native adults. These comparisons reinforce the commonly known observation that Mexicans in the United States are substantially less educated than U.S. natives, but they also point to the lesser-known fact that Mexican-born females in the United States are educated at least as well as Mexican-born males.

Combining the Mexican data with the U.S. data permits us to calculate rates of out migration or probabilities of leaving Mexico by education level and gender. Figure 1.12 shows that about 9 percent of all persons born in Mexico who have completed no more than a primary education are living in the United States. By contrast, 20 percent of Mexicans with a high school degree have migrated. Interestingly, the proportion of those with a bachelor's degree is lower (8 percent). Yet, at the upper extreme, about 36 percent of all persons born in Mexico who have completed a doctoral (Ph.D.) or professional degree live in the United States. In other words, a Mexican Ph.D. is almost four times as likely to move and remain in the U.S. as is a Mexican with a primary education.

This "selectivity" of Mexican migrants (i.e., that highly educated Mexicans are more likely to migrate than are lesser skilled Mexicans) may seem implausible. This pattern may be confusing at first blush because it is well-known that the greatest *number* of Mexican migrants have little education. But the educational pyramid of Mexico has a very broad base.

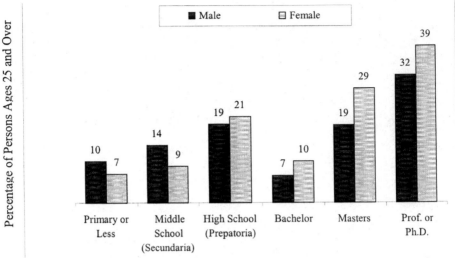

Figure 1.12.   Percentage of All Mexican-Born Adults Residing in the United States by Level of Completed Education, 2000

Source: Mexican and U.S. Census Microdata

Even a small percent of this large numerical base moving to the United States generates a large number of migrants. Thus, even though there are a large number of Mexican immigrants with little education in the United States, they are only a small fraction of those who could have moved. On the other hand, there are rather few highly educated persons in Mexico, and because they are likely to migrate, a much higher share of them end up in the United States.

Educational selectivity is greatest for female migrants at all but the lowest educational levels and is particularly so among the college educated. Men's migration rates increase more slowly with education than do the rates for women.[65] To demonstrate this pattern we compute the proportion of Mexican-born persons of a given educational level who reside in the United States.[66] About 10 percent of Mexico's women with a bachelor's education reside in the U.S. as compared with 7 percent of Mexico's males with the same. Even more strikingly, 29 percent of Mexico's women with a masters and 39 percent of those with a Ph.D. reside in the United States, as compared with a lesser but still significant 19 percent of Mexico's males with a masters and 32 percent of those with a Ph.D.

Highly educated persons are the most prized asset of any nation in today's post-industrial economy, and they are the workers who are increasingly favored by employers over the past three decades. Our analysis shows that on this basis Mexican migration has its greatest effect on Mexico in terms of a substantial loss of the best educated. The loss is also apparent at the lower end of the educational spectrum, with significantly a higher proportion of those who have completed high school migrating, as compared with those with only a primary education. This is rather the opposite conclusion reached by most observers.

CONCLUSIONS

The late 1990s saw a significant increase in Mexican migration, above and beyond the already substantial growth seen in the prior two and one-half decades. Practically all observers agree that the major impetus behind the 1990s boom in migration was facilitated by two decades of migration that set the stage, and the 1987–1988 U.S. legalization that anchored men and their families in the United States. Legalization enabled the now-legal U.S. residents to sponsor generous numbers of legally approved migrants, as well as to host new unauthorized Mexican migrants in subsequent years.[67] Yet other observers also attribute some of the migration growth to border enforcement that induced some migrants to stay in the United States rather than return to Mexico because it made crossing more difficult. But, rates of return migration actually increased in 1997–2002 while border enforcement intensified its buildup. In reality, the spike in migration that occurred between 1996 and 2000, for the most part, can be readily traced to the booming U.S. "new economy." The decades-old demand for Mexican labor deepened in metropolitan areas such as Los Angeles with a market that restructured for low-skill labor, as well as in a diverse array of states where demand for Mexican labor had also begun to emerge in the late 1980s.[68]

The trend toward diversity of migrant destinations in the United States accelerated in the 1990s, and by 2006 almost one-third of all Mexican migrants live in states other than the four major states of settlement—or well more than double the share in 1990. At the same time, the Mexican population in Los Angeles doubled to 1.5 million in 2000 and half of all Mexican migrants live in just twelve U.S. metropolitan areas. So dispersion to new states has gone hand in hand with a growing scale in the number of migrants who tend to concentrate in a rather few cities. Although there has been much discussion about a parallel dispersion of migrants leaving Mexico from new sending areas, we find that broad regional patterns have remained reasonably stable, but that some evidence points to shifts for a few states. Shifting origins is thus more of a trend worth watching rather than a significant change on the same scale as the new dispersion of destinations. Likewise, there has been much speculation about the feminization of Mexican migration. However, we find that female migrants in the late 1990s are somewhat less likely to participate in the northward flow while being somewhat more likely to settle in the United States than male migrants. The final trend that we investigate is that of migrants' education, which indicates that, contrary to most assumptions, Mexican migrants are disproportionately drawn from the better educated college and especially post-baccalaureate populations. While Mexican migrants represent a large population with low skills relative to the U.S. population, migrants represent a significant loss of persons with high skills to the Mexican population.

While we review projections on the future of Mexican migration, we leave an elaboration of that discussion to a later chapter. The major governmental projections agree that migration will begin to taper off in the coming decade, but that trend is merely the result of assumptions; it is by no means a prediction and it is far from certain that it will occur. But the fact that trends in Mexican migration are responsive to economic conditions in Mexico and the United States suggests that future declines in the northward flow are quite possible. Indeed, most research finds that migration responds more to economic conditions in Mexico that have tended to trump conditions in the United States. So as Mexican demographic growth slows, there is a real opportunity for home-based demand to create enough formal-sector jobs attractive to potential migrants. Of course, if the United States offers large-scale legalization to Mexican migrants that may well echo the past IRCA-legalization and generate follow-up migration, although it may induce some to restart a pattern of circular mobility. And if a large-scale guest worker program leading to residency is instituted and further deepens employer demand for low-skilled labor, increased migration of both a temporary and permanent nature will likely follow.

NOTES

1. The figures on Mexican-born include an edit to assign persons with country of birth "unknown" to countries based on reported Hispanic origin and country of birth of parents. These data differ slightly from published numbers.

2. The estimates are drawn from Jeffrey Passel, "Unauthorized Migrants: Numbers and Characteristics," report (Washington, D.C., Pew Hispanic Center, 2005), http://pewhispanic.org/files/reports/46.pdf and a forthcoming update (2007). A discussion of the methodology is in Jeffrey Passel, Jennifer Van Hook, and Frank D. Bean, "Estimates of legal and unauthorized foreign born population for the United States and selected states, based on Census 2000," report to the Census Bureau (Urban Institute, 2004), http://www.sabresys.com/i_whitepapers.asp.

3. Although the U.S. decennial Census and Current Population Survey are known to undercount immigrants, the residual estimates of Passel (2005) and Passel, Van Hook, and Bean (2004) explicitly incorporate an allowance for omissions. These corrections are based on the work of Enrico Marcelli and Paul Ong, "2000 Census Coverage of Foreign-born Mexicans Residing in Los Angeles County: Implications for Demographic Analysis" (paper presented at the Meetings of the Population Association of America, Atlanta, May 2002), who found that the 2000 Census missed

about 10–11 percent of unauthorized Mexican immigrants and 4–8 percent of legal Mexican immigrants. In its residual estimates, the Census Bureau has assumed undercount rates for Hispanics generally to be no more than 6.7 percent or, overall of 15 percent for the residual foreign born. Kevin E. Deardorff and Lisa M. Blumerman, "Evaluating Components of International Migration: Estimates of the Foreign-Born Population by Migrant Status in 2000" (Washington, D.C.: U.S. Census Bureau, 2001). On the basis of these studies, there appears to be no empirical foundation for claims such as 20 million total unauthorized persons in the United States. Robert Justich and Betty Ng, "The Underground Labor Force Is Rising to the Surface" (Bear Stearns Asset Management, January 3, 2005). Thus, we are confident in the 11.5 million figure. This already substantial figure reflects a level of unauthorized migration in line with other estimates using similar methodologies. Frank D. Bean and Gillian Stevens, *America's Newcomers and the Dynamics of Diversity* (New York: Russell Sage, 2003); Joseph Costanzo, Cynthia J. Davis, Caribert Irazi, Daniel M. Goodkind, and Roberto R. Ramirez, "Evaluating Components of International Migration: The Residual Foreign Born" (Washington, D.C.: U.S. Census Bureau, 2002).

4. Various administrative requirements and bottlenecks mean that it takes time to process applications for immigration benefits. Some individual applicants may enter and stay illegally in the country while waiting for the approval and issuance of a resident visa. The U.S. Citizenship and Immigration Services (USCIS) reports on the number of persons whose applications are in process for immigration benefits such as work authorization, permanent residency, and naturalization. The processing backlog had reached a high of 3.8 million cases at the outset of 2004, but as of Fall 2004 was reduced to 1.5 million cases. USCIS, "Backlog Elimination Plan: Fiscal Year 2004, 4th Quarter Update" (Washington D.C.: U.S. Citizenship and Immigration Services, 2005). However, the "quasi-legal" population discussed here includes not only some such persons in the backlog, but many others with more or less "permanent" temporary statuses including TPS or "temporary protected status." The portion of persons who are Mexican is not known.

5. Costanzo et al., "Evaluating components of international migration."

6. Costanzo et al. ("Evaluating components") estimate 1.7 million "quasi-legals" of three types: the legalizing population waiting to adjust status (900,000); refugees/asylum applicants who are, likewise, waiting for administrative adjustment (600,000); and migrants deported during the decade (200,000). In the residual estimates cited in the text, virtually all of the refugees are in the legal categories. Between June 2002 and May 2003, the Department of Homeland Security (DHS) issued Employment Authorization Documents (EADs) to many persons who fall into the residual population. Some examples include the backlogs noted above as person with applications for green cards pending (about 700,000); persons with applications for asylum pending, those with TPS, and those with TPS applications pending (700,000). Most in the first group will eventually become legal whereas most in the second will probably not. The former group probably includes a significant number of Mexicans but the latter probably includes few. David Martin, "Twilight Statuses: A Closer Examination of the Unauthorized Population" (Migration Policy Institute, 2006) http://www.migrationpolicy.org/ ITFIAF/publications .php.2006.

7. The estimates through 2004 taken from Elena Zúñiga and Paula Leite, "Estimaciones de CONAPO con base en INEGI, Encuesta Nacional de la Dinámica Demográfica (ENADID), 1992 y 1997 y Encuesta Nacional de Empleo (ENE) módulo sobre migración, 2002" (Mexico City: CONAPO, 2004) are, in turn, taken from U.S. data-based estimates made by the Binational Study, *Binational Study: Migration Between Mexico and the United States* (Washington, D.C.: U.S. Commission on Immigration Reform, 1997), http://www.utexas.edu/ lbj/uscir/binational.html. The estimate for the late 1990s is made by CONAPO which is Mexico's lead statistical agency.

8. At the time this was written we are aware of, but unable to evaluate, two estimates of the Mexican emigrant population residing in the United States. Mexico's Instituto Nacional de Estadistica Geografia y Informaticia (INEGI) reports 1.6 million Mexican emigrants between 1995 and 2000 or a yearly average of 320,000 (see http://www.inegi.gob.mx/est/contenidos/espanol/rutinas/ept.asp?t=mpob67&c =3244). However, another estimate generates net yearly migration of 530,000 between 2000 and 2005, numbers more in line with those made by U.S. demographers, perhaps because it partly draws upon U.S. data sources; see unpublished estimates by CONAPO (Virgilio Partida, Mexico City, 2006).

9. There are two reasons for this. The first is that when an entire household migrates from Mexico to the U.S., it leaves no trace in the Mexican census. The second has to do with the specific method used by INEGI in the 2000 Census adjustment, which imputed population in a portion of the dwellings that did not respond to the census.

10. Passel, "Unauthorized Migrants."

11. Roberto Suro and B. Lindsay Lowell, "Highs to Lows: Latino Economic Losses in Today's Recession," report (Pew Hispanic Center, 2002), http://pewhispanic.org/ files/reports/1.pdf .

12. See Jeffrey Passel and Robert Suro, "Rise, Peak, and Decline: Trends in U.S. Immigration 1992–2004," report (Washington, D.C.: Pew Hispanic Center, 2005), http://pewhispanic.org/files/reports/53.pdf, for a detailed description of the methodology. The yearly values for 1992–2004 are a simple average of the estimates available for each year restricted to figures consistent with Census 2000. The averaged estimates are: (a) Census 2000 estimates based on year of arrival for 1992–2000; (b) average ACS estimates based on year of arrival for 1992–2004; (c) average CPS 2000-based estimates based on year of arrival for 1992–2004; (d) average ACS estimates based on residence abroad 1 year ago for 1999–2004; and (c) average CPS 2000-based estimates based on residence abroad 1 year ago for 1999–2004.

13. See Pew Hispanic Center, "Indicators of Recent Migration Flows from Mexico," Fact Sheet (Pew Hispanic Center, 2007), http://pewhispanic.org/factsheets/ factsheet.php?FactsheetID=33, which describes a slowing down in the rate of growth of the Mexican-born population entering since 1990, the flow of remittances from the United States to Mexico, and the employment of foreign-born Hispanics.

14. Douglas S. Massey and Rene Zenteno, "The Dynamics of Mass Migration," *Proceedings of the National Academy of Sciences* 96, no. 8 (1999): 5325–335.

15. *Binational Study.*

16. Total fertility rates represent the average lifetime fertility of a woman; and a replacement level TFR is about 2.05-2.1.

17. The differing underlying fertility, mortality, and emigration assumptions also lead to significant differences in the projected Mexican population: 129.6 million for CONAPO, 140.2 million for the U.N. (medium), and 147.9 million for the U.S. Census Bureau.

18. See the discussion of the effects of Mexico's demography/and economy on future labor demand/emigration in Alba in this volume.

19. Most observers believe the decline was real, since IRCA removed many individuals from the unauthorized inflow by giving them legal status in the United States and thus permitting them to cross legally. Beyond this impact, any "IRCA-effect" was mostly psychological and very short lived. Frank D. Bean, Barry Edmonston, and Jeffrey Passel, eds., *Undocumented Migration to the United States: IRCA and the Experience of the 1980s* (Washington, D.C.: RAND and The Urban Institute, 1990); Douglas S Massey, Jorge Durand, and Nolan J. Malone, *Beyond Smoke and Mirrors: Mexican Immigration in an Era of Economic Integration* (New York: Russel Sage Foundation, 2003).

20. The Mexican repatriation counts are less than the U.S. apprehension counts, most likely because they include only individual Mexicans caught at the border who are returned to Mexican authorities. In line with this, the authors learned from the Mexican National Migration Institute that, while many returnees are formally returned to Mexican authorities, the U.S. Immigration and Customers Enforcement also releases migrants without reporting them to the authorities.

21. Joseph Nevins, "Thinking Out of Bounds: A Critical Analysis of Academic and Human Rights Writings on Migrant Deaths in the U.S.-Mexico Border Region," *Migraciones Internacionales* 2, no. 2 (2003): 171–90; CLINIC (Catholic Legal Immigration Network, Inc.), "Chaos on the U.S.-Mexico border: A report on migrant crossing deaths, immigrant families and subsistence-level laborers," report no. 5, 2004.

22. Karl Eschbach, Jacqueline Hagan, and Nestor Rodríguez, "Deaths during Undocumented Migration: Trends and Policy Implications in the New Era of Homeland Security," *Defense of the Alien* 26 (2003): 37–52. These data, while the best available, are thought to be conservative, i.e., they too low to the extent that deaths in remote areas are undercounted. Mexican and U.S. authorities collect data on deaths from different sources, as do other parties that independently attempt to tabulate border deaths. Still, the volume of deaths from the different sources is, broadly speaking, within the same order of magnitude.

23. U.S. General Accountability Office, "Illegal Immigration Border-Crossing Deaths Have Doubled Since 1995; Border Patrol's Efforts to Prevent Deaths Have Not Been Fully Evaluated," report (Washington D.C.: GAO, 2006), www.gao.gov/cgi-bin/getrpt?GAO-06-770. Note, however, that research suggests that official data undercount true mortality; see Binational Migration Institute, "The 'Funnel Effect' and Recovered Bodies of Unauthorized Migrants Processed by the Pima County Office of the Medical Examiner, 1990–2005," report (Mexican American Studies & Research Center, University of Arizona, 2006).

24. Massey, Durand, and Malone, *Beyond Smoke and Mirrors.* Deaths per apprehension hit a high of 0.6 in 1988 and then continuously sank to a low of 0.2 in

1999, only to then rise to 0.4 in 2003 as the overall number of apprehensions fell precipitously (authors' tabulations using Eschbach, Hagan, and Rodríguez, "Deaths during Undocumented Migration" and UCSIS, "Backlog Elimination Plan" data).

25. Eschbach, Hagan, and Rodríguez, "Deaths during Undocumented Migration."

26. Indeed, the larger concern might be that mortality rates in border communities are higher than elsewhere. Note, too, that accidents are the second leading cause of male death in Sister Communities on the Mexican side of the border, the third leading cause of male death on the U.S. side, and the leading cause of death among young men; see PAHO (Pan American Health Organization), "Leading Causes of Mortality on the United States-Mexico Border," *Epidemiological Bulletin* 20, no. 2, (June 1999): 1–5. The problem is exacerbated by the growing financial stress of the unreimbursed care of unauthorized persons in border emergency rooms. MGT of America, "Medical Emergency: Costs of Uncompensated Care in Southwest Border Counties," report (Washington, D.C.: United States/Mexico Border Counties Coalition, 2002).

27. Bean and Stevens, *America's Newcomers*.

28. Roberto Coronado and Pia M. Orrenius, "The Impact of Illegal Immigration and Enforcement on Border Crime Rates," The Federal Reserve Bank of Dallas–El Paso Branch, Working paper 0303, 2003.

29. Massey et al., *Beyond Smoke and Mirrors*.

30. Christina Gathmann, "The Effects of Enforcement on Illegal Markets: Evidence from Migrant Smuggling along the Southwestern Border," IZA Discussion Paper No. 1004, 2004, analyzes Mexico survey data from the Mexican Migration Project (see also Massey et al., *Beyond Smoke and Mirrors*).

31. Pia Orrenius, "The Effect of U.S. Border Enforcement on the Crossing Behavior of Mexican Migrants," in *Crossing the Border: Research from the Mexican Migration Project*, ed. Jorge Durand and Douglas S. Massey (New York: Russell Sage Foundation, 2004), 281–90.

32. Frank D. Bean, Roland Chanove, Robert G. Cushing, Rodolfo de la Garza, Gary P. Freeman, Charles W. Haynes, and David Spener, *Illegal Mexican Migration and the United States/Mexico Border: The Effect of Operation Hold the Line on El Paso/Juarez* (Population Research Center, University of Texas at Austin and U.S. Commission on Immigration Reform, 1994); Gathmann, "The Effects of Enforcement on Illegal Markets." See also Mark G. Guzman, Joseph H. Haslag, and Pia M. Orrenius, "Coyote Crossings: The Role of Smugglers in Illegal Immigration and Border Enforcement," The Federal Reserve Bank of Dallas, Working Paper 0201, 2002.

33. Belinda I. Reyes, "U.S. Immigration Policy and the Duration of Undocumented Trips," in *Crossing the Border: Research from the Mexican Migration Project*, ed. Jorge Durand and Douglas S. Massey (New York: Russell Sage Foundation, 2004), 299–320.

34. Douglas S. Massey, "Backfire at the Border: Why Enforcement without Legalization Cannot Stop Illegal Immigration" (Washington, D.C.: CATO Institute, 2005); see also Massey et al., *Beyond Smoke and Mirrors*; Belinda I. Reyes, Hans P. Johnson, and Richard Van Swearingen, *Holding the Line? The Effect of Recent Border Build-up on Unauthorized Immigration* (San Francisco: Public Policy Institute of California, 2002).

35. Fernando Riosmena, "Return versus Settlement among Undocumented Mexican Migrants," in *Crossing the Border: Research from the Mexican Migration Project*, ed. Jorge Durand and Douglas S. Massey (New York: Russell Sage Foundation, 2004), 265–80; Belinda I. Reyes, "U.S. Immigration Policy."

36. Frank D. Bean and B. Lindsay Lowell, "NAFTA and Mexican Migration to the United States," in *NAFTA's Impact on North America*, ed. Sidney Weintraub (Washington, D.C.: Center for Strategic and International Studies, 2004), 263–84.

37. Of course, using just Mexican data introduces a selectivity bias into the analysis. One attempt to address this combines Mexican and U.S. data. It found that the rates of net stay for all migrants in the United States decreased between 1992 and 1997, while rates of return increased for working migrants. Lindsay Lowell and Frank D. Bean, "Does the Wave Change? Reinvestigating Mexican Migration in the 1990s" (paper presented at the Meetings of the Population Association of America, Atlanta, May 2002). This supports the observation that IRCA's legalization stabilized family members residing in the United States while the new economy created a boom in job opportunities for primarily young, male Mexican workers.

38. Massey et al., *Beyond Smoke and Mirrors*.

39. Reyes, "U.S. Immigration Policy."

40. Elzbieta Gozdziak and Susan F. Martin, eds., *New Immigrant Communities: Addressing Integration Challenges* (Lanham, MD: Lexington Books, 2005).

41. Jeffrey Passel and Wendy Zimmerman, "Are Immigrants Leaving California? Settlement Patterns of Immigrants in the Late 1990s" (paper presented at the meetings of the Population Association of America, Los Angeles, 2000).

42. In other cases, government programs sought to disperse new immigrants to new communities with growing economies. The Office of Refugee Resettlement (ORR), for example, provided grants to voluntary resettlement agencies to encourage dispersion to such places as Fargo, North Dakota; Charlotte, North Carolina; and Lincoln, Nebraska. Thus, Asian refugees were often the first wave of labor in new settlement areas, establishing new rural-based industries, and were later replaced by more plentiful Mexican workers.

43. Michael Broadway and Terry Ward, "Recent Changes in the Structure and Location of the U.S. Meatpacking Industry," *Geography* 75, no. 1 (1990): 76–79; Donald D. Stull, Michael J. Broadway, and David Griffith, *Any Way You Cut It: Meat Processing in Small-Town America* (Lawrence: University Press of Kansas, 1995).

44. Lindsay Lowell, "Circular Mobility, Migrant Communities, and Policy Restrictions: Unauthorized Flows from Mexico," in *Migration, Population Structure, and Redistribution Policies*, ed. Calvin Goldsheider (Boulder: Westview Press, 1992), 137–58.

45. Edward J. Taylor, Phil L. Martin, and Michael Fix, *Poverty amid Prosperity: Immigration and the Changing Face of Rural California* (Washington, D.C.: The Urban Institute Press, 1997).

46. Authors' tabulations from U.S. 2000 Census microdata.

47. Dowell Myers, "The Impact of Ebbing Immigration in Los Angeles: New Insights from an Established Gateway" (paper presented at the Population Association of America, Philadelphia, April 2005) notes that some 400,000 long-term residents of Los Angeles left during the 1990s (pre-1990 arrivals from all countries, not just Mexico). Despite the significant growth of the Mexican population, he characterizes Los

Angeles as an "ebbing gateway" city which has meant some lessening of poverty and increasing homeownership for the average foreign-born resident.

48. Wayne A. Cornelius, "California Immigrants Today," in *California Immigrants in World Perspective: The Conference Papers* (Institute for Social Science Research, 1990), http://repositories.cdlib.org/issr/volume5/10; Enrico Marcelli and Wayne A. Cornelius, "The Changing Profile of Mexican Migrants to the United States: New Evidence from California and Mexico," *Latin American Research Review* 36, no. 3 (fall 2001): 105–31.

49. Jorge Durand, Douglas S. Massey, and Fernando Charvet, "The Changing Geography of Mexican Immigration to the United States: 1910–1996," *Social Science Quarterly* 81, no. 1 (2000): 1–15.

50. *Binational Study.*

51. Bean, Edmonston, and Passel, *Undocumented Migration to the United States;* Marcelli and Cornelius, "The Changing Profile of Mexican Migrants."

52. Shawn M. Kanaiaupuni, "Reframing the Migration Question: An Analysis of Men, Women and Gender in Mexico," *Social Forces* 78, no. 4 (June 2000): 1311–348.

53. Ivonne Szasz, "La Perspectiva de Género en el Estudio de la Migración Femenina en Mexico," in *Mujeres, Género, y Población en México,* ed. Brígida García (Mexico City: El Colegio de México/Sociedad Mexicana de Demografía, 1999), 167–210.

54. Ivonne Szasz, "La perspectiva de genero en el Estudio de la Migración."

55. Durand, Massey, and Charvet, "The Changing Geography of Mexican Immigration."

56. Authors' tabulations of the U.S. March Current Population Survey from various years; and of the Mexican *Conteo de Población,* 1995 (Mexico City: INEGI, 1996); ENADID (Mexico City: INEGI, 1997); *XII Censo General de Población y Vivienda 2000* (Mexico City: INEGI, 2000); and the ENE 2002 (Mexico City: INEGI, 2002).

57. We did not find substantive differences in the trend of relative female migration by age group.

58. Authors' tabulations of Mexican ENE 2002 data. This phenomenon also shows up in either U.S. or Mexican data when comparing, at one point in time, the female share of migrants by prior year of departure/arrival. Females are an increasing share of earlier arriving cohorts and a lesser share of the most recent arrived cohort. This reflects the fact that males are highly represented in the dynamic, circular migration flow and are captured as "recent migrants," but they have higher rates of return than females and so drop out of earlier-arrived cohorts of more stably resident women.

59. Unless otherwise attributed, figures in this paragraph are based on the authors' tabulations of ENE 2002 microdata.

60. See Marcela Cerrutti and Douglas S. Massey, "On the Auspices of Female Migration from Mexico to the United States," *Demography* 38, no. 2 (2001): 187–200.

61. Authors' tabulations from Mexican Census 2000 microdata.

62. In Mexico, current enrollment levels in grades 7–9 and 10–12 are even by gender. But among the population that has left school, the gender gap remains.

63. Nicole Stoops, "Educational Attainment in the United States: 2003," *Annual Social and Economic Supplement,* U.S. Census Bureau (2004): 20–550.

64. Author's tabulations from U.S. Census 2000 microdata.

65. Kanaiaupuni, "Reframing the migration question."

66. These are measures of "cumulative loss," e.g., the numerator is all Mexican-born migrants of given education in the U.S. and the denominator is the sum of Mexicans in Mexico and the United States.

67. The U.S. provided special numbers for legal family reunification with legalized persons, as well as the so-called 245-I provisions of U.S. law, which permitted additional unauthorized residents within the U.S. to petition for legal admission.

68. Research also indicates that while NAFTA did not restrain potential migration, it also did not appear to stimulate it. Bean and Lowell, "NAFTA and Mexican Migration."

2

The Mexican Economy and Mexico-U.S. Migration

A Macro Perspective

Francisco Alba, El Colegio de México

INTRODUCTION

Although the main analytical justification for the North American Free Trade Agreement (NAFTA) was the quest for better regional use of productive factors and resources derived from a reallocation of the respective nations' activities, the "political" acceptance of NAFTA, particularly in the United States, was based largely on the assumption (whether genuine or merely strategic) that trade liberalization would have significant collateral implications for the emigration of Mexicans to the United States. In their discussions and debates on NAFTA, the governments of Presidents Salinas and Bush, Sr. argued that by encouraging investment, creating employment, and raising incomes in Mexico, thus fostering economic convergence between the two countries, trade liberalization would discourage the flow of Mexicans to the United States.

NAFTA's terms of reference regarding the relations between trade, development, and migration are those of mainstream international economic theory, which postulate that trade liberalization produces a trend toward the equalization of the prices of productive factors within the economic area that is advancing toward integration, as a result of which, free movement of goods and capital acts as a substitute for the mobility of the labor force.[1] This position was at the basis of the international consensus, prevalent in the late 1980s and early 1990s, which posited that the countries' economic development depended on their integration into the world economy. The principal mechanism in the process that would narrow the gap between rich and poor countries would be investment, which, under conditions of openness to world markets, would flow toward the latter. Trade liberalization and investment flows, both domestic and foreign, would help create more jobs and increase wages, leading toward convergence with salary levels in other countries. This, in turn, would reduce the incentives that lead migrants to abandon their countries of origin.[2]

More than ten years after the ratification of NAFTA, the migratory issue continues to be highly controversial—both domestically and bilaterally—as are the implications of NAFTA and the opening up of the Mexican economy. As a matter of fact, the emigration of Mexicans to the United States continues to be one of the thorniest issues in the bilateral relationship, and the frequent subject of discrepancies and conflicts. One of the main complicating factors is undocumented migration, that which occurs outside of formal agreements between the two countries on the mobility of people and workers within North America, and on their rights and obligations. Unlike the "trade vision" embedded in the NAFTA accords, the agreement contains no comparable "migration vision."[3] Thus, partly in response to this situation, the two governments have engaged in dialogue and negotiations with the aim of finding mutually acceptable ways of dealing with the migration issue.

Within this context it is also important, and part and parcel of the issue, to bring into focus the determinants or driving forces that underlie this migratory phenomenon. Managing migration in the broad sense of the term, and from a long-term perspective, also implies dealing with the root causes of the phenomenon. It is from this perspective that the Mexican economy is examined here, as part of that which constitutes the "economic aspects of migrations." It is important to note, however, the behavior of the U.S. economy and its labor demands are also key constituent parts of these "economic aspects."

The most general framework for analyzing migration dynamics includes demand and supply factors, as well as their interaction (migration takes place as a response to conditions in both the country of origin and the destination country). In the countries of origin, economic conditions are difficult, to say the least, while in destination countries there is, in general, both an absolute and a relative scarcity of workers or, at least, of certain types of workers. However, most scholars also accept that once migration flows start they tend to continue, almost regardless of the economic conditions that gave rise to them in the first place, by virtue of the dynamics of the social networks that develop and the social capital that migrants and entrepreneurs accumulate (which also involve the countries of origin and destination). These conditions make it difficult for states to regulate migration.

In the following three sections, I attempt to provide an answer to this question: Are economic, demographic, social, and political conditions in Mexico and the United States conducive to the emergence and continuance of migration pressures and migratory flows from Mexico to the north? First, I review the record of the Mexican economy since the early 1980s, when the country adopted a new development path by abandoning the Import Substitution Industrialization (ISI strategy) and opening up its economy. Second, given that economic liberalization is assumed to produce effects of convergence between the integrating economies, the economic trends between Mexico and the United States are explored, looking specifically at the effect of closer economic integration on migration between Mexico and the United States. Third, in order to contextualize the potential of the current development path to produce significant changes in contemporary migration trends, the record of past development paths and Mexican migration is briefly reviewed.

A fourth section argues that NAFTA has influenced the migratory strategies implemented, and the responses provided, by governments since 1994. This section also briefly explores potential future developments in the management of the migratory issue, bearing in mind the terrorist attacks of September 11, 2001, and their consequences, events that have profoundly altered previously existing scenarios and contexts. A final section addresses some of the policy implications and recommendations that can be derived from a review of Mexico's economic conditions.

THE MEXICAN ECONOMY SINCE 1982

The main purpose of this section is to draw a picture of some of the principal macroeconomic variables of a non-monetary nature, the conditions of which affect migration decisions. Another objective is to examine the potentials and limitations in matters of economic growth and development that the Mexican economy has shown since its acceptance of the global challenge. It is not the purpose of this chapter to undertake an evaluation of this experience or to advocate a return to past policies; however, some lessons can be drawn from even a broad description of this record, with a view toward improving its performance.

The Mexican economy began to open up aggressively more than twenty years ago. According to other historical experiences (particularly in certain countries in Europe and Asia), this period is long enough to have had a significant impact on development change and people's lives (wellbeing). Against this background, the Mexican record is rather poor in many respects, or key dimensions, although not in others. This section attempts to explore this record.

This twenty-year period is divided into three subperiods in order to include the transition and consolidation stages of this new direction in Mexico's development strategy and political economy. These major periods are:

1982–1987	(Transition)
1987–1993	(Opening and Liberalization)
1994–present	(Free Trade in North America)

In addition, the last period is subdivided into two subperiods—1994–2000 and 2001–2006—to take into account the behavior of the Mexican economy once it achieved closer integration into much larger economies, particularly that of the United States.

The year 1982 marks a turning point in the political economy of Mexico's development, as it moved from a relatively closed to a relatively open economy. With Mexico's adherence to GATT in 1986, this new direction was locked in. Then, in 1994, NAFTA came into effect. Around the year 2000, economic growth began to slow in the U.S. There are two interesting coincidences here: in 1986, IRCA became an important piece of U.S. immigration law, and in 1993–1994, the physical closing of the U.S.-Mexico border became a key strategy for deterring unauthorized migrants from crossing into the United States.

Trends in GDP

Salient features: economic growth is weak and unstable; growth was fastest during the initial phase of NAFTA (1993–2000); the Mexican economy faltered (2000–2006), at a time when the economies of the partner countries slowed and there was lack of leadership in Mexico. The manufacturing sector best exemplifies the above features (see Table 2.1). For the

Table 2.1. Mexico: Gross Domestic Product by Selected Divisions of Economic Activity (Average annual growth rate)

	PERIOD				
	1982–1986	1986–1993	1993–2000	2000–2006	1982–2006
All divisions	−0.3	3.1	3.5	2.0	2.3
Farming, forestry, and fisheries	1.3	0.9	1.5	2.5	1.5
Manufacturing	−0.8	3.9	5.4	0.7	2.7
Construction	−5.9	3.9	1.8	2.6	1.3
Electricity, gas, and water	4.5	3.2	3.9	2.3	3.3
Commerce, restaurants, and hotels	−3.2	3.5	3.6	2.0	2.0
Transport, storage, and communication	0.4	3.7	6.4	6.0	4.5

Source: INEGI, "Databank of Economic Information," Instituto Nacional de Estadística Geografía e Informática, http://dgcnesyp.inegi.gob.mx.

entire 1982–2006 period, the average GDP annual growth rate of 2.3 percent translated into approximately a mere 0.5 percent growth in *per capita* terms.

Demographic Trends

Demographic growth was still relatively fast in Mexico in the 1980s and 1990s, totaling an average of 1.7 percent annually in the latter decade (see Table 2.2). For the same period in the United States, meanwhile, the average annual growth rate was just 1.1 percent. However, the rate registered in Mexico is lower than the real index of its natural growth, due to emigration (while that of the United States is proportionally higher, due to immigration). The estimated natural population growth rate in Mexico for the 1990s is in the range of 2.0 percent annually (almost three times that of the estimated U.S. rate of 0.7 percent).[4]

However, even more significant than the growth rates of the total population is the expansion of the working-age population (usually between the ages of fifteen and sixty-five) and. more particularly, of the population between fifteen and forty-four, among whom there is a greater propensity to migrate. During the 1990s, this latter population group grew at a mean annual rate above 2.0 percent (as opposed to just 0.3 percent in the United States). As shown in Table 2.2, the absolute increase of this population group in Mexico approached 10 million in the 1990s (vs. less than 4 million in the United States). However, Mexican demographic trends are expected to slow down significantly in the early decades of the twenty-first century (see Tables 2.2 and 2.17).

Labor Market Conditions

Formal private sector employment follows the trends of GDP, but its fluctuations are more pronounced. Employment creation (3.6 percent, as shown in Table 2.3) in this sector of economic activity falls within the range of the growth of the population in the fifteen to sixty-four age group; however, that rate of formal private employment creation did little to absorb all those who entered the economically active population, not to mention its scant impact on the trends of those employed in informal occupations.

Wages in Mexico have shown an uneven record since the restructuring and opening of the economy. For the 1982–2006 period, the record is dismal (see Table 2.4), while during the NAFTA subperiod (1994–2006) it is somewhat mixed: in the early years (1993–2000), wage contraction continued strong, although during the later years of this subperiod (2000–2006) the contraction was only slight. However, there was some improvement of

Table 2.2. Mexico: Total Population by Age Groups, 1980–2005 (thousands)

Age groups	Year					
	1980	1985	1990	1995	2000	2005
	Population					
TOTAL	67,569	75,464	83,225	91,143	98,933	106,943
0–14	30,494	31,926	32,089	32,759	33,465	33,161
15–44	27,924	32,992	38,804	43,889	48,124	52,772
45–64	6,587	7,747	9,038	10,584	12,608	15,378
65 and more	2,564	2,799	3,295	3,913	4,737	5,630
15–64	34,511	40,739	47,842	54,473	60,732	68,150

Mexico: Total Populations by Age Groups, 1980–2005 (average annual rate of change %)

Age groups	1980–1985	1985–1990	1990–1995	1995–2000	2000–2005
			Rate		
TOTAL	2.23	1.98	1.83	1.65	1.57
0–14	0.92	0.10	0.41	0.43	-0.18
15–44	3.39	3.30	2.49	1.86	1.86
45–64	3.30	3.13	3.21	3.56	4.05
65 and more	1.77	3.32	3.50	3.90	3.51
15–64	3.37	3.27	2.63	2.20	2.33

Source: United Nations, *World Population Prospects: The 2002 Revision, Vol. II: The Sex and Age Distribution of Populations* (New York: United Nations Population Division, 2002). For 2005, CELADE, http://www.eclac/cl/celade/ proyecciones/ basededatos-BD.htm.

Table 2.3. Permanent Employees Registered in the IMSS (Mexican Social Security Institute) by Selected Sectors of Economic Activity (average annual growth rate)

	PERIOD				
	1982–1986	1986–1993	1993–2000	2000–2006	1982–2006
All sectors	4.3	4.0	5.5	0.5	3.6
Farming, forestry and fisheries	−1.1	−3.1	−0.8	−1.2	−1.6
Manufacturing	3.4	2.8	6.2	−3.3	2.3
Construction	6.2	11.0	18.1	4.9	10.7
Electricity, gas, and water	1.4	2.6	4.5	1.0	2.5
Commerce, restaurants and hotels	3.9	4.2	4.3	1.5	3.5
Transport, storage, and communication	2.1	2.9	4.2	1.1	2.6

Source: Own elaboration with data from IMSS, http://www.inegi.gob.mx.

the wages among workers in the formal economy (see Table 2.5). This seems paradoxical, because of an apparent disconnect between the behavior of wages and that of the economy.[5]

In 2000, permanent employment in the formal private sector represented close to one quarter of the total economically active population (estimated at 40 million people). However, as can be inferred from the figures in Table 2.6, labor market conditions are rather poor for the majority of the Mexican population.

Table 2.4. Mexico: Real Minimum Wage (1994 pesos)

Period	Average Annual Growth Rate
1982–1986	−7.7
1986–1993	−5.7
1993–2000	−3.7
2000–2006	−0.2
1982–2006	24.1

Source: Own elaboration with data from Comisión Nacional de los Salarios Mínimos (CONASAMI), http://www.conasami.gob.mx/.

Table 2.5.   Wages of Permanent Workers Affiliated to the IMSS (average annual growth rates)

	1994–2000	*2000–2006*	*1994–2006*
All sectors	−3.4	2.8	−0.3
Farming, forestry, and fisheries	−4.0	0.4	−1.8
Manufacturing	−3.6	4.5	0.5
Construction	−5.0	5.8	0.4
Electricity, gas, and water	−1.6	4.2	1.3
Commerce, restaurants, and hotels	−4.1	4.1	0.0
Transport, storage, and communication	−3.5	1.4	−1.1

Source: Own elaboration with data from STPS, http://www.stps.gob.mx/.

NAFTA, Investment, and Regional Disparities in Mexico

The passage of NAFTA has effectively translated into significant changes in Mexico's commercial trends. According to many observers, and the promoters of the agreement themselves, the evolution of commercial trends has exceeded even the most optimistic expectations.[6]

The growing importance of trade in the Mexican economy can be gauged by comparing, for the 1984–2001 period, the rates of growth of international trade (exports and imports)—which averaged over 10 percent (in real terms)—with those of other key economic variables, such as private consumption, which grew by just over 3 percent (in real terms), or investments, which increased by over 5 percent (in real terms). At the same time, bank financing decreased by approximately 5 percent (also in real terms). The growing internationalization of the Mexican economy is also reflected in the rising percentage of foreign trade (exports and imports) in relation to total GDP. In 1993, foreign trade totaled 88 billion

Table 2.6.   Mexico: Labor Market Conditions

	1991–1993	*1995–2000*
Open unemployment	2.3	2.7
Employed at less than minimum	31.7	32.5
Employed part-time	21.9	16.81
Employed without Social Security	62.2	63.9

Source: Brígida García, "Medición del empleo y el desempleo. Indicadores complementarios," *DEMOS: Carta demográfica sobre México*, no. 5 (2002): 5–6.

Table 2.7. Distribution of Mexican Exports and Imports by Country

	Exports		Imports	
Year	U.S.	Year	U.S.	Canada
1990	79.2	0.6	74.6	1
1993	82.7	3	69.3	1.8
2000	88.7	2	73.1	2.3
2006	84.9	2.1	51.1	2.9

Source: Mexican Ministry of Economy, http://www.economia.gob.mx/

dollars, accounting for 22 percent of GDP, whereas by 2006 it had risen to 506 billion dollars and accounted for 60 percent of GDP. Trade liberalization has thus effectively proven to be an important factor in Mexico's development path.

It should also be noted that, since NAFTA came into effect, the share of Mexico's exports to the U.S. has increased to very high levels, while imports from the United States have declined as a significant share of total imports (see Table 2.7). This divergent trend explains the huge trade surplus vis-à-vis the United States. Since NAFTA was introduced, imports from Canada to Mexico have gained relevance.

The changes in the composition of Mexico's exports indicate that, to a significant degree, the objectives pursued have been achieved, namely a deepening of the manufacturing sector's integration into the world economy (see Table 2.8). In this process, the "maquila industry" continues to play a very important role. However the profound structural transformation of Mexico's exports has, so far, not translated into an equivalent transformation of Mexico's pattern of economic growth, with favorable domestic implications, either in terms of economic dynamism or distribution, as Mexico's economy continues to be highly segmented and predominantly low-wage.

Another one of NAFTA's objectives was to increase the flow of direct foreign investment toward Mexico. This has in fact taken place, as shown in Table 2.9. Current annual FDI averages more than ten times the levels at the beginning of the opening up of the economy, and today's levels are several times higher than the pre-NAFTA ones. Table 2.9 also shows that FDI in the manufacturing sector has grown at a more stable pace. However, the shares of U.S. and Canadian FDI have not changed significantly, as shown in the second half of Table 2.9.

It is interesting to note that in the context of the opening up of the Mexican economy, and specifically since NAFTA, FDI seems to be associated with increasing regional disparities inside the country,[7] though this association may well have existed before the opening up of the economy.

Table 2.8. Distribution of Mexican Exports (Millions of constant 1994 dollars, mean by period)

	PERIOD				
	1982–1986	*1987–1994*	*1995–2000*	*2001–2003*	*2004–2006**
Total exports	37,031	46,499	106,895	132,713	217,409
Without Maquila	30,771	29,244	60,182	68,965	—
Without Oil	16,694	37,343	97,050	120,165	185,883
Without Maquila and Oil	10,434	20,088	50,337	56,417	—
Manufacturing	13,591	34,427	93,037	116,384	178,573
Maquila Industry	6,261	17,255	46,713	63,748	—
Traditional	7,330	17,172	46,324	52,636	—

Source: Own elaboration with data from the Mexican Ministry of Economy, http://www.economia.gob.mx/
*For 2004–2006 current U.S. dollars

Distribution of Mexican Exports

	PERIOD				
	1982–1986	*1987–1994*	*1995–2000*	*2001–2003*	*2004–2006**
Without Maquila	83.1	62.9	56.3	52	—
Without Oil	45.1	80.3	90.8	90.5	85.4
Without Maquila and Oil	28.2	43.2	47.1	42.5	—
Manufacturing	36.7	74	87	87.7	82.1
Maquila Industry	16.9	37.1	43.7	48	—
Traditional	19.8	36.9	43.3	39.7	—

Source: Own elaboration with data from the Mexican Ministry of Economy, http://www.economia.gob.mx/.
*For 2004–2006 current U.S. dollars

The state-by-state analysis of FDI in Mexico during the period 1994–2003 provides an indirect approach to the issue of the effects of NAFTA on Mexico's regional development, assuming that this investment has been made largely as a component of trade liberalization. The distribution of FDI by state (excluding the Federal District) is positively and significantly associated with variables such as manufacturing occupation, educational achievement, and telephone lines per inhabitant, variables that are among the indicators most commonly used to measure economic conditions, human resources, and infrastructure.[8] The correlation between FDI and Gross State Product *per capita* is also positive and significant. Further, a positive association was found between FDI and the North Zone of Mexico, a dummy variable intended to explicitly capture the effects of proximity to the United States.[9]

Table 2.9. FDI (Foreign Direct Investment) in Mexico, 1982–2006 (U.S. Dollars) (Millions, annual average)

Period	Total	Manufacturing
1982–1986	1,378.6	1,066.5
1987–1994	4,497.9	2,023.5
1995–2000	11,778.3	6,762.5
2001–2006	20,036.6	9,094.1

Foreign Direct Investment, 1982–2006 (distribution %)

Period	U.S.	Canada	Rest of the World
1982–1986	60	2	38
1987–1994	57.1	3.1	39.7
1995–2000	64.2	3.7	32.1
2001–2006	60.2	2.2	37.6
1982–2006	60.2	2.7	36.8

Sources: Mexican Ministry of Economy
1982–1983: http://www.inegi.gob.mx
1994–2006: http://www.economia.gob.mx/
Own elaboration with data from the National Institute of Statistics, Geography and Informatics (INEGI), http://www.inegi.gob.mx.
For the years 1994–2006: >Statistical information>Bank of economic information (BIE)> Consult by Subject >Direct foreign investment> By country> Past method
For the years 1982–1993: >Statistical information>Bank of economic information(BIE)> Consult by Subject >Direct foreign investment> By country> New method.

The spatial rearrangement of productive activities due to the opening up of the economy and NAFTA has presumably concentrated more opportunities for development in the north and in certain areas of the center of the country, while placing the rest of Mexico, particularly the south, at a disadvantage with regard to occupational opportunities in modern sectors and local possibilities for economic and social mobility. The above analysis suggests that the policies of economic liberalization and NAFTA are acting as elements of a regressive domestic regional policy that favors the states with greater resource availability and lower transaction and information costs. Thus, these policies have not proven particularly effective in fostering the development of the more backward states, or in offsetting preexisting regional imbalances.[10] This is hardly surprising, however, since the Mexican economy as a whole is profoundly heterogeneous in terms of infrastructure, social, and human capital.[11]

NAFTA and Migration

Mexican and U.S. positions coincided in their expectation that NAFTA would trigger a tendency toward economic convergence that would struc-

Table 2.10.   Correlation Matrix of Variables Related to FDI (Data for 31 Mexican states, Federal District excluded)

	FDI	GSP	MEAP	PRIM	NZ	TEL
FDI	1					
GSP	0.7118***					
	0.0000	1				
MEAP	0.4889***	0.3826**				
	0.0039	0.025565	1			
PRIM	0.6553***	0.7055***	0.5685***			
	0.000038	0.000005	0.000568	1		
NZ	0.6735***	0.5062***	0.3720**	0.5746***		
	0.00002	0.002561	0.031983	0.000482	1	
TEL	0.8149***	0.7430***	0.4679***	0.8262***	0.6067***	
	0.0000	0.000001	0.005739	0	0.00019	1

FDI   Foreign Direct Investment per thousand inhabitants.
       By the author with data from XII Censo General de Población y Vivienda (INEGI, 2000) for popula-
       tion, and data from the Mexican Ministry of Economy, Dirección General de Inversión Extranjera for
       foreign direct investment.
GSP   Gross State Product per capita in Mexican pesos. By the author with data from XII Censo General de
       Población y Vivienda (INEGI, 2000) for population, and INEGI.
MEAP   Percentage of population working in manufacturing.
PRIM   Percentage of population 15 years and older or more who completed primary school.
NZ   States in the north of Mexico: Baja California, Baja California Sur, Coahuila, Chihuahua, Durango,
Nuevo León, Sinaloa, Sonora and Tamaulipas.
TEL   Number of telephone lines per thousand inhabitants.

***Significant at 1%
** Significant at 5%
* Significant at 10%

turally transform the Mexican economy, as a result of which the emigration of Mexican workers toward the U.S. would eventually diminish. However, the evolution of *per capita* production in these two countries—the most general indicator of comparison—does not suggest that NAFTA has yet produced any tendency toward convergence at all. In 1993—in terms of 1990 U.S. dollars—per capita production in Mexico was equivalent to 14.3 percent of U.S. production, while in 2000, the index for Mexico was equivalent to just 13.5 percent of the U.S. figure. In 2006, this diminished even further, to only 13.0 percent. The first part of Table 2.11 presents estimates of per capita production in Mexico, the United States, and Canada, in terms of 1990 U.S. dollars, for various years between 1982 and 2006, while the second part of Table 2.11 exhibits the ratio of per capita production in Mexico in relation to that of the other two countries.

However, a more significant comparison might be one based on *per capita* production estimated in terms of purchasing power parity.[12] On the basis of this indicator, in 1993, per capita production in Mexico was equivalent to 28 percent of the U.S. figure, but by 2005, it had decreased to 25.8 percent.

Table 2.11.   GDP per capita, 1982–2006 (1990 U.S. dollars)

Year	Canada	Mexico	U.S.
1982	17,487	3,352	17,877
1986	19,518	3,021	20,629
1993	20,197	3,288	22,931
2000	24,923	3,730	27,712
2006	27,889	3,997	30,634

Source: Own elaboration with data from IMF, Global Econ Data >IMF International Financial Statistics, http://www.un.org/, and U.N., Economic and Social Development >UNSTATS>National Accounts Main Aggregates Database/Data Selection, http://unstats.un.org/unsd/default.htm.

Per Capita GDP in Mexico as a Percentage of U.S. and Canadian GDP

Year	Canada	U.S.
1982	19.2	18.8
1986	15.5	14.6
1993	16.3	14.3
2000	15.0	13.5
2006	14.3	13.0

Source: Own elaboration with data from IMF, Global Econ Data >IMF International Financial Statistics, http://www.un.org/, and U.N., Economic and Social Development >UNSTATS>National Accounts Main Aggregates Database/Data Selection, http://unstats.un.org/unsd/default.htm.

Table 2.12 "explains" the main factor that accounts for the above behavior: the fact that the Mexican economy has been growing at a slower pace than those of its partners, even though just the opposite had been expected; i.e., if regional economic convergence was really the goal, then Mexico should have grown more rapidly. This unexpected and adverse behavior is observed for the entire 1982–2006 period, as well as for the two NAFTA subperiods.

Nonetheless, isolating the effects of NAFTA on the process of convergence among the member countries from other factors is no easy methodological task, particularly in the context of national economies with very different behaviors.[13] During the 1990s, the U.S. economy experienced one of its longest cycles of prolonged growth, while Mexico's underwent broad restructuring and experienced a profound crisis at mid-decade.[14] Indeed, the events of 1994 and 1995—political assassinations, Zapatista uprising, and peso devaluation—and their consequences weighed heavily upon the subsequent evolution of the macroeconomic aggregates of the Mexican economy.[15]

Table 2.12.   Per Capita, GDP 1982–2006 (average annual growth rate)

Period	Canada	Mexico	U.S.
1982–1986	2.8	−2.6	3.6
1986–1993	0.5	1.2	1.5
1993–2000	3	1.8	2.7
2000–2006	1.9	1.0	1.7
1982–2006	2.0	0.9	2.2

Source: Own elaboration with data from United Nations and the International Monetary Found, Global Econ Data >IMF International Financial Statistics, http://www.un.org/, and http://unstats.un.org/unsd/default.htm

Regarding the convergence issue, the different trends of wages in the United States and Mexico are certainly worth noting. Wages have stagnated, or even declined, in the United States during the past two decades, as is the case of the minimum wage (see Table 2.13), which remained static between 1997 and 2007. Table 2.14 reveals that U.S. wages in important industrial sectors where sizeable numbers of Mexican workers obtain employment—such as manufacturing, construction, and the service sector—have remained relatively stable. Both of these trends contrast with the deteriorating situation in Mexico since the early 1980s, as shown previously (see Tables 2.4 and 2.5).[16]

Although trends in international trade can be downplayed and their role qualified, trade has undoubtedly played a significant role in changing the Mexican economy. The assumptions implicit in NAFTA led both governments to expect that this development would have a restricting influence on migration. Migratory trends, however, have failed to develop as expected, and still reflect much greater continuity than change when compared to the trends observed prior to the passage of NAFTA. Permanent emigration continues to rise and the geographical origin of migrants has expanded well be-

Table 2.13.   U.S. Minimum Wage (dollars 1994)

Period	Average Annual Rate of Change (%)
1982–1986	−3.1
1986–1993	−0.5
1993–2000	0.2
2000–2006	−2.4
1982–2006	−1.3

Source: Own elaboration with data from the Department of Labor, http://www.bls.gov/home.htm

Table 2.14. U.S. Change in Real Average Hourly Earnings of Production Workers (average annual rate of growth)

Period	Construction	Manufacturing	Leisure and Hospitality
1982–1986	0.24	−0.69	−0.25
1987–1994	−0.92	−1.41	−0.74
1995–2000	0.39	0.76	1.31
2001–2006	1.75	2.18	2.14
1982–2006	0.31	0.18	0.59

Source: U.S. Department of Labor, http://www.bls.gov/home.htm.

yond traditional emigration regions to include other areas of the country that have only recently become incorporated into migratory flows, and where this phenomenon is rapidly becoming consolidated.

At the same time, the heterogeneity and diversification of migrants' work and occupational experience has also been increasing, though these emerging dynamics have certainly not replaced the "older" components of migration, such as circularity, the traditional areas of origin, and the peasant element.[17]

As for the geographical origin of migrants, some authors prefer to highlight the still considerable relative importance of traditional migrant-sending regions,[18] while others emphasize the growing territorial expansion of migration in the context of the continuity of the phenomenon itself.[19] In any case, given its increasing extension migration has clearly become a national phenomenon, as can be deduced from Table 2.15.

Migrants now come from urban areas as well as rural zones, and not only from the agricultural sector but also from industry and the service sector. While in the United States, they engage in unskilled, semi-skilled, and even highly skilled jobs, as their levels of education are rather heterogeneous (see Table 2.16). It seems that emigration now affects, albeit to varying degrees, the entire spectrum of the country's social and occupational groups.

In short, NAFTA does not appear to have had a significant effect on either the economic convergence between the two countries or on reducing the flow of Mexicans towards the United States, though it must be recognized that both of these aims were difficult to achieve in any case. Regarding the first aim, the explanation is probably related to factors associated with Mexico's very low economic growth, such as the lack of a sustained structural transformation and of fiscal and other policies geared toward strengthening economic activity. With respect to the second aim, it was never going to be an easy task to transform a deeply rooted, well-established migratory system, such as the one that exists between Mexico and the United States.

The modification of this complex migratory system was a very ambitious purpose imposed on NAFTA and trade liberalization, neither of

Table 2.15.   Mexico: The Ten Principal Migrant–Sending States

1968–1970[a]		1993–1994[b]	
State of Residence	*Percentage*	*State of Residence*	*Percentage**
Chihuahua	18.5	Guanajuato	12.9
Durango	9.9	Michoacán	10.8
Michoacán	8.3	Chihuahua	9.6
Guanajuato	8.3	Jalisco	8
Jalisco	7.5	Zacatecas	7
San Luis Potosí	7.3	Coahuila	5.4
Zacatecas	6.9	Durango	5.3
Nuevo León	6.1	Sinaloa	4.7
Tamaulipas	5.1	Tamaulipas	4
Coahuila	4.9	Oaxaca	3.8
Others	17.2	Others	28.4

[a]Source: Julián Samora, *Los Mojados. The Wetback Story* (University of Notre Dame Press, 1971).
[b]Source: *Encuesta sobre Migración en la Frontera Norte de México* (Secretaría del Trabajo y Previsión Social / Consejo Nacional de Población / El Colegio de la Frontera Norte, 1993–1994)
*Migrants over 12 years old

Ten States with the Highest Number of Migrants Who Did Not Return from the United States (1995–2000)

State of Residence	*Percentage*
Guanajuato	10.6
Jalisco	10.4
Michoacán	10.4
México	8.2
Veracruz	5.3
Guerrero	5.1
Puebla	4.8
San Luis Potosí	4.2
Zacatecas	4.1
Hidalgo	4
Others	32.9

Source: CONAPO's estimates based on 10 percent sample of the *XII Censo General de Población y Vivienda 2000* (INEGI, 2000).

which addressed the necessary changes in the broader socioeconomic environment, nor in other sector-specific policies, in either Mexico or the United States.[20]

In addition to the abundant supply of Mexican workers, the system's enormous dynamism is based on the sustained demand for immigrant workers by the U.S. economy, fueled both by structural demand and by conjunctural demand during the up side of the economic cycles.[21] The United States created 15 million new jobs between 1993 and the year 2000.[22]

Table 2.16.   Selected Characteristics of Mexican Migrants (around 2000)

Sector of activity in U.S. (%)*	
Primary	12.1
Secondary	36.6
Tertiary	51.2
Permanent migrants' level of education (%)**	
Less than elementary school	18.8
Elementary school	23.8
High school and higher	57.3
Temporary migrants' level of education (%)**	
Less than elementary school	28.9
Elementary school	25.6
High school and higher	45.6

Source: *Conapo estimates based on Bureau of Census, *Current Population Survey (CPS)*, 2000
** Conapo estimates based on STyPS, CONAPO, INM, and COLEF, *Encuesta sobre migración en la Frontera Norte de México (EMIF)* (Secretaría del Trabajo y Previsión Social /Consejo Nacional de Población / El Colegio de la Frontera Norte, 1998–1999, 1999–2000, and 2000–2001).

Throughout that period, U.S. economic growth was sustained and dynamic, rising to nearly 4 percent between 1994 and 2000.

In addition to the economic forces and demographic factors that create extremely strong migratory pressures, the enormous inertial momentum of the social relations associated with mature migratory systems and their broad social networks based on family and community also point toward the continuity of Mexican migratory flows.[23]

The inertial momentum of Mexican migration increased substantially precisely during the 1990s, as a legacy of the Immigration Reform and Control Act (IRCA) of 1986, which enabled over two million Mexicans to regularize their migratory status. As a large part of this population became either permanent immigrants or U.S. citizens, they also acquired rights related to immigration, such as the right to sponsor family members as immigrants, and to "family reunification" in general. With time, these circumstances permitted a constant influx of Mexican population into the United States that reinforced the "transnationalism" of family and social networks.[24]

The continuity of migration, and its increase in the years since NAFTA, is not, however, incompatible with the expected migratory results, as long as it is a transitory phase. The transitory nature of an increase in migration has been described as a "migratory hump," since migratory flows initially rise above their traditional trajectory (as a result of closer economic integration associated with significant processes of economic restructuring and the availability of higher incomes, which make it possible to afford migration) only to decline subsequently (in the medium and long term) once a certain threshold of economic development has been crossed.[25]

However, more than ten years after the implementation of NAFTA, there is still no indication of any downward change in migration trends, other than the one probably associated with the slow-down in the U.S. economy in 2001–2004, or the more recent downward trend arguably associated with stringent measures to curb nonauthorized immigration. One could argue, then, that trade liberalization has been insufficient or incapable of significantly modifying the factors that contribute to Mexican-U.S. patterns of migration, and that economic integration has been insufficient to transform the current Mexican economy based, as indeed it is, on low wages.

PUTTING THINGS IN PERSPECTIVE

The future trajectories—some uncertain, others more predictable—of the factors that underpin Mexico-U.S. migration patterns suggest the continuity of powerful migration pressures in the medium- to long-term. On the U.S. side, most observers agree that the structural demand for immigrant workers will continue in the immediate future. By the same token, if the weakness and stagnation of Mexico's economic growth persist and no solution is found to overcoming its low capacity for absorbing labor despite its high degree of integration into the U.S. economy, then strong migratory pressures will persist.[26] Looking toward the immediate future, the persistence of profound economic and social asymmetries between the two countries (as well as the intensity of their trans-border social relations) will continue to influence migratory outcomes in the context of the growing integration and interdependence of Mexico and the United States.

Thus, the basic scenario regarding migration pressures and trends would seem to be "more of the same." This scenario is made all the more credible if one looks back and adopts a long historical perspective. With the exception of only a few years, Mexican migration to the U.S. was a constant during the twentieth century. Moving closer to current conditions, the long period of stable and sustained economic growth and development in Mexico (1940s to 1960s) was accompanied by migration to the United States. Later, the shorter—but unstable and unsustainable—period of high economic growth in the 1970s, was also accompanied by migration. Finally, since the 1980s, as shown in previous sections, the weak, unstable economic growth and poor development record experienced since the opening up of the economy and the implementation of NAFTA have also been accompanied by migration.

Certainly, the intensity, trends, and patterns of migration have all changed through these periods. In the first, most migrants came from a relatively well-circumscribed area in west-central Mexico. Those workers were temporary migrants and the phenomenon was sustained and characterized by a circular movement. During the second epoch, this rotating pattern began to change toward one of longer stays and more permanent migration. In the third phase, this "permanent" character has been consolidated at the same time as the spread of the migratory experience has attained national proportions in both countries.

The possibility of a different scenario—one of diminishing migration pressures—will depend on drastically modified economic and development patterns in Mexico (and on equally novel measures and policies in the United States). But even assuming that a new development path takes hold, its effects on the factors underling migration will take some time to materialize. For this reason, it is time to begin charting a new course, and the sooner the better.

The outlook for demographic factors is more predictable. The demographic context is prone to create migratory pressures for at least two more decades, given the differentials in population trends in the two countries. Mexico's population in the fifteen to forty-four age group will increase by 1.6 percent annually in the first decade of the twenty-first century (see Table 2.17), much more quickly than the corresponding sector of the U.S. population, which is estimated to grow at just 0.2 percent. The absolute increase in this group in the first decade will be over 7 million people in Mexico, compared to just above 2 million in the United States.

The increases in Mexico's working-age population will certainly be less significant in the second and third decades. That larger population group, however, will continue to be an important factor in creating migration pressures in the future, as Mexico's working-age population will increase from 60 million in 2000 to 85 million in 2020 (see Table 2.18).

Table 2.17.   Population Growth Rates (annual average)

	PERIOD				
Age Groups	*1980–1985*	*1990–1995*	*2000–2005*	*2010–2015*	*2020–2025*
TOTAL	2.23	1.83	1.46	1.09	0.74
15–44	3.39	2.49	1.63	0.91	−0.002
45–64	3.3	3.21	3.99	3.32	2.7
15–64	3.37	2.63	2.14	1.53	0.84

Source: United Nations, *World Population Prospects, The 2002 Revision, Vol. II* (New York: United Nations Population Division, 2002), 616–17.

Table 2.18.   Mexico: Population by Age Group (thousands)

Age Groups	1980	1990	2000	2010	2020
TOTAL	67,569	83,225	98,933	113,320	125,176
15–44	27,924	38,804	48,124	55,808	59,230
45–64	6,587	9,038	12,608	18,242	25,451
15–64	34,511	47,842	60,732	74,050	84,681

Source: United Nations, *World Population Prospects: The 2002 Revision, Vol. II: The Sex and Age Distribution of Populations* (New York: United Nations Population Division, 2002), 616–617.

NAFTA AND RESPONSES TO MIGRATION

NAFTA created an important institutional framework for the economic integration of the three member countries. Moreover, since its implementation in 1994, NAFTA's influence has permeated the migratory relations and discussions that have taken place between Mexico and the United States.[27]

As a result of this agreement, various currents of opinion in Mexico hold that trade and investment liberalization should be accompanied by a liberalization of labor or, at least, that Mexican migration should be the object of negotiations and agreements.[28] A variant of this opinion is a position that considers that once governments and societies accept the realities of greater economic integration (which usually include trade and investment, as in the case of NAFTA), subsequent events will lead to a more open attitude toward the liberalization of the mobility of persons and workers—in this case, of the Mexican labor force.[29]

Later, the institutionalization of a "migratory dialogue" under the Zedillo and Clinton administrations was credited with transforming the context of Mexican-U.S. relations that began with the constructive engagement of the two nations during the NAFTA negotiating process and thereafter.[30] However, the migratory dialogue notwithstanding, the Clinton administration unilaterally started and consolidated the strategy of "border enforcement" to deter unauthorized migrants from entering U.S. territory.

Without NAFTA, it would have been much more difficult for the United States and Mexico to sit down at the negotiating table to discuss migration. NAFTA facilitated the acknowledgement, on the part of the United States, of the existence of sustained demand for Mexican migrant workers and of their contribution to the economy. This, in turn, justified the appropriateness of engaging in negotiations.[31] In 2001, the two presidents met for the first time, after elections in the U.S. and Mexico, and agreed to initiate negotiations. The so-called "Guanajuato Proposal" explicitly suggests "reaching short- and long-term agreements . . . that will enable migration to be dealt with constructively . . . " and pledges to establish "an orderly scheme of migratory flows . . . "

This proposal also states the need to pay particular attention to efforts aimed at "reducing the economic gap between, and within, both societies, and consolidating a North American economic community that will benefit the less developed zones of the region and the most vulnerable social groups."

However, the bilateral relationship was substantially affected by the events of September 11, 2001, which caused the United States to shift its priorities toward national security concerns, border security, and the fight against terrorism. The whole question of migration has experienced a return of sorts to the largely ineffectual responses and policies that both countries maintained in the past. Attempts to pass comprehensive immigration legislation that would have, in addition to helping secure and control U.S. borders, included temporary workers programs and some mechanisms to bring into the open many of those undocumented Mexican migrants who are already part and parcel of the U.S. economy and society, have failed.

Policy Implications and Recommendations

The analysis presented in the previous sections suggests that dynamic migratory trends and strong pressures will frame the possibilities (efficacy) of any policy options regarding the management of migration. In other words, once an objective for migration is established (whatever it may be) policy options will have to be commensurate with the existing and estimated migratory pressures.

There is every indication (based on the analysis of the Mexican economy, of the role of demand forces in the United States, and of the strong cumulative causation that is already built into current Mexico-U.S. migration) that migratory pressures will continue to be very strong in the near future. In such circumstances, and given the social and political circumstances and perceptions in the U.S. regarding undocumented migration, one can only assume that the issue of managing migration will fall somewhere between two "extreme scenarios." The first of these would include a migration objective of "zero tolerance" (though not necessarily zero migration), while the second assumes some kind of "borderless economic space." Between these two scenarios, a "realistic" or "compromise" scenario could be one based on the primary migration objective of attempting to phase down and abate massive migratory flows.

In support of this realistic scenario one could enlist at least three important considerations. The first has to do with the acceptance of the current situation and of the multiple causes behind it that endow it with a built-in momentum. The second consideration refers to the clear need to bring these flows into some kind of order. Finally, the third consideration relates to recognizing that there are limits to the public policies that states can implement with respect to migration issues (as in other domains) and that, therefore, sufficient "avenues for migration" should exist within the system.[32]

In such a realistic scenario, the success in reaching the stated objective of *gradually* reducing nonauthorized flows implies a multidimensional and multiphase strategy—in other words, a complex set of policies to manage migration.

What, then, can be said regarding the proposals being made in the United States, particularly from the perspective of what the Mexican government should attempt to do? One major implication is that any pragmatic and realistic approach should be of a bilateral nature, with both governments considering and weighing the consequences that would occur if they do not act together. Another is that a "gradualist approach" should dominate the strategies, policies, and measures of the two governments. However, U.S. discussions in Congress and elsewhere are being carried out in an atmosphere of unilateral attitudes and actions.

Under normal circumstances, managing migration implies achieving migratory flows that are legal, orderly, and safe, because access to U.S. labor market is neither free nor unlimited today, and probably will not be so in the near future. Under these scenarios, there is a clear preference in the United States for temporary workers. Realistic policies must, therefore, take into account these opportunities and constraints. In this context, the priority should be given to institutionalize rules for the orderly flow of temporary workers. In that way, Mexico would be ready to take advantage of the opportunities—even limited ones—that will be available if changes are made in U.S. immigration laws, particularly regarding temporary worker programs.

Currently, a substantial portion of the demand for additional workers in the U.S. economy is no longer of a temporary nature, though this does not mean that the U.S. society and government are willing to bring in new workers as "permanent" migrants or immigrants. On this point, however, there is a potential contradiction, as many of the additional jobs created by a growing U.S. economy are of a "permanent" nature whereas newcomers would arrive with limited-time visas. This implies that the United States can by no means take for granted the volume of this flow of rotating temporary workers. Indeed, to rely exclusively on such a rotating system to fill those permanent jobs would be a risky venture. Thus, provisions should be made for those migrants who qualify, under certain rules, to become permanent residents and immigrants, if they wish to do so and if they comply with the established regulations.

In this context, the Mexican government should be willing to play according to any new rules that are established, notwithstanding that there certainly is, and will probably be in the near future, an oversupply of candidates who are willing to work, either temporarily or permanently, in the U.S. This means a willingness on the part of the Mexican government to assure that those migrant workers who leave the country have the proper documentation. The Mexican government must be well aware that any avenues for migration—negotiated or not—may well put additional pressure on Mexican labor markets, as any agreed ceiling would almost certainly involve smaller numbers of workers than the current number of potential migrants.

Regarding the Mexican population that already lives in the United States, it is clear that the Mexican economy has nowhere near the capacity to absorb most of them in a productive and orderly manner. From an economic point of view, it is also clear that the great majority of those who now work in the United States, even if undocumented and unauthorized, perform all sorts of normal and regular jobs. Regularizing such populations (or large portions of them) should not represent any major problem for the U.S. economy, because it is already functioning with those people as part of its available labor supply, or as a component of its labor markets. Regularization is, of course, a decision of a very delicate political and social nature.

The above policy recommendations—derived primarily from economic considerations—address some of the important questions regarding broad aspects of Mexico–U.S. migration management. However, it is also clear from these same economic considerations that, given the very long historical interdependence of the Mexican and U.S. economies and labor markets, bringing migration to more manageable volumes implies some common strategy or shared strategies for development in Mexico, if the long-term aim is, indeed, to gradually disengage those secular labor and migration relations, and to reduce current migration flows.

From a development perspective, Mexico must do a great deal more, and adopt an explicit policy to "absorb" its workers and citizens and deactivate a deeply entrenched emigration mentality. In general, Mexico's development experience in the twentieth century shows that all the different development periods and paths have been accompanied by relatively massive migration flows. Thus, quantitative and qualitative changes are needed in Mexico's economic policy in order to hasten the pace of economic growth and narrow regional and social gaps. It is imperative to raise the standards of living of the Mexican population and to improve employment opportunities in Mexico, and not only in the poorest parts of the country.

However, the United States also has an important role to play in supporting Mexico's development. The two governments have to find a meaningful interpretation of the initiatives that refer to a "Partnership for Prosperity." Both sides must recall the fact, implicitly incorporated into NAFTA's economic vision and into the Security and Prosperity Partnership of North America, that only development will discourage migration. Once this idea is recovered, bilateral discussions on migration could be redirected toward less visible but perhaps more effective grounds: the search for mechanisms to shift the Mexican economy toward economic convergence with the other partner countries in the North American bloc. It is only within broad-based regional development that the massive flows of Mexicans to the United States can be reduced. If the North American region were to effectively begin to move toward shared prosperity, this would increase the possibilities of reaching agreements on the orderly mobility of workers.

If the conviction exists that development is the long-term solution to reducing massive Mexican migration towards the United States, then the argument originally implicit in NAFTA would recover its central role, albeit in a modified form, since economic and trade liberalization would be supported by active policies designed to achieve economic convergence. From the perspective of a comprehensive view of development, a strategy that leans toward shared prosperity and economic convergence should also incorporate changes in Mexico in the spheres of education, infrastructure, social investment, and poverty reduction, among others.

Given that social and migratory relations between the two countries are expected to continue for a long period as structural components of a complex bilateral relationship, the explicit aim of any bilateral (regional) initiative should be to reduce economic and wage gaps in North America. This is a great challenge, indeed, but by adopting a long-term vision the two governments would be better equipped, in the years ahead, to deal with a difficult relationship that is so distinctly marked by intense migratory pressures.

NOTES

1. This argument is based on the results of the standard Heckscher-Ohlin international trade model regarding the trend toward the equalization of the prices of productive factors and the substitutability of migration by trade. Robert A. Mundell, "International Trade and Factor Mobility," *American Economic Review* 47, no. 1 (June 1957): 321–35.

2. Doris Meissner, "Managing Migrations," *Foreign Policy*, no. 86 (Spring 1992): 66–83; The Trilateral Commission (A Report to . . .), *International Migration Challenges in a New Era* (New York: The Trilateral Commission, 1993); Commission for the Study of International Migration and Cooperative Economic Development, *Unauthorized Migration: An Economic Development Response* (Washington, D.C.: U.S. Government Printing Office, 1990).

3. NAFTA did include migration in Chapter XVI. It is however restricted to a select group of professionals, and is remarkably under-utilized.

4. Natural growth rates are estimates.

5. Real Minimum Wages are for the whole country: wages by economic activity are those reported in the formal private sector. See Tables 2.4 and 2.5.

6. Carlos Salinas de Gortari, "TLC ayer, hoy y mañana," *Enfoque, Reforma*, December 15, 2002.

7. Gerardo Esquivel and Miguel Messmacher, "Economic Integration and Subnational Development: The Mexican Experience with NAFTA" (Paper presented at the Conference *Spatial Inequality in Latin America*, Universidad de las Américas-Puebla/WIDER/Cornell/LSE, November, 2002).

8. If the Federal District is included in the calculation, the positive and significant correlation with the level of manufacturing occupation disappears. The Federal District is the main service center of the country.

9. If the Federal District is included in the calculation, the positive association with regional location vanishes. Most multinationals have their headquarters in the Federal District.

10. Francisco Alba, "El Tratado de Libre Comercio, la migración y las políticas migratorias," in *Diez años del TLCAN en México. Una perspectiva analítica*, ed. Enrique R. Cásares and Horacio Sobarzo (México: Fondo de Cultura Económica, 2004), 215–42.

11. A case in point is Mexican agriculture, where the capacity to adapt to the new context has been extremely limited, with the resulting stagnation in the creation of jobs and continuing low wages, though this performance obviously cannot be attributed solely to the effects of economic liberalization and NAFTA. Antonio Yúnez-Naude, "Cambio estructural y emigración rural a Estados Unidos," *Comercio Exterior* 50, no. 4 (April 2000): 334–39.

12. This measure attempts to take into account different lifestyles and levels of relative prices, in addition to correcting biases that might occur due to variations in exchange rates.

13. The lack of convergence between the economies does not in any way suggest an inverse causality in the sense of attributing little or no convergence to trade liberalization and capital flows.

14. Mexico's GDP fell by 6.2 percent in 1995. According to many analysts, NAFTA enabled Mexico to recover quickly from this recession.

15. On the profound and prolonged effects of the financial crises on economic conditions and the population's well-being, see Peter Fallon and Robert E. B. Lucas, "The Impact of Financial Crises on Labor Markets, Household Incomes, and Poverty: A Review of Evidence," *The World Bank Research Observer* 17, no. 1 (2002): 21–45.

16. Economic liberalization and NAFTA have affected the composition of the demand for labor by the Mexican economy in very different ways. For example, the demand for certain professionals and skilled workers, of whom there is a limited supply, has apparently been very dynamic and accompanied by steady and increasing salaries.

17. It is estimated that the circular flow of Mexican workers during the period from 1995 to 2000 was in the range of half a million migrants a year on average, if transmigrants or border migrants are excluded. The chapter on demography in this volume covers the changing characteristics of migration more extensively.

18. Jorge Durand, Douglas S. Massey, and René M. Zenteno, "Mexican Immigration to the United States: Continuities and Changes," *Latin American Research Review* 36, no. 1 (2001): 107–26.

19. Francisco Alba, "Migración internacional: consolidación de los patrones emergentes," *DEMOS: Carta demográfica sobre México*, no. 13 (2000): 10–11.

20. Even before NAFTA came into effect, various studies and sectorial analyses strongly questioned the wage convergence hypothesis and the inhibiting effects of NAFTA on migration. Raúl Hinojosa-Ojeda and Sherman Robinson, "Labor Issues in a North American Free Trade Area," in *North American Free Trade: Assessing the Impact*, ed. Nora Lustig, Barry P. Bosworth, and Robert Z. Lawrence (Washington, D.C.: The Brookings Institution, 1992), 69–108; Clark W. Reynolds, "Will a Free Trade Agreement Lead to Wage Convergence? Implications for Mexico and the United States," in *U.S.-Mexico Relations: Labor Market Interdependence*, ed. Jorge Bustamante, Clark W. Reynolds, and Raúl Hinojosa-Ojeda (Stanford, CA.: Stanford University Press, 1992), 477–86; Santiago Levy and Sweder van Wijnbergen, *Labor Markets, Migration and Welfare: Agriculture in the Mexico-USA Free Trade Agreement* (Washington, D.C.: World Bank, 1991).

21. On the issue of "structural demand" (not associated to the economic cycle) for migrant workers and the demand derived from the segmentation of the U.S. labor market, see Alejandro Portes and Robert L. Bach, *Latin Journey: Cuban and Mexican Immigrants in the United States* (Berkeley: University of California Press, 1985).

22. Figures refer to civil jobs.

23. This phenomenon of social relations has been conceptualized as "social capital" or "migratory capital." On social and migratory capital accumulated by the Mexican population, see Douglas S. Massey, Kirstin E. Espinosa, and Jorge Durand, "Dinámica migratoria entre México y Estados Unidos," in *Población, desarrollo y globalización*, ed. René Zenteno (Mexico City: Sociedad Mexicana de Demografía/El Colegio de la Frontera Norte, 1998), 49–67.

24. Another feature that contributes to the transnationalism of the migratory system was the change in Mexican law concerning the non-loss of Mexican nationality (i.e., the acceptance of dual nationality), which eliminated certain social and psychological ties that could have divided migrants' loyalties, keeping them distant from becoming American.

25. Philip Martin, *Trade and Migration: NAFTA and Agriculture* (Washington, D.C.: Institute for International Economics, 1993); Philip Martin, "Migration and Development: The Mexican Case," in *La migración internacional y el desarrollo en las Américas*, edited by CEPAL (Santiago, Chile: CEPAL, 2001), 181–98.

26. It is estimated that even a moderate and sustained economic growth rate in Mexico, say of 5 percent annually, will not significantly stem the number of emigrants during the early decades of the twenty-first century. Rodolfo Tuirán, Virgilio Partida, and José Luis Ávila, "Las causas de la migración hacia Estados Unidos," in *Migración México-Estados Unidos. Presente y futuro*, ed. Rodolfo Tuirán (Mexico City: Consejo Nacional de Población, 2000), 53–75. See also CIR/SRE (Commission for Immigration Reform/Secretaría de Relaciones Exteriores), *Binational Study of Mexico-U.S. Migration*, (Washington, D.C., Mexico City, 1997).

27. This section is largely based on Francisco Alba, "El Tratado de Libre Comercio," in *Diez años del TLCAN en México* (see note 10).

28. This appears to have been the Mexican position when negotiations began. Manuel García y Griego, "La emigración mexicana y el Tratado de Libre Comercio en

América del Norte: dos argumentos," in *Liberación económica y libre comercio en América del Norte,* ed. Gustavo Vega (Mexico City: El Colegio de México, 1993), 291–304.

29. Francisco Alba, "El Tratado de Libre Comercio y la emigración de mexicanos a Estados Unidos," *Comercio Exterior* 43, no. 8, (August 1993): 743–49. The logic in favor of liberalizing labor mobility is similar to that underlying trade liberalization agreements. In terms of conventional economic analysis, this would entail benefits for all the parties involved: destination countries, countries of origin, and migrants themselves. The editorial of an influential, liberal international journal, *The Economist,* translated this analytical perspective into the following terms: "The gap between earnings in the poor and rich worlds is vastly greater than the gap in the prices of traded goods . . . the potential economic benefits to the world of liberalising migration dwarf those from removing trade barriers." However, like other forces of globalization, immigration also entails costs and readjustments in receiving societies. Migrants carry with them social and cultural legacies, which is why quite often countries have placed multiple obstacles to the mobility of labor and persons; "Immigration. Opening the Door," 365, no. 8297 (November 2002): 11.

30. On the "NAFTA-spirit" and its implications for the migration issue, see *Binational Study of Mexico-U.S. Migration.*

31. For one example, see *The New York Times* editorial, July 23, 2001.

32. This consideration implies that the notion of sovereignty cannot be absolute in the contemporary, profoundly globalized, world.

3

Managing Mexico-U.S. Migration

Economic and Labor Issues

Philip Martin, University of California-Davis

INTRODUCTION

This chapter reviews U.S. economic and labor trends, the diffusion of Mexican-born workers throughout the U.S. labor market, and the options being discussed to deal with the arrival and employment of Mexican-born workers. Chapter 4 assesses Mexican economic and labor force trends, the diffusion of the origins of Mexican migrants, and Mexican proposals to improve the status of Mexican workers employed in the United States.

Migration was the central feature of Mexico-U.S. relations for most of the twentieth century, but the volume of cross border flows rose remarkably in the 1990s—a third of all legal Mexican immigrants admitted in the twentieth century and a third of twentieth-century apprehensions were in the 1990s. The roots of Mexico-U.S. migration lie in the U.S.-government approved recruitment of about 5 million Mexican workers during two Bracero eras, 1917–1921 and 1942–1964. The result was distortion and dependence in parts of the U.S. economy such as agriculture: some U.S. farmers made investment decisions that assumed there would be a continued influx of Mexican workers, and some Mexicans became dependent on U.S. jobs and earnings, making it hard to stop Mexico-U.S. migration when government-approved recruitment ended.

The networks created during these Bracero programs facilitated rising levels of Mexico-US migration in the 1970s, 1980s, and 1990s. A combination of increased demand-pull pressures in the United States, especially during the job booms of the late 1980s and late 1990s, and increased supply-push pressure in Mexico, especially after economic crises in the mid-1980s and mid-1990s, helped to spread Mexican migrants throughout the United

States, a process accelerated by the legalization of 2.3 million Mexicans in the late 1980s. The 2004 U.S. labor force of 148 million included 19 million Hispanics (13 percent), including perhaps a third born in Mexico.

The major trends in the U.S. economy and labor market include relatively rapid economic and productivity growth but slower employment growth. Total U.S. employment[1] was about 146 million in 2007, a slower than usual recovery from the 2001 recession. The Hispanic share of net labor force and employment growth over the past decade, 44 percent, is far higher than the Hispanic share of the labor force, which is 13 percent.[2] Data on how many of these additional Hispanics are immigrants are not available.[3]

What is to be done about the growth and diffusion of Mexican-born workers? There are two extreme policy options: give up on trying to manage Mexico-U.S. migration because it is deeply ingrained in both countries and follows a logic of its own that defies government control, versus make continued incremental additions to border enforcement efforts that eventually reduce unauthorized entries. The U.S. government has embraced the second option, but many policymakers recognize that the presence of 12 million unauthorized foreigners, and the addition of perhaps 500,000 a year, will require additional actions. Most of the additional actions being debated would legalize some of the unauthorized foreigners who have U.S. employers, but they differ on whether and how the newly legalized could become permanent residents of the United States.

EVOLUTION OF MEXICO-U.S. MIGRATION

Migration has been a defining feature of Mexico-U.S. relations for most of the twentieth century, but legal immigration remained low until recently. Some 36 percent of twentieth-century Mexican immigrants arrived in the 1990s, and 34 percent of the apprehensions of unauthorized Mexicans were in the 1990s (Table 3.1). During most of the twentieth century, Mexican migrants were negatively selected, meaning that Mexican emigrants usually had less education and fewer skills than the average Mexican, largely because U.S. farmers recruited rural Mexicans willing to accept seasonal farm jobs.[4] There were bilateral agreements to regulate Mexico-U.S. labor migration between 1917–1921 and 1942–1964, but most twentieth-century, Mexican-born workers in the U.S. labor market arrived and were employed outside these guest worker or Bracero programs.

From Braceros to IRCA

Many Mexicans and Americans continue to associate Mexicans in the United States with Braceros (strong arms), the workers who arrived with

Table 3.1. **Mexican Immigration and Apprehensions: 1890–2003**

Decade	Immigrants Annual Average	Decade Total	Decade as Percent of Total 1890–2003	Apprehensions Annual Average	Decade Total	Decade as Percent of Total 1890–2003
1890–1900	97	971	0%	na	na	na
1901–1910	4,964	49,642	1%	na	na	na
1911–1920	21,900	219,004	3%	na	na	na
1921–1930	45,929	459,287	7%	25,697	256,968	1%
1931–1940	2,232	22,319	0%	14,746	147,457	0%
1941–1950	6,059	60,589	1%	137,721	1,377,210	3%
1951–1960	22,981	229,811	3%	359,895	3,598,949	8%
1961–1970	45,394	453,937	7%	160,836	1,608,356	4%
1971–1980	64,029	640,294	10%	832,150	8,321,498	19%
1981–1990	165,584	1,655,843	25%	1,188,333	11,883,328	26%
1991–2000	224,942	2,249,421	34%	1,466,760	14,667,599	33%
2001–2003	180,557	541,670	8%	1,008,017	3,024,052	7%
Total		6,582,788	100%		44,885,417	100%

Source: INS Statistical Yearbook and Yearbook of Immigration Statistics
Notes:
a. Apprehensions record events, so one person caught three times is three apprehensions. Mexicans are 95–98 percent of those apprehended.
* Apprehension data for 1921–30 is calculated as twice the reported 1925–30 figure (128,484).

U.S. government approval during and after the First and Second World Wars to work on farms and in some cases railroads. Mexican Braceros were admitted by making "exceptions" to U.S. immigration laws that otherwise would have blocked their entry, that is, the head tax and the literacy test was waived for Western Hemisphere nationals coming to the United States "for the purpose of accepting employment in agricultural pursuits." The number of Mexican workers admitted peaked after WWI ended—18,000 were admitted in 1917, and 52,000 in 1920. A U.S. recession in 1921 and Mexican government dissatisfaction with the treatment of Braceros in some states and on some U.S. farms allowed the program to end.

Mexicans who continued to migrate north found few obstacles to entry, in part because the U.S. Border Patrol was not established until 1924. Mexican-born workers became the core of the seasonal farmwork force in California's expanding agriculture during the 1920s; it was estimated that 70 to 80 percent of the 72,000 seasonal farmworkers in California were Mexican by 1930.[5] The Great Depression led to "repatriations" of Mexicans in the United States to free up jobs for unemployed Americans, and there were fewer Mexican-born U.S. residents in 1940 (378,000) than there had been in 1930 (641,000), according to the U.S. Census.

During the 1930s, the farm labor system in southwestern agriculture, dependent on seasonal workers who "came with the wind and went with the dust," came under attack. John Steinbeck's 1939 novel, *The Grapes of Wrath*, gave an emotional impetus to the call for farm labor reform—namely, to restructure southwestern agriculture in a manner that reduced its dependence on migrant and seasonal workers. Alternatively, if factories in the fields persisted, reformers wanted farmworkers to be treated as factory workers and covered under nonfarm labor standards and labor relations laws that guaranteed workers minimum wages, unemployment insurance, and the right to form unions.

Restructuring a major industry, agriculture, which employed a third of U.S. workers in the mid-1930s, was risky, and decades of low farm wages had been capitalized into higher land prices, giving landowners an economic incentive to oppose labor changes that might result in higher wages and lower land prices. The outbreak of World War II allowed farmers to win a new Bracero program, which eliminated the need to restructure agriculture or to treat farmworkers as factory workers. Between 1942 and 1945, Braceros, prisoners of war, interned Japanese, and state and local prisoners "supplemented" the U.S. hired farmwork force, sending an unmistakable signal: to get ahead in the U.S. labor market, ambitious young Americans had to get out of farmwork, which was relatively easy to do during WWII.

The Bracero program expanded in the 1950s, when federal and state irrigation projects opened new land for farming in the southwest, the cost of shipping produce by truck from west to east fell with the completion of the interstate highway system, and the baby boom increased the U.S. demand for fruits and vegetables. Western farmers who assumed that Mexican or other foreign workers would continue to be available at minimum wages made business decisions reflecting this assumption, which raised land prices and allowed California to replace New Jersey as the garden state in the eastern time zone, still home to almost 60 percent of Americans.

Farmers argued that the U.S. should not end the Bracero program because, without foreign workers, labor-intensive agriculture would shrink and make the U.S. dependent on imported commodities during the Cold War. Their predictions of what would happen without Braceros proved to be wrong. The tomatoes used to make catsup, known as processing tomatoes, were in the spotlight during debates over whether to continue the Bracero program. In 1960, over 80 percent of the 45,000 peak harvest workers employed to pick the 2.2 million ton processing tomato crop in California were Braceros.[6] In a very close congressional vote in 1963, urban legislators persuaded by unions and civil rights groups that Braceros in the fields held down wages and slowed the upward mobility of Mexican Americans, voted to end the Bracero program. Contrary to expectations, the harvest was mechanized rapidly, production of processing tomatoes expanded, and prices fell because plant scientists and engineers collaborated to develop tomatoes that ripened simultaneously and a machine to cut and shake ripe tomatoes from the plants. Four decades after the Bracero program ended, 5,000 workers ride machines in California to sort 12 million tons of tomatoes; that is, a ninth as many workers harvest six times more tomatoes.

Labor-saving mechanization was spurred by the higher wages that followed the end of the Bracero program, and was facilitated by federal and state governments that subsidized labor-saving research. Mechanization resulted in fewer and larger tomato farms, and the University of California was sued by worker groups alleging that taxpayer monies intended to improve rural communities wound up displacing farm workers and small farmers. The suit was eventually settled with an agreement to have worker advocates review plans for labor-saving research, but a combination of less government research money and rising unauthorized Mexico-U.S. migration dulled employer interest in labor-saving agricultural mechanization.

Mexico-U.S. migration was relatively low between the end of the Bracero program in 1964 and peso devaluations in the late 1970s, the "golden age" for U.S. farmworkers and the only time in the twentieth century that U.S. farm wages rose faster than nonfarm wages. Cesar Chavez and the United Farm Workers won a 40 percent wage increase for grape pickers in 1966, increasing entry-level wages from $1.25 to $1.75 an hour amid predictions that an expanding UFW could become one of the largest U.S. unions by organizing most of the 3 million U.S. hired farmworkers (the federal minimum wage was $1.25 an hour in 1966). However, some ex-Braceros became U.S. immigrants during the 1960s, when U.S. immigration law allowed employers to issue letters asserting that a foreigner was "essential" to fill even a seasonal farm job, enabling the foreigner to get an immigrant visa. Ex-Braceros who became immigrants in this manner received visas printed on green cards, and many became green-card commuters who lived in Mexico and worked seasonally in the United States.

The UFW called strikes in support of another 40 percent wage increase in 1979 in a bid to raise the entry-level farm wage from $3.75 to $5.25 at a time when the federal minimum wage was $3.35. Growers along the Mexico-U.S. border, where the strikes began, resisted, pointing out that, in a time of high inflation, President Carter had asked that wage increases be limited to a maximum 7 percent. The growers turned to farm labor contractors (FLCs) to get replacement workers for strikers, including some who were green-card commuters that returned to their villages to recruit workers, prompting the UFW to establish "wet patrols" on the border and complain that the Border Patrol was failing to do its job of preventing unauthorized migration. Many of the FLCs stayed in business after the strikes were settled, and they soon replaced the UFW as the major supplier of farmworkers—the number of workers under UFW contract fell from 70,000 in 1978 to 7,000 by 1986.[7]

Mexicans were encouraged to migrate north by a peso devaluation in 1982, the first time in forty years that the Mexican economy did not grow.[8] The Mexican government declared a moratorium (but did not default) on repaying the $88 billion foreign debt that had been incurred in the hope that oil prices would continue rising, and had to sharply reduce government spending when oil revenues fell. Real wages in Mexico fell and inflation rose, making work in the United States more attractive, and the movement of more Mexican workers north was reflected in sharply higher apprehensions.[9]

From IRCA to NAFTA

In 1986, the United States enacted the Immigration Reform and Control Act (IRCA), whose purpose was to reduce illegal immigration by imposing sanctions on U.S. employers who knowingly hired unauthorized foreigners and by legalizing some unauthorized foreigners in the United States. Contrary to expectations, the IRCA increased legal and unauthorized Mexico-U.S. migration.

The IRCA included two legalization or amnesty programs, and over 70 percent of the applicants in each were from Mexico (Table 3.2). Residence-based legalization allowed those in the United States "continuously" since January 1, 1982, to legalize their status during a twelve-month period in 1987–1988, while the employment-based Special Agricultural Worker (SAW) program permitted unauthorized foreigners who did at least ninety days of farmwork in 1985–1986 to legalize during an eighteen-month period in 1987–1988.[10] The SAW program, had easier eligibility requirements and was rife with fraud because it allowed foreigners to present one-sentence affidavits from farm employers or labor contractors asserting that the applicant did at least ninety days of farmwork. The burden of proof then shifted to the U.S. government to disprove the applicant's claimed work, which it was not prepared to do. Other features of the program encouraged the entry and employment of unauthorized workers. Border Patrol raids on fields stopped, employer sanctions enforcement did not begin until after legalization ended, and over 100,000 Mexicans were allowed to come to U.S. ports of entry, assert they did qualifying farmwork and needed to enter the United States to obtain proof from their past employers, and were admitted with temporary work permits.

The 1 million Mexican men who eventually became U.S. immigrants under the SAW program were equivalent to a sixth of the adult men in rural Mexico in the mid-1980s. Their families were deliberately excluded from legalization, under the theory that rural Mexican men wanted to commute to seasonal U.S. farm jobs from homes in Mexico, as had earlier green-card commuters. However, many SAWs soon found nonfarm jobs and settled in U.S. cities with their families. As outlays for education, health, and other

Table 3.2. IRCA Legalization Applicants in 1987–88

Characteristic	LAW(a)	SAW(b)
Median Age at Entry	23	24
1. Age 15 to 44 (%)	80	93
2. Male (%)	57	82
3. Married (%)	41	42
4. From Mexico (%)	70	82
5. Applied in California (%)	54	52
Total Applicants	1,759,705	1,272,143

Source: U.S. Immigration and Naturalization Service, *1991 Statistical Yearbook of the INS*, 1992, 70–74.
(a) Persons in the U.S. since January 1, 1982 filing I-687 legalization applications
(b) Persons who did at least 90 days of farmwork and filing I-700 legalization applications.
About 80,000 farmworkers applied under LAW.

public services rose, especially during the early 1990s recession, state and local governments sued the federal government, seeking reimbursement for the costs of educating and caring for unauthorized foreigners. The result was a series of studies that demonstrated that the taxes paid by low-income immigrants accrued to the federal government, while the costs were borne primarily by state and local governments. This federal-state difference in taxes collected and services provided, as well as controversy over the balance of taxes paid and benefits received, set the stage for California's Proposition 187 in 1994 and federal welfare reforms in 1996 that restricted the access of legal and unauthorized foreigners to tax-supported benefits.

IRCA's legalization programs encouraged more Mexico-U.S. migration during a time of rapid change in Mexico. Mexico traditionally defined itself in opposition to the United States, exemplified by the saying, "poor Mexico, so far from God, and so close to the U.S."[11]

However, beginning in the mid-1980s, Mexico's economic policies changed from inward-oriented import substitution and minimal foreign investment and trade to an outward-oriented East Asian model, which meant that the Mexican government encouraged foreign investors to create jobs in factories producing goods to be exported. The Mexican government's continued push for economic integration with its northern neighbors was symbolized by the North American Free Trade Agreement (NAFTA) which, over the strong objections of U.S. unions and 1992 presidential candidate Ross Perot, went into effect on January 1, 1994, to lock into international agreement policies that lowered barriers to trade and investment between Canada, Mexico, and the United States.[12]

NAFTA was expected to increase trade, employment, and wages in all three countries, which was eventually expected to reduce Mexico-U.S. migration. However, many migration specialists warned that the economic dislocations associated with restructuring in Mexico would initially increase Mexico-U.S. migration, as previously protected sectors such as agriculture were exposed to cheaper imports.[13] Foreign investors, on the other hand, needed time to create factory jobs, and when they did, many were far from the rural areas experiencing labor displacement. Most of the new factories, many of which assembled imported components into products that were exported, hired mostly young graduates rather than displaced farmers.

Mexico-U.S. migration increased in the 1990s: the number of unauthorized Mexicans in the United States rose from an estimated 2.5 million in 1995 to 4.5 million in 2000, an increase of 400,000 a year. Between 1991 and 2000, some 2.2 million Mexicans were admitted as legal immigrants, over 200,000 a year. Those who argue that the 1990s are likely to have seen the peak of the Mexico-U.S. migration hump pin their hopes on Mexican demographic and employment trends—there are fewer labor force entrants and there may be faster jobs growth—while those who think that the Mexico-U.S. migration peak has not yet been reached stress the strength of the migration networks bridging the border and the diffusion of the origins and destinations of Mexican migrants, so that more migrants coming from and going to more places will be harder to control.[14]

Developments since 2000

In 2000, about 10 percent of 110 million persons born in Mexico, 14 percent of the 47 million Mexican-born workers, and 30 percent of the 21 million Mexican-born workers with formal-sector jobs, were in the United States (Table 3.3). The Mexican government is committed to creating jobs in Mexico so that emigration eventually is unnecessary, but its major priority until there is stay-at-home development is to improve conditions for Mexicans in the United States; job creation in Mexico has lagged.

Elections in 2000 were expected to usher in a new era for Mexico-U.S. migration policy. Newly elected Mexican President Vicente Fox and U.S. President George Bush agreed early in 2001 to devise "an orderly framework for [Mexico-U.S.] migration that ensures humane treatment [and] legal security, and dignifies labor conditions." Fox subsequently proposed a four-point migration plan that included legalization for unauthorized Mexicans in the United States, a new guest-worker program, cooperative measures to end border violence, and changes in U.S. law that would exempt Mexicans from U.S. immigrant visa ceilings. In presenting Mexico's proposal, Foreign Minister Jorge Castañeda said: "It's the whole enchilada or nothing."[15]

The September 11, 2001, terrorist attacks shifted Mexico-U.S. migration discussions away from legalization and toward security, with an emphasis on ensuring that foreign terrorists do not arrive legally or illegally. The movement of the Immigration and Naturalization Service to the new De-

Table 3.3. Mexico-US Population and Labor Force (1970–2050)

	Mexico	U.S.
Population in 1970 (millions)	53	203
Labor force in 1970 (millions)	15	83
Percent of population	28%	41%
Population in 2000 (millions)	100	281
Labor force in 2000 (millions)	40	141
Percent of population	40%	50%
Labor force increase 1970 to 2000 (percent)	167%	70%
Population in 2050 (millions)	151	414
Labor force in 2050 (millions)	70	207
Percent of population	46%	50%
Labor force increase 2000 to 2050 (percent)	75%	47%
Employment in 2000		
Formal Sector Jobs (millions)	15	125
Filled by Mexicans (millions)	15	6
Employed in Agriculture (millions)	6	3
Filled by Mexicans (millions)	6	2

Sources: US Census and CONAPO, 2050 projections from PRB, IMSS (Instituto Mexicano del Seguro Social), Subdirección General de Finanzas.

partment of Homeland Security on March 1, 2003, and recession in both Mexico and the United States slowed changes in Mexico-U.S. migration policy. Despite stepped-up border controls, unauthorized Mexico-U.S. migration continued at historically high levels, and the Mexican government took steps to improve conditions for Mexicans in the United States by, *inter alia,* issuing *matricula consular* documents to Mexicans so that they have the government-issued ID card needed to open bank accounts, rent apartments, and fly or enter government buildings in a security-conscious United States.

There have been many proposals to deal with the growing number of unauthorized Mexicans in the United States, especially those employed in agriculture. As the share of workers employed on U.S. crop farms that were believed to be unauthorized topped 50 percent in the mid-1990s, there were calls for a new agricultural guest worker program, but union, ethnic group, and presidential opposition prevented their enactment in Congress.[16] During the summer of 1999, however, some of those traditionally opposed to guest workers advanced proposals that reflected what growers had been seeking for the previous two decades, a way to employ foreign workers without having the U.S. Department of Labor supervise individual farmer efforts to recruit U.S. workers and elimination of the requirement to provide housing for out-of-area workers. In December 2000, worker and grower representatives reached a compromise that included an earned legalization concept: unauthorized workers who did at least 100 days of farmwork could receive a temporary legal status, which they could convert to full immigrant status by continuing to do farmwork for at least 360 more days in the next six years, including at least 240 days of farm work in the first three years of their temporary resident status. Worker advocates found the compromise acceptable, since unauthorized workers and their families eventually became immigrants, and employers accepted the compromise because experienced farmworkers would not leave the farmwork force immediately.

As discussed in further detail in chapters 5 and 6, Congress remains deadlocked on immigration reform legislation. Despite support within both houses of Congress for the compromise negotiated between growers and migrant advocates in the form of the Agricultural Job Opportunity, Benefits, and Security Act (AgJOBS), the legislation has stalled and does not appear likely to pass in the 110th Congress.

U.S. ECONOMIC AND LABOR TRENDS

This section reviews trends in U.S. economic and labor force growth. Mexico-U.S. migration may have become less sensitive to U.S. macroeconomic indicators, that is, Mexico-U.S. migration may have continued at about the same pace during the 1998–2000 boom as during the 2001–2002 recession, although in 2007 the number of new Mexican entrants appears to have dropped. The apparent stability of Mexico-U.S. migration even as macroeconomic circumstances changed suggests that there is a "structural demand" for Mexican-born workers, especially in particular "niches" of the U.S. labor market such as agriculture, construction, meat processing and other non-durables manufacturing, and a widening range of services.

The 1990s began with an economic recession in the United States and ended with the lowest unemployment rates in decades. There were recessions in 1991 and 2001, defined as periods in which real GDP shrinks, and the unemployment rate, 7.5 percent in 1992, fell to 4 percent in 2000. The rate of productivity growth almost doubled, from about 1.5 percent a year from the mid-1970s to mid-1990s, to over 2.5 percent a year in the late 1990s, reflecting unprecedented business investment in high-tech capital such as computers as well as high levels of consumer and housing investment in an era of low interest rates.[17]

The stock market boomed amid assertions that the United States had entered a new economic era in which old rules and parameters did not apply. The Wilshire 5000 index tripled between late 1994 and late 1999, and the

Nasdaq rose four fold. Business investment and employment growth began to stall in 2000–2001, and an economic recession began before the September 11, 2001, terrorist attacks. Economic recovery was slow in 2002–2003 despite substantial tax cuts and low interest rates, a result attributed to corporate governance problems (accounting scandals) in 2002 and the uncertainties due to the war with Iraq in 2003.[18]

The major puzzle of the 2002–2004 recovery was the persisting high unemployment rate despite a resumption of economic growth, although unemployment fell in 2005. The explanations range from continued immigration to the outsourcing of U.S. jobs to fast productivity growth—the Economic Report of the President favors the faster productivity growth explanation, suggesting that firms decided to better utilize the workers and capital they had rather than to hire and buy more.[19] The "jobless recovery" of 2002–2003 meant that President Bush was the first president since Herbert Hoover to seek reelection with lower employment than when he began his term.[20]

The U.S. labor force includes all persons 16 and older who are employed or actively looking for work. It expanded from 126 million in 1990 to 151 million in 2006. The average growth of 1.6 million a year was less than the rise in employment, so that the unemployment rate fell from a peak 7.5

Table 3.4.   U.S. Real GDP and Unemployment, 1990–2005

	Real GDP	Unemployment rate
	$ bills	Percent
1990	7,113	5.6
1991	7,101	6.8
1992	7,337	7.5
1993	7,533	6.9
1994	7,836	6.1
1995	8,032	5.6
1996	8,329	5.4
1997	8,704	4.9
1998	9,067	4.5
1999	9,470	4.2
2000	9,817	4.0
2001	9,891	4.7
2002	10,049	5.8
2003	10,301	6.0
2004	10,704	5.5
2005	11,049	5.1

Source: Economic Report of the President, 2007

percent in 1992 to 4.6 percent in 2006. Perhaps the most remarkable employment change was the jump in the employment-population ratio, the percentage of persons 16 and older who were employed, which rose from 63 percent in 1990 to over 64 percent in 2000—each additional one percent means another two million persons employed.

Generally favorable economic and labor market developments during the 1990s helped to boost average hourly earnings for U.S. private sector workers from $10 in 1990 to $14 in 2000, not adjusted for inflation. The federal minimum wage was $3.80 an hour in 1990, $4.25 between 1991 and 1996, $5.15 between 1997 and 2006; it rose to $5.85 an hour in 2007, and is scheduled to rise to $6.55 in July 2008. Many states including California have higher minimum wages ($6.75 since 2002), and some cities have even higher "living wage" laws that cover workers employed under city contracts with private employers.

There is considerable disagreement about the state of the U.S. labor market. On the one extreme are those who argue that, with continued rapid increases in productivity, U.S. economic competitiveness and real wages and employment can continue to increase. At the other extreme are those who argue that outsourcing abroad and the impacts of deregulation in industries such as airlines at home have shifted a great deal of bargaining power to employers, who have responded by holding down wages and reducing or ending pension and health benefits.

Downward pressures on wages and benefits is evident in many industries, but is especially pronounced at the bottom of the labor market, where many workers have less than a college education. Former Federal Reserve chairman Alan Greenspan repeatedly warned that the United States faced a growing mismatch between the oversupply of low-skilled workers on the one hand, and the unmet demand for people with specialty training on the other. Greenspan called for increases in spending on community colleges and vocational training schools to improve worker employability and productivity. The number of U.S. workers twenty-five and older who do not have a high-school diploma has fallen, so that immigrants have become a larger share in that category. In 1980, about 17 million of 80 million U.S. workers did not have a high-school diploma; in 2000, it was 12 million of 120 million.

Two issues have dominated recent U.S. labor market discussions: immigrant and U.S. worker employment and outsourcing/offshoring. There are about 16 million foreign-born workers in the U.S. labor force, including five to six million who are unauthorized, and one of the most-debated issues is the effects of their presence on U.S. workers—economic theory suggests that the presence of foreign workers in U.S. labor markets depresses wages and/or increases unemployment. However, it has been very hard to measure any wage depression due to immigration. The usual study compares wage trends

Table 3.5. U.S. Labor Force, Employment, and Unemployment 1975–2006

	Pop.15	Labor Force Total	Employment Ag	Non-Ag[1]	Unemployment	Not in Labor Force	Percentage LFPR[2]	Percentage Emp/Pop Ratio	Percentage Unemploy Rate
1975	153,153	93,775	3,408	82,438	7,929	59,377	61.2	56.1	8.5
1976	156,150	96,158	3,331	85,421	7,406	59,991	61.6	56.8	7.7
1977	159,033	99,009	3,283	88,734	6,991	60,025	62.3	57.9	7.1
1978	161,910	102,251	3,387	92,661	6,202	59,659	63.2	59.3	6.1
1979	164,863	104,962	3,347	95,477	6,137	59,900	63.7	59.9	5.8
1980	167,745	106,940	3,364	95,938	7,637	60,806	63.8	59.2	7.1
1981	170,130	108,670	3,368	97,030	8,273	61,460	63.9	59.0	7.6
1982	172,271	110,204	3,401	96,125	10,678	62,067	64.0	57.8	9.7
1983	174,215	111,550	3,383	97,450	10,717	62,665	64.0	57.9	9.6
1984	176,383	113,544	3,321	101,685	8,539	62,839	64.4	59.5	7.5
1985	178,206	115,461	3,179	103,971	8,312	62,744	64.8	60.1	7.2
1986	180,587	117,834	3,163	106,434	8,237	62,752	65.3	60.7	7.0
1987	182,753	119,865	3,208	109,232	7,425	62,888	65.6	61.5	6.2
1988	184,613	121,669	3,169	111,800	6,701	62,944	65.9	62.3	5.5
1989	186,393	123,869	3,199	114,142	6,528	62,523	66.5	63.0	5.3
1990	189,164	125,840	3,223	115,570	7,047	63,324	66.5	62.8	5.6
1991	190,925	126,346	3,269	114,449	8,628	64,578	66.2	61.7	6.8
1992	192,805	128,105	3,247	115,245	9,613	64,700	66.4	61.5	7.5
1993	194,838	129,200	3,115	117,144	8,940	65,638	66.3	61.7	6.9
1994	196,814	131,056	3,409	119,651	7,996	65,758	66.6	62.5	6.1
1995	198,584	132,304	3,440	121,460	7,404	66,280	66.6	62.9	5.6
1996	200,591	133,943	3,443	123,264	7,236	66,647	66.8	63.2	5.4
1997	203,133	136,297	3,399	126,159	6,739	66,837	67.1	63.8	4.9

(continued)

Table 3.5. *(continued)*

	Pop.15[1]	Labor Force Total	Employment Ag	Non-Ag	Unemployment	Not in Labor Force	LFPR[2]	Percentage Emp/Pop Ratio	Unemploy Rate
1998	205,220	137,673	3,378	128,085	6,210	67,547	67.1	64.1	4.5
1999	207,753	139,368	3,281	130,207	5,880	68,385	67.1	64.3	4.2
2000	212,577	142,583	2,464	134,427	5,692	69,994	67.1	64.4	4.0
2001	215,092	143,734	2,299	134,635	6,801	71,359	66.8	63.7	4.7
2002	217,570	144,863	2,311	134,174	8,378	72,707	66.6	62.7	5.8
2003	221,168	146,510	2,275	135,461	8,774	74,658	66.2	62.3	6.0
2004	223,357	147,401	2,232	137,020	8,149	75,956	66.0	62.3	5.5
2005	226,082	149,320	2,197	139,532	7,591	76,762	66.0	62.7	5.1
2006	228,815	151,428	2,206	142,221	7,001	77,387	66.2	63.1	4.6

Source: Economic Report of the President, 2007
[1]Population 15 and Older
[2]Labor Force Participation Rate

for demographic groups believed to compete with migrants in cities with different shares of migrants, such as blacks and women in Los Angeles, where the immigrant share of the labor force is over a third, and Atlanta, where the immigrant share is under 10 percent.

Such wage-comparison studies have found little wage depression that can be attributed to the presence of immigrant workers. The generally low unemployment rates in cities with higher shares of immigrant workers has been attributed to the fact that immigrants are attracted to areas with jobs, and that U.S. workers who may have been displaced by immigrants tend to move away rather than stay and remain unemployed. The failure to find the expected wage depression has been attributed to immigrants being attracted to booming cities and to U.S. workers in immigrant cities often being employed in different labor markets from the immigrants. For example, if U.S. blacks and women are disproportionately employed in government, and there are few immigrants employed by government, then the different wage-setting processes in government and non-government jobs can make it hard to find wage depression for U.S. workers who are similar in education, age, etc. to the immigrants in cities with higher shares of immigrant workers.

The other labor market issue is outsourcing, which means moving jobs out of the firm for which they are done (some analysts distinguish outsourcing from offshoring, which means moving jobs outside the United States). Democratic presidential candidate John Kerry in 2004 called U.S. corporate leaders who offshored jobs "Benedict Arnolds," or traitors to their country, and proposed a six-point plan to reduce offshoring, including new requirements that U.S. employers tell their workers at least three months in advance if their jobs are to be eliminated because of offshoring and eliminating tax credits for firms that move jobs overseas. Then-Federal Reserve chairman Alan Greenspan said in March 2004 that improved education was the best long-term solution to the U.S. job losses caused by globalization, the same remedy proposed to deal with immigrant workers.

MEXICANS IN THE U.S. LABOR MARKET

There are several reasons for the presence of an increasing number of Mexican workers in the U.S. labor market during the 1990s and first half of the 2000s. Fewer returns of those who enter illegally (due in part to the high cost of illegal reentry) increased the stock of Mexican migrants. In 1992, an estimated 20 percent of unauthorized Mexicans in the United States returned to Mexico within six months; by 1997, the return rate was down to 15 percent within six months, and by 2002, only 7 percent. At the same time, some U.S. employers demonstrated a distinct preference for hiring Mexican workers regardless of their legal status. The preference is particularly high in sectors of the economy that require lesser-skilled workers with relatively low levels of education. CPS data suggest that a third of Mexican-born workers are employed in U.S. jobs that require little education. For example, Mexican-born workers are 20 percent of those employed as landscapers and groundskeepers, 14 percent of food preparation workers and 11 percent of janitors.

It has been very hard to find evidence that the presence of immigrants generally reduces the wages of U.S. workers or increases their employment in "immigrant cities." However, macro analyses suggest that there are employment-increasing and wage-depressing effects of immigrant workers, and the result is that the U.S. economy receives a net benefit due to immigration.

Figure 3.1 illustrates the net benefit of immigration to the U.S. economy in the mid-1990s. If there were no migrant workers at E, the U.S. would

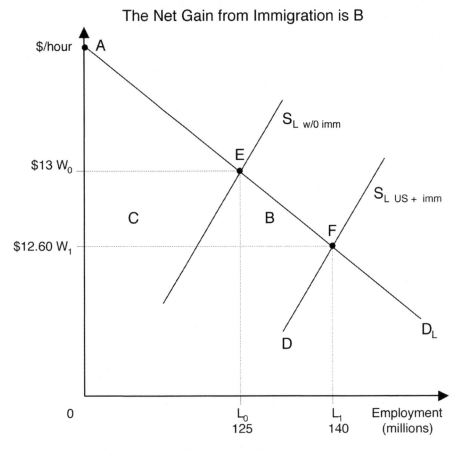

Figure 3.1.   **The Net Economic Effects of Migration**

have had 125 million U.S.-born workers earning, according to the best estimates, $13 an hour. Total income, represented by the rectangle *AE L0*, includes the wages paid to workers plus the triangle above the wage line, which is the share of national income going to owners of capital and land. The United States had 15 million foreign-born workers in the mid-1990s, which shifted the labor supply to the right, to 140 million at *F*, and lowered average hourly earnings according to most estimates by 3 percent to $12.60.

The movement from *E* to *F* creates two rectangles, *C* and *D*, as well as triangle *B*. Rectangle *C* represents the reduced wages paid to U.S. workers. These reduced wages do not disappear, but are transferred to the (U.S.) owners of capital and land in the form of higher profits and rents, many of which flow to higher-income Americans. Because of immigration, the U.S. economy expands by rectangle *D* and triangle *B*, with migrant workers getting most of the benefits of this economic expansion in the form of their wages (rectangle *D*).

The net economic gain from immigration is triangle *B*. Its size can be estimated in percentage-of-national-income terms as ½ × (estimated 3 percent decrease in U.S. wages due to immigration × 11 percent immigrant share of U.S. labor force × 70 percent share of labor in U.S. national income, or 0.001), which means that U.S. national income was about ¹⁄₁₀ of 1 percent or about $8 billion higher in 1997 because of immigration.[21] To put this economic gain in perspective, if the $8 trillion U.S. economy in the mid-1990s grew at 2 percent a year, economic output rose by $160 billion a year, which makes the gain due to immigration equivalent to about 20 days of "normal" economic growth.[22]

It is worth noting that, if there is no wage depression, there is no net economic gain due to immigration; without wage depression, the economy expands with immigration but immigrants get the expansion in the form of their wages. Borjas estimated that the wage depression due to immigration between 1980 and 2000 was 3.7 percent for all U.S.-born male workers and 7.4 percent for U.S.-born workers who did not complete high school, with half of this 7.4 percent attributed to unauthorized Mexican migrants.[23] These estimates are consistent with others that find a 10 percent increase in labor supply associated with a 4 percent drop in wages, although there are studies that show a 10 percent increase in the supply of labor associated with less than a 1 percent drop in wages. Indeed, there are models that assume immigration shifts out both the supply and demand for labor, minimizing any wage-depressing effect of immigration.

The New Immigrant Survey tracks a sample of 9,600 foreigners receiving immigrant visas or green cards in 2003 to determine their income gains as a result of immigration. The pilot survey for the NIS examined those admitted in 1996, and found that immigrant wage gains were lower than would be suggested simply by comparing average per capita GDPs in the country of origin and the United States. For immigrants marrying U.S. citizens and those sponsored by U.S. employers with less than twelve years schooling, the average difference in per capita GDP between countries of origin and the U.S. was about $21,000 in 1996, but the average U.S. earnings gain was only $7,000. For those who had at least sixteen years of schooling, average GDP per capita differences were $18,000, and the average earnings gain was $16,000. For legal Mexican immigrants in 2003–2004, the earnings gain after immigration averaged $10,000 a year, but the per capita income difference was about $26,000.

U.S. GUEST WORKER PROGRAMS

The purpose of nonimmigrant or guest worker programs is to add workers temporarily to the labor force, but not settled residents to the population; the guest adjective implies that the foreigner is expected to leave the country when his job ends. In most cases, guest workers are expected to be a transitional presence in an industry or occupation, employed until jobs are mechanized or replaced by trade or until additional workers are trained locally.

The United States has over twenty programs that permit foreigners to enter and work. These programs are often referred to by the type of nonimmigrant visa issued to the foreigner, such as *E* for treaty traders and investors, *H* for workers, and *L* for intra-company transferees. The three major worker visas are H-1B for specialty workers (capped at 65,000 a year, and raised to 85,000 a year beginning in 2005, with the extra 20,000 visas available to foreign graduates of U.S. universities with M.S. or Ph.D. degrees), H-2A for agricultural workers (no cap), and H-2B for non-farmworkers (capped at 66,000 a year). In addition, Mexicans and Canadians with at least a B.A. degree may enter the United States (and Americans may go to Canada and Mexico) in response to written job offers in over sixty occupations requiring at least a B.A. degree under the NAFTA TN visa system.

Most Mexican guest workers arrive with H-2A (farm) or H-2B (nonfarm) visas, and the fastest growth in recent years has been in H-2B arrivals. Both the H-2A and H-2B programs admit foreigners to fill temporary U.S. jobs, generally defined as those lasting less than 12 months.[24] Both programs are based on U.S. Department of Labor certification, meaning that employers must have their need for H-2A and H-2B foreign workers certified before they can go abroad and recruit guest workers. However, the H-2A program erects more hurdles for employers than the H-2B program by requiring farm employers, *inter alia*, to offer out-of-area workers free and approved housing and to pay the guest workers' inbound transportation costs; the H-2B program does not.

Table 3.6. Admissions Under H-Worker visas, 1992–2005

1992–94 = 100	1992–94 Average	1995	1996	1997	1998	1999	2000	2001	2002	2003	2004	2005
H-1B Specialty occupations	105,828	100	111	137	228	286	336	363	350	341	366	385
H-2A Ag Workers	16,486	80	69	58	166	196	202	168	95	85	134	
H-2B Nonfarm Unskilled	18,114	87	78	79	137	198	284	400	480	568	480	374*

Source: *Yearbook of Immigration Statistics.*
*The 2005 Yearbook of Immigration Statistics does not distinguish between the H-2A and H-2B workers.

H-2A admissions have been rising. Many U.S. farmers say they would like to obtain legal guest workers under the H-2A program, but do not because of the requirement to provide housing and the threat of litigation. SAMCO, a custom harvester of citrus, brought thirty-eight H-2A Mexican workers to California to harvest lemons in March–April 2002 in what it said was a humanitarian act to save Mexicans from attempting to enter the United States via Arizona deserts illegally. SAMCO was sued for failing to pay overtime wages to the H-2A workers, not providing rest periods and lunch breaks, and not reimbursing some workers fully for expenses they incurred traveling to and from Mexico.[25] Other workers are not entitled to reimbursement, and unauthorized workers are.

The H-2B program admits foreign workers to fill seasonal jobs for which U.S. workers cannot be recruited at the prevailing wage. In 2002, DOL certified 121,665 U.S. jobs as needing to be filled by H-2B workers, and immigration statistics reported that 72,387 workers with H-2B visas were admitted.[26] A fourth of the H-2B certifications were for landscape laborers, 10 percent were for forestry workers, 7 percent were for housekeepers in hotels and motels, and 4 percent each were for stable attendants and tree planters.

Admissions of H-2B workers rose almost fivefold in the 1990s, and the program has come under scrutiny as a result of problems, especially in forestry. In September 2002, fourteen Honduran and Guatemalan H-2B workers died when the van driven by their foreman went off a bridge on a private Maine road. Their workplace was 2.5 hours each way from their housing, and the men were charged $84 a week to ride in the van. Their employer was fined the maximum amount for not registering the driver, but continued to bring H-2B workers into the U.S. for reforestry work, much of which is done on public land at government expense.

The number of H-2B visas issued rose from 10,000 in 1995 to more than 60,000 in 2002 and on March 10, 2004, the 66,000 limit on H-2B visas was reached for the first time since the program was created in 1990, largely because winter ski resorts requested more H-2B workers. Employers formed an organization seeking an "emergency" increase in the cap, and labor brokers have begun to advertise the availability of H-2B workers to employers.[27]

The number of U.S. admissions of Canadians and Mexicans with TN visas tripled between 1995 and 2002 to 74,000 and in 2004 the 5,500 a year limit on TN-visas for Mexican professionals ended.[28] The sixty-plus NAFTA freedom-of-movement professions, listed in chapter 16 of the treaty, range from accountant to zoologist, and the program is supposed to allow Mexicans and Canadians to appear at U.S. ports of entry with proof of citizenship and education and a U.S. job offer and receive their TN visas.

CONCLUSIONS: MUTUALLY BENEFICIAL MIGRATION MANAGEMENT

In an ideal world, the 2,000-mile-long Mexico-U.S. border would resemble the longer Canada-U.S. border, a relatively open border with large trade flows and little unwanted migration. The question is what the Mexican and U.S. governments can and should do now to achieve such a border relationship.

Unlike the Philippines and some other labor-sending countries that aim to expand labor emigration by "marketing" their workers abroad, the Mexican government's announced goal is to achieve the economic development, human security, and confidence in the future that eventually makes emigration unnecessary. The major tool for achieving developed country status is a new economic policy that stresses investment, job creation, and trade while tapping the migrant diaspora to participate in development at home via remittances. Until Mexicans feel that emigration is unnecessary, the Mexican government aims to improve the status of Mexicans in the United States.

The U.S. government aims to remain open to immigrants and nonimmigrants, but to reduce illegal migration. There are several major challenges, including what to do about the 10 million unauthorized foreigners in the United States and how to change the attitudes of both migrants and employers who have found it easier to work outside rather than inside the legal migration system. Changing the perception that illegal is easier than legal will require some combination of carrot and stick that makes it easier for migrants and employers to participate in legal programs, but that also increases penalties for operating outside legal channels. The challenge for the U.S. government is to find the correct balance of carrots and sticks to govern behavior inside its borders, and to cooperate with Mexico to encourage legal migration and economic development.

APPENDIX: NAFTA AND THE MIGRATION HUMP REVISITED

Poverty is seen as a root cause of migration, and development or a reduction in poverty as the solution for unwanted migration. For this reason, attacking the "root causes" of migration is widely heralded as the surest path to decrease illegal and unwanted migration.

Economic theory teaches that the root causes of poverty and migration can be attacked in a way that promotes economic convergence via freer trade and investment, so that trade can be a substitute for migration. The U.S. Commission for the Study of International Migration and Cooperative

Economic Development, in searching for "mutually beneficial" ways to reduce unwanted migration, concluded that freer trade was preferable to more migration as a way to promote the convergence that would reduce unwanted migration: "expanded trade between the sending countries and the United States is the single most important remedy."[29]

Trade means that a good is produced in one country, taken over borders, and bought and consumed in another. Economic theory teaches that trading dictated by each country's comparative advantage increases global income. If each country specializes in producing those goods in which it has relative advantage because of its resources, location, or capital-labor costs, then even if one country can produce all goods cheaper than another, both are still better off specializing in the production of the goods they can produce most efficiently, exporting some, and importing goods they cannot produce as efficiently. Trade can also lead to economies of scale, which lowers the cost of production as output increases for a larger market.

However, there can be job-displacement in emigration areas in response to freer trade, as when TV factories in the U.S. close and reopen in lower-wage Mexico, or as Mexican farmers quit growing corn because of cheaper imports. The displaced U.S. workers are not likely to migrate to Mexico, but since rural Mexicans were migrating to the U.S. before there was freer trade, more may emigrate as a result of freer trade. The U.S. Commission anticipated this temporary increase in migration, warning that "the economic development process itself tends in the short to medium term to stimulate migration." Thus, there can be a migration hump, a temporary increase in migration that accompanies freer trade.[30]

Most political leaders assume that, if the trade and migration are substitutes in the long-run, they are also substitutes in the short-run. This is why then-Mexican President Salinas, in arguing in favor of NAFTA in the early 1990s, asserted that that freer trade means "more jobs . . . [and] higher wages in Mexico, and this in turn will mean fewer migrants to the United States and Canada. We want to export goods, not people."[31]

The Migration Hump

A migration hump in response to economic integration between labor-sending and -receiving countries leads to a paradox: the same economic policies that can reduce migration in the long run can increase it in the short run or, in the words of the U.S. Commission, there is "a very real short-term versus long-term dilemma" to persuade a skeptical public that freer trade is the best long-run way to reduce unwanted migration.[32] Political leaders can explain that the short-run increase in migration associated with freer trade is a worthwhile price to pay for policies that reduce unwanted immigration in the long run, but they must first understand why trade and migration can rise together.

The steadily rising line in the figure below represents the status-quo migration flow, and the hump line depicts the additional migration associated with freer trade and economic integration; the number of migrants is measured on the Y-axis and time on the X-axis. Without economic integration, migration rises in the status-quo scenario because of faster demographic growth and slower economic growth in emigration countries. Economic integration, on the other hand, leads to a temporary increase in migration, represented by **A**. However, economic integration should also speed up economic and job growth, and the downside of the hump is shown in the movement toward **B**. As economic integration accelerates convergence, area **C** represents the migration avoided by economic integration, while area **D** represents the migration transition, which occurs when a net migrant sending country becomes a net receiving country.

The critical policy parameters are A, B, and C—how much does migration increase as a result of economic integration (A), how soon does this hump disappear (B), and how much migration is "avoided" by economic integration (C)? Generally, three factors must be present to create a migration hump: a continued demand-pull for migrants in the destination country, an increased supply-push in the origin country as a result of labor displacement and slow job growth, and migration networks that can move workers across borders. The usual comparative static economic analysis involves comparisons of equilibrium points before and after economic changes, not the process of adjustment to a new equilibrium; the

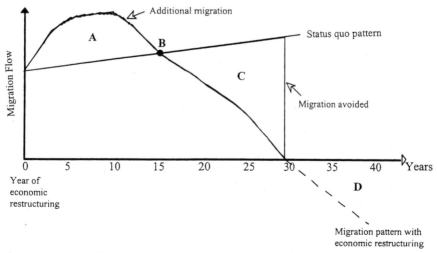

Figure 3.2.   The Migration Hump

migration hump is precisely this process of adjustment. It is important to emphasize that, once wage differences narrow to 4 to 1 or less, and job growth offers opportunities at home, the "hope factor" can deter especially irregular migration—most people prefer to stay near family and friends rather than cross national borders, especially if their migration is irregular.[33]

NAFTA at 10

The North American Free Trade Agreement was ten years old on January 1, 2004. In the early 1990s, NAFTA was controversial in the U.S., with presidential candidate Ross Perot asserting there would be a "giant sucking sound" of jobs leaving the U.S. for Mexico. President Clinton overcame opposition from the AFL-CIO[34] and congressional Democrats with the promise that NAFTA would increase prosperity "from the Yukon to the Yucatan."

The major promise of NAFTA was to increase trade, and this has occurred. Trade between the U.S. and its NAFTA partners increased sharply between 1993 and 2001—U.S. exports to Canada went from $107 billion to $145 billion, and U.S. exports to Mexico rose from $47 billion to $91 billion. U.S. imports rose even faster: from Canada, from $129 billion to $217 billion, and from Mexico imports rose from $45 billion to $131 billion.

NAFTA was also expected to create jobs in Mexico, raise wages, and eventually decrease unauthorized Mexico-U.S. migration. U.S. Secretary of State Warren Christopher in November 1993 said: "As Mexico's economy prospers [under NAFTA], higher wages and greater opportunity will reduce the pressure for illegal migration to the United States." However, Mexico's per capita economic growth was 1 percent a year between 1994 and 2003, compared to 7 percent in China. The best estimate is that the number of unauthorized Mexicans in the U.S. rose from 2 million in 1990 to 4.8 million in 2000.

NAFTA got off to a promising start in Mexico, where employment rose in 1994. However, in December 1994, just before President Zedillo was inaugurated, there was an economic crisis—the peso fell sharply, and the U.S. provided emergency funds to stabilize Mexican government finances. Job growth resumed in 1996, and formal Mexican employment peaked in 2000, as employment in maquiladoras, which expanded under NAFTA, reached 1.3 million, or 10 percent of formal sector jobs.

When the U.S. went into recession in 2000–2001, maquiladora employment fell, and remains below peak levels, because many of the border assembly factories, especially those producing textiles and apparel, moved to China and other countries with lower wages. Of the 700,000 new maquiladora jobs generated in NAFTA's first seven years, 300,000 were eliminated between 2000 and 2003, and there is a consensus that Mexico must upgrade worker skills and productivity or risk losing more assembly-type jobs to lower-wage countries. Maquiladoras produced $78 billion in exports during 2002, nearly two-thirds of that from American parts assembled in Mexico and re-exported to the United States.

Critics charge that NAFTA devastated Mexican agriculture, which generates about 5 percent of Mexican GDP. However, 25 percent of Mexicans live in rural areas, and 20 percent are mainly employed in agriculture, and the alleged NAFTA villain is increased imports of low-cost U.S. corn. Corn is planted on 50 percent of the Mexican land that is farmed, and much of this land is not irrigated. Some three million Mexicans depend at least partially on corn production, but most of the poorest corn farmers produce white corn that is used to make tortillas for their own consumption. However, the ready availability of cheaper U.S. corn sends a clear signal that there is no future in small-scale and rain-fed corn production in Mexico.[35]

There are many evaluations of NAFTA. Ex-President Salinas in January 2004 said that recession and a lack of Mexican reforms prevented Mexico from achieving NAFTA's promises. He said "The problem for Mexico lies inside, not outside." The World Bank's Daniel Lederman, co-author of "NAFTA Is Not Enough," argued that, to benefit more from NAFTA, Mexico must invest more in innovation, education, telecommunications, and do more to reduce corruption, concluding that free-trade agreements are not substitutes for development strategies. However, the World Bank concluded that Mexico would have been worse off without NAFTA. With NAFTA, Mexico's per capita income was $5,900 in 2002; without NAFTA, it would have been $5,600.

NAFTA speeded up changes in Mexico, creating jobs in services and manufacturing, especially in the northern border states, and raising the demand for and wages of skilled workers. However, as growing competition with China for assembly-line manufacturing jobs attests, Mexico has relatively high labor costs for unskilled workers. Mexico's period as a subcontractor for the U.S. proved to be short-lived, roughly from the mid-1990s to 2001. Further south inside Mexico, NAFTA's tariff reductions combined with other Mexican policies to speed the displacement of labor from agriculture, but there was little job creation and wage growth for less skilled workers, including those leaving the farm.

Many of the evaluations of NAFTA's first decade conclude that trade-led growth was not sufficient to bring prosperity to Mexico: real wages in Mexico were lower in 2001 than in 1994 despite higher productivity, income inequality was greater, and Mexico-U.S. migration rose. Poverty remains widespread: half of the 104 million Mexicans are considered poor, including 42 million who have less than $2 a day (the daily minimum wage is about $4 a day). One report concluded: "It takes more than just trade liberalization to improve the quality of life for poor people around the world."

NOTES

1. Employment means at least one hour of paid work during the survey week.

2. The U.S. labor force rose by an average 1.7 million a year in the past decade, from 131 million to 148 million, and employment by an average 1.6 million a year, from 123 million to 139 million, with Hispanics workers and employment rising by 700,000 a year, from 11 million in 1994 to 18 million in 2004.

3. One study, based on assumptions about the interactions of immigration and employment, estimated that two million more immigrants were employed in 2004 than 2000. If true, this study suggests fewer U.S.-born workers employed in 2004 than in 2000.

4. Philip L. Martin, *Trade and Migration: NAFTA and Agriculture* (Washington, D.C.: Institute for International Economics, 1993).

5. Philip L. Martin, *Promise Unfulfilled: Unions, Immigration, and Farm Workers* (Ithaca: Cornell University Press, 2003), chapter 2.

6. Philip L. Martin and Alan L. Olmstead, "The agricultural mechanization controversy," *Science* 227, no. 4687 (February 1985): 601–6.

7. Philip L. Martin, *Promise Unfulfilled*.

8. The Mexican peso dropped from $1 to 14 pesos in 1982 to $1 to 150 pesos in 1984.

9. A peak 1.8 million Mexicans were apprehended in 1986, and the Border Patrol was apprehending an overage of 3 Mexicans a minute, 24 hours a day, 7 days a week. Apprehensions record events, so the same person caught three times is three apprehensions.

10. Philip L. Martin, "Good intentions gone awry: IRCA and U.S. agriculture," *The Annals of the Academy of Political and Social Science* 534 (July 1994): 44–57.

11. Alan Riding, *Distant Neighbors: A Portrait of the Mexicans* (New York: Alfred A. Knopf, 1985).

12. Gary Hufbauer and Jeffrey Schott, *North American Free Trade: Issues and Recommendations* (Washington: Institute for International Economics, 1992).

13. P. Martin, *Trade and Migration*.

14. Douglas Massey, Jorge Durand, and Nolan Malone, *Beyond Smoke and Mirrors: Mexican Immigration in an Era of Economic Integration* (New York: Russell Sage, 2002).

15. Cited in "Bush Meets Fox," *Migration News* 8, no. 10 (October 2001). http://migration.ucdavis.edu/mn/archive_mn/oct_2001-02mn.html.

16. The U.S. Commission on Immigration Reform concluded in June 1995 that: "a large-scale agricultural guest worker program . . . is not in the national interest . . . such a program would be a grievous mistake." "CIR Recommends Less Immigration," *Rural Migration News* 1, no. 3 (July 1995), http://migration.ucdavis.edu. President Clinton issued a statement: "I oppose efforts in this Congress to institute a new guestworker or '*Bracero*' program that seeks to bring thousands of foreign workers into the United States to provide temporary farm labor." White House Press Release, June 23, 1995. Clinton's statement continued: "If our crackdown on illegal immigration contributes to labor shortages . . . I will direct the departments of Labor and Agriculture to work cooperatively to improve and enhance existing programs to meet the labor requirements of our vital agricultural industry consistent with our obligations to American workers."

17. Economic Report of the President (ERP), 2004, 46, http://www.gpoaccess
.gov/usbudget/fy05/pdf/ 2004_erp.pdf.

18. ERP, 33–45.

19. ERP, 47.

20. Employed persons have employers or are self-employed, and the U.S. collects data on employees from employers, the household survey, and from workers. The monthly employer or establishment survey asks 160,000 businesses and government agencies with 400,000 work sites about their roughly 40 million employees, while the separate monthly household survey collects data from 60,000 households and 100,000 workers. The household survey includes several types of workers not in the establishment survey, such as the self-employed and unpaid family and farmworkers. The establishment survey, which covers almost a third of U.S. payroll jobs and is considered more accurate, showed that employment had not yet returned to its pre-recession 2001 peak by fall 2004, while the household survey showed a new peak in employment. Some say that the reason why the household and establishment surveys have been diverging is unauthorized workers, who are counted in the household survey, but not in the establishment survey.

21. The data for Figure 3.1 are derived from James P. Smith and Barry Edmonston, eds., *The Immigration Debate: Economic, Demographic and Fiscal Effects of Immigration* (Washington: National Research Council, 1997). The increase in national income due to immigration–triangle **B** will be larger if (1) there are more migrant workers and/or (2) if the wage depression effect of migrant workers is larger. For example, if the migrant wage-depression impact doubled to 6 percent, and the migrant share of the work force doubled to 22 percent (as in California in the late 1990s), the income increase due to migration by $\frac{1}{2} \times 0.06 \times 0.22 \times 0.7 = 0.005$, or $\frac{5}{10}$ of 1 percent, four times larger.

22. The economic gain may be larger if there are positive externalities, as might occur if immigrants are entrepreneurial or the risk taking that encouraged them to migrate inspires Americans to work more productively. On the other hand, if there are negative externalities from migration, as when immigration is associated with crime or crowding in schools, for example, the gains are smaller.

23. "The Labor Demand Curve is Downward Sloping: Re-examining the Impact of Immigration on the Labor Market," *Quarterly Journal of Economics* 118, no. 4 (November 2003): 1335–74.

24. There are exceptions, for example H-2A sheepherders, who are allowed to remain in the U.S. up to thirty-six months.

25. One reason why it is relatively easier to sue H-2A employers is that the job recruitment offers they are required to submit to the Employment Service become contracts that provide a benchmark against which workers and their lawyers can assess actual wages and conditions. Many U.S. and unauthorized workers in similar jobs have only oral contracts, which makes it much harder to determine exactly what the employment contract is/was.

26. One worker could fill more than one H-2B job, and a worker who left the U.S. and returned within one year counts as two admissions.

27. For example, Amigos Labor Solutions (www.amigos-inc.com/) in Dallas says it provided 2,000 H-2B workers to employers in thirty-four states in 2002.

28. In 2000 and 2001, there were about 2,000 admissions a year of Mexicans with TN visas.

29. *Unauthorized Migration: An Economic Development Response* (Washington, D.C, 1990), xv.

30. *Unauthorized Migration*, xvi.

31. Quoted in "Bush letter to Congress," May 1, 1991, 17.

32. *Unauthorized Migration*, xvi.

33. South Korea made one of the world's fastest migration transitions, sending 200,000 workers abroad in the early 1980s and having over 300,000 migrants today. However, some Koreans still want to emigrate, and about 11,000 a year do so. Private firms such as the Emigration Development Corporation advertise emigration opportunities to Koreans, and collect fees for helping Koreans who want to emigrate to navigate the Canadian point system.

34. The AFL-CIO made defeat of NAFTA its number one priority in 1993, and AFL-CIO President John J. Sweeney said in November 2003 that: "We really feel that the record is clear after 10 years that NAFTA has failed American and Mexican workers."

35. Rural Mexico is dominated by *ejidos*, the communal farms that include 103 million hectares, or 56 percent of the arable land and 70 percent of the forests. In order to ensure that peasants had land, until the early 1990s, *ejido* land could not be sold, which limited productivity-increasing investments. The 29,162 *ejidos* became synonymous with rural poverty, and in 1992 the Mexican constitution was amended to allow the sale or rental of *ejido* land.

4

Determinants of the Migration Decision in Mexico

Liliana Meza González, Universidad Iberoamericana

INTRODUCTION

The Mexican economy has gone through a series of transformations since the mid-1980s that have been accompanied by political turmoil and demographic transitions. This has profoundly affected the way Mexican labor markets work, and has promoted more emigration than at any other period in recent history. As the demographics chapter in this study shows, between 1970 and 2004, the Mexican-born population living in the United States grew an amazing fifteen fold.[1]

There are many factors associated with this outstanding increase in Mexican migration flows. Mexican and American societies are now more integrated than ever, and several economic and social institutions have evolved to keep pace with this development. Capital, goods, and technology are now transferred across the border with minimal hindrance, but a major exception to this trend concerns the migration of labor. According to the Mexican National Employment Survey 2002, almost 80 percent of all Mexican international emigrants turn to the United States as an option to improve their standard of living through labor. This implies that Mexican emigration is primarily economic in the sense that it is mainly driven by differences in economic opportunities between the two countries. Recent information suggests that the rate of growth of the migration flow started to decrease after 2001, when the U.S. economy started to slow down. During this period the Mexican economy experienced relative economic stability accompanied by slow growth, and the combination of these factors seems to have exerted a small but significant migration-deterring effect, which may also be associated with the lesser "pull" of U.S. jobs at the time.[2]

In fact, a recent study by Richter, Taylor, and Yúñez-Naude, using retrospective data on the migration decision in Mexican rural households, points out that increases in the Mexican GDP seem to deter female rural emigration significantly, while increases in the U.S. GDP appear to promote more male emigration from rural Mexican communities.[3] In their study, the authors analyze the long-term effect of three specific policies on the dynamics and trends of rural migration: NAFTA (North American Free Trade Agreement), IRCA (the 1986 U.S. Immigration Reform and Control Act), and the intensified enforcement along the southern U.S. border. These three policies were aimed—wholly or partially—at curtailing the flow of unauthorized Mexico-U.S. migration, but the authors argue that the theoretical impact on migration of these policies is ambiguous and that it is necessary to estimate the real effect econometrically. To control for macroeconomic conditions in both the sending and the receiving countries, they include in their estimation the rate of growth of both the United States and Mexico GDP, and the change in the peso/dollar real exchange rate.

In their study, data from Mexican rural households show an upward trend in rural migration to the United States between 1980 and 2002, both for males and females, and conclude this trend is mainly driven by past migration, reflecting the central role of migration networks. The trend is steeper for males than for females, but the data show a steady increase in rural female migration in the twenty-three-year time span. Their results suggest that policy variables strongly influence migration, but not as much as macroeconomic variables, and certainly not as much as the network effect embodied in past migration. They argue NAFTA and IRCA seem to have exerted some impact on curtailing migration, while increased border enforcement appears to have had the opposite effect. These results support the belief that economic factors influence the migration decision of Mexicans, and suggest again that the economic changes in Mexico might have had an impact on the recent increase in the urban migration flow. In this sense, it is important to mention that although rural areas show the highest rate of emigration in the country, Mexico is 76 percent urban, and what happens in urban areas is also important to understand the migration dynamics, since they contribute to roughly half the total flow.

If migration is driven by economic forces, we might hypothesize that changes in the urban labor markets are affecting individual and family decisions about migration. Migration, in turn, affects the labor market through changes in the supply, causing dynamics that are worth studying in order to understand the economic effects of the phenomenon. This chapter is organized as follows. In the next section, I describe the main changes experienced by the Mexican economy and urban labor markets; I then describe the main economic theories that explain the migration decision at an individual and at a household level. The following three sections analyze how some of the economic changes may have affected the international migration decision of urban workers. I then estimate econometrically the migration decision of urban individuals and families, taking into account the labor conditions each individual or head of household faces prior to the migration decision, starting from the assumption that labor conditions are main determinants of emigration. This is followed by conclusions.

Mexican Economic and Labor Trends

In the mid-1980s, Mexican authorities unilaterally, but under severe external pressure, decided to liberalize the economy and to open it up to international trade and financial investment flows, just after a deep economic crisis. Development strategies were set aside, along with social protection policies, and the government concentrated on its stabilizing efforts. Trade and financial liberalization were accompanied by privatization, decentralizations, and deregulation policies, causing an important displacement of workers from formal and secure jobs in big firms and the government to less structured labor markets characterized by poor job conditions. In the rural sector, subsidies to basic produce started to be dismantled, contributing to promote rural emigration to urban areas.

The development strategy of the years previous to the 1980s was based on import substitution of consumption goods, and on imports of capital and intermediate inputs. The foreign currency needed to finance the imports came, in the after WWII period, mainly from agricultural exports. Mexican produce at that time was highly demanded in the U.S. market. Agricultural workers not producing for the foreign market were provided with guaranteed prices, so the agricultural sector was protected. In the urban areas, the industrialization efforts of the government, along with the political system—characterized by a corporative structure—also protected less skilled workers from risks, and migration to the United States was not considered an option by the vast majority of workers. Between 1940 and 1960 the economy grew at record rates due to the industrialization and accumulation efforts promoted by a highly interventionist government. In 1965 the Mexican and the U.S. governments agreed on allowing *maquiladoras*[4] to establish in Mexican territory, and the economy started to produce for the international market in isolation from the rest of the productive sector. The main attraction of maquiladoras was the low cost of labor.

But the economic model based on import substitution was gradually less successful at promoting growth. It started to show signs of exhaustion when the international economy slowed down and prices of Mexican produce dropped to unprecedented levels by the mid-1970s. In 1976 Mexico experienced the first of a series of crises, characterized by low levels of growth, high inflation, and devaluation of the domestic currency.

By the late 1970s, authorities argued that a new economic model was needed, and that government intervention had been a source of negative externalities and market failures that only a freer market could correct. At that time, government intervention and physical accumulation were severely questioned as sources of growth by recognized scholars, given the experience of Asian economies, growing mainly through liberal policies. However, the decision to open up the Mexican economy was postponed by the authorities when huge oil fields were discovered and oil prices reached record levels. The government contracted an enormous external debt in international currency that reached an unprecedented peak, arguing that income from oil sales would be sufficient to cover the service. The economy experienced another economic crisis in 1982, after oil prices dropped, causing a significant decrease in the average wage. Wage levels of 1981 have not been reached since.

Between 1981 and 1988 the Mexican economy grew at an average annual rate of only 1.8 percent, with a drop of 5.3 percent in 1983. Inflation reached its highest level in 1987, when it grew more than 150 percent. All this affected the working conditions of the average Mexican worker severely, not only because real wages and the number of formal jobs decreased, but also because jobs became more unstable in the sense that they were created in short-lived small firms. In 1985 Mexico joined the GATT (General Agreement of Tariffs and Trade), the predecessor of the World Trade Organization (WTO). In 1986 another crisis hit the Mexican economy when international interest rates increased and oil prices decreased again. A stabilization plan was put in place in 1987, and inflation went down dramatically. The stabilization process itself imposed another cost on workers because real wages were used as anchors of inflation. Between 1989 and 1994 the economy grew at relatively high levels, and new social programs were implemented to protect the poorest of the poor, mainly in rural areas. In 1992 Mexico entered the OECD (Organization for Economic Cooperation and Development), and optimism reigned, but a series of political events caused capital to flee the country and that triggered, in late 1994, another crisis that once again affected growth and inflation and, of course, wages and unemployment rates. In 1994 the North American Free Trade Agreement (NAFTA) was enacted, reducing trade barriers further and locking-in economic reforms.

The transition from a highly protected to a more liberal economy in Mexico, as in other countries, seems to have represented a very high cost for the working class in both rural and urban areas, although a thorough analysis is needed to clearly understand the dynamics behind the labor market transformations. Mexico has recently experienced increases in the return to capital and other inputs, at the expense of wages and employment oppor-

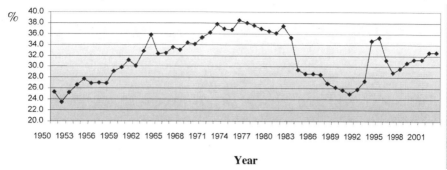

Figure 4.1. Worker Remunerations as a Proportion of GDP
Source: Banco de México

tunities. Figure 4.1 shows the proportion of GDP absorbed by workers. It is clear that in the period previous to 1980 it had an increasing trend, which is clearly reversed after 1982. It is important to point out that economic crises are closely correlated to decreases in this series, suggesting they impose a heavy burden on the working class.

According to various authors, the economic crisis of the 1980s led to the increase of low-wage jobs, and the jobs created were, in general, unprotected.[5] In short, the crisis awoke the infamous *informal* economy, despite the important amounts of foreign direct investment received. Workers affected by the implementation of the new economic model and the series of economic crises were not provided with any kind of social protection, and the new formal jobs created were not sufficient to absorb the increasing number of entrants to the labor market. The prescriptions of the Washington Consensus were followed without questioning, but it seems that the gains in economic efficiency were partly outweighed by costs in earnings volatility, uncertainty for workers, job losses, and decreases in well-being of a large proportion of the population. Figure 4.2 shows the trend in the Mexican average wage between 1965 and 1997. The graph shows the indicator drops in 1982 and does not recover to previous levels.

In 2000 a new democratic government took office, and the economy grew at high rates for a few months, mainly promoted by manufacturing exports. The deceleration of the U.S. economy since 2001 negatively affected the Mexican economy, but more reasonable economic policies have avoided another crisis. Real wages and the average proportion of GDP dedicated to workers' remunerations have slightly recovered in the last few years, but the labor market still exhibits its two main characteristics: an important amount of the labor force is inserted in the informal sector, holding insecure and volatile jobs, and significant amounts of workers turning

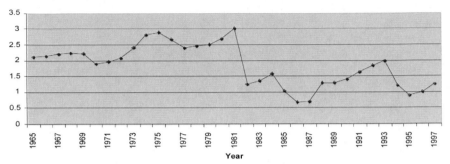

Figure 4.2. Real Average Mexican Wage
Source: Mexican Migration Project

to the U.S. labor market looking for opportunities they cannot find at home. Nevertheless, it is important to mention that the slight recovery of real wages and salaries coincides with the highest increase in migration flows, suggesting other forces are also behind this phenomenon.

When NAFTA was negotiated, it was said that its purpose was to "boost the confidence of foreigners investing in plants and equipment in Mexico"[6]—that is, its main purpose was to promote the flow of foreign direct investment (FDI), in order to decrease the movement of labor across the borders into the United States. But migration was not deterred, and boomed along with FDI and trade, at least during the late 1990s.

Analytically, it is hard to disentangle the effect of the economic transition on the Mexican labor market, and especially on migration, because there are many factors affecting them at the same time. Economic transition implied not only trade and financial liberalization but also a reduction in the size of the government and the elimination of a series of benefits for certain population groups. The Mexican population is also more educated now than it was twenty years ago, and more skilled workers are choosing to migrate, rather than to wait for a formal urban job. Women are participating more in the labor market as well, meaning there is more labor competition. Demographically we observe considerable impact coming from young workers entering for the first time in the labor market, which are a consequence of the highest fertility rates in the country twenty years ago. In the political arena, bureaucratic discretion has not been completely eliminated, and institutions do not work as they were supposed to for the reforms to be considered successful in terms of increasing growth. All this should have affected labor markets and migration in many different ways, as the new economic model was expected to reduce migration, but it did not do so. In the following section I present different versions of the economic theories of migration and, based on them, I elaborate some material to try to understand why urban migration increased in the late 1990s, despite the different changes the economy has experienced.

THE MIGRATION DECISION

Economics proposes several theories to explain the migration decision. The neoclassical basic microeconomic theory of migration states that an individual migrates based on a cost-benefit analysis of the decision, where benefits and costs accrued to migration can be pecuniary or non-pecuniary. In this scheme, individual rational actors decide to migrate because the cost-benefit calculation leads them to expect a positive net return from movement.[7] International migration is then conceptualized as a form of investment in human capital; people choose to move where they can be most productive, given their skills, but before they can capture the higher wages associated with greater labor productivity they must undertake certain costs. Assuming individuals maximize income, and that the flow of net income can be expressed in present value, the theory states that a positive weighted wage differential will make individuals migrate, i.e., the theory predicts that a potential migrant will go to where the expected returns to migration are the greatest. In this model, the attitude toward risk of the economic actors is not taken into account, meaning the model assumes risk neutrality of all individuals involved in a migration decision. This assumption is certainly not realistic given the characteristics of the current U.S. migration policy. In this context, it is more realistic to assume migrants are less risk averse than the rest of the population, but this does not mean they are not averse to risk at all, as it was assumed in the income maximization models.

This basic economic theory of migration takes into account the fact that the individual decision to migrate is greatly influenced by current and past migration experiences of the individual migrant social network. As Davis, Stecklov, and Winters put it, "networks influence migration because potential migrants use their network connections to obtain information that alters the returns to migration and, if the decision to migrate is taken, use these networks for direct assistance in the migration process, thus lowering the cost of migration."[8] Networks, therefore, serve an important theoretical function in economic models as they alter the expected income gains from migration as well as the uncertainty associated with it.

A relatively new economic theory of migration assumes that the migration decision represents a once-and-for-all relocation of the individuals or of the entire households. Mexico-U.S. migration usually initiates as a temporary allocation of household labor, meaning it can be viewed as one component of the household "labor portfolio" in which some members migrate to the United States while others migrate to destinations in Mexico to combine domestic wage work with work in the household.[9]

These models can be combined to develop a theoretical framework in which the migration decision within a household is taken in steps. First, families decide to send a member to another destination in Mexico, expecting him/her to obtain a formal job in the urban labor market. If this is not accomplished soon, families may decide to send the same individual abroad, with a view to have remittances to help support the family. In 1978, Calvo developed a model of internal rural-urban migration under uncertainty that assumes risk aversion of migrants that can be modified to incorporate the international migration decision easily.[10] In this model, the urban labor market is characterized by two sectors, one formal and another informal. The informal sector offers lower wages and lower quality jobs relative to the formal, but the rural migrant takes into account different probabilities of obtaining a job in either of the two sectors when deciding to migrate. A higher probability of getting a formal job implies a higher probability of migration to the urban area, given a particular rural income.

The recent changes in the Mexican economy have created a more insecure and uncertain labor market, while the U.S. economy experienced a high growth period. It is precisely in this moment when migration flows from Mexico to the United States have increased the most. This coincidence deserves an analysis, and the following sections of this article will try to shed some light on the role that a more insecure labor environment in the source country plays in promoting migration. In the following sections I describe the main changes in the Mexican labor market that might have affected the migration decision and the number of Mexican emigrants in the late 1990s.

MIGRATION AND THE INFORMAL SECTOR

The Mexican labor market has been under strong demographic and social strain during the last ten to fifteen years. First, new generations of young workers were born in the periods of highest fertility rates in the country. The Mexican population growth rate peaked at 3.3 percent in 1970, and in 1974 the government launched a family planning program that helped birth rates to fall: fertility dropped from an average of seven children per woman in 1965 to 2.5 by 2000.[11] Additionally, more women are now entering the labor force, competing for jobs mainly with younger and unskilled workers. Another strain has come from rural migration, which has steadily incorporated workers into urban labor markets since the 1960s.[12] Considering these factors, the number of urban formal sector jobs created in the last few years has not been enough to absorb the increasing Mexican urban labor force. In this context, the informal sector has become a refuge for a number of workers that do not find opportunities in the domestic formal labor market. Some models of internal migration and economic development state that the informal employment sector is a temporary staging post for new migrants on their way to formal sector employment.[13] If the number of formal jobs created in the economy is not enough to absorb the domestic labor force, at least part of this labor force will be stuck for long periods in informal, low-quality jobs, characterized by volatility and insecurity, which means they are not protected by laws and are victims to the changes in the market by way of supply and demand.[14]

Assuming rural workers or newcomers to the labor market look for job opportunities either in the urban sector of their home country or in a foreign country, we can model the role of the informal sector in the international migration decision. According to a certain kind of migration model, migration is a two-stage phenomenon in which migrants initially spend some time in the "urban informal" sector or remain unemployed before finding a job in the "formal" sector. We could add to this model the idea that a worker can look for a job either in the urban formal sector or in a foreign country. Furthermore we could argue that the worker first looks for a job in the urban formal sector of his/her home country and when the search is not successful he/she looks for a job abroad. In this case, employment in the informal sector serves as a means of financing the period of search for formal sector or for foreign country employment. In their decision to migrate, potential migrants balance the probability of unemployment or informal sector employment against the real income differential between the urban formal sector or the foreign country and the rural area. The main assumptions underlying this probabilistic migration model are:

1. The urban labor market is divided into two sectors: a high-wage formal sector in which the wage rate is set above the market clearing level and is downwardly rigid, and a low wage informal sector which is characterized by a high rate of turnover and freedom of entry.
2. The foreign labor market is not segmented and wages are determined by a competitive mechanism.
3. Migrants are attracted to the urban center and the foreign country by opportunities and the associated wage structure in both.
4. Search for urban jobs is conducted in the urban center, while search for jobs abroad can be conducted anywhere.

5. Participation in the informal sector does not interfere significantly with search in the formal sector and the foreign country.
6. Social networks play an important role in the process of searching in the foreign country.
7. Mobility from the informal sector to the other sectors takes place.

The model would predict that lower probabilities of finding a formal job in the urban center will promote more migration, while longer periods in the informal sector will imply higher probabilities of international migration. Increases in the number of formal jobs in the urban center will then deter migration, and economic crisis will promote more migration because of the destruction of formal sector opportunities.

MIGRATION AND ECONOMIC INTEGRATION

One of the main changes the Mexican economy has experienced during the last fifteen years is the increasing integration with the world economy and, more specifically, with the North American economy. Although this integration has not formally implied enormous changes in terms of freer movement of labor across borders, the freer movement of goods has indeed promoted changes in relative wages, relative prices, and in employment rates that might have affected the migration decision of a good number of individuals. Standard trade theory does not have a prediction about the way migration changes with trade liberalization. Under certain assumptions migration is assumed to increase with trade, i.e., migration is supposed to complement trade and specialization, while under others it is assumed to decrease (or substitute trade). The effects can differ in the short and in the long run, and they depend on the capital flows trade liberalization promotes. I now proceed to explain the possible changes the migration flow can suffer when economic integration takes place.

First, when exposed to international competition, countries tend to specialize in the production of goods that use the abundant factor more intensively, and to displace inputs from import-competing industries. The relative demand for the abundant factor of production is then assumed to increase with specialization along with its relative price. If we simplify the theory and assume the abundant factor in Mexico is labor relative to capital, we might then have predicted less migration with trade. This result, however, lies on an assumption of perfect competition in all markets before the trade liberalization reform. In Mexico, several markets were not characterized by competition prior to the trade liberalization reform, so this result may or may not hold depending on the market conditions. According to Feliciano, the markets most affected by the trade liberalization reform were exactly those where labor was more protected, causing trade to induce decreases in prices and wages in labor intensive industries, and not increases as it was expected.[15] A clear example of this situation is maize,[16] whose production accounts for the largest share of employment in rural areas. Maize protection was Mexico's de facto rural employment and anti-poverty program before NAFTA was enacted,[17] and although the maize market was not liberalized immediately when NAFTA was signed, Mexican authorities unilaterally decided to decrease warranty prices paid to producers in the early 1990s, inducing a major rural-urban migration and/or the impoverishment of a great number of rural households.

Now, labor is not a homogeneous factor, and this may mask the migration results. If we consider labor can be classified according to skills, we could assume unskilled labor is the relatively abundant factor in Mexico while skilled labor is relatively scarce. If the relative demand for unskilled labor increases with trade, we could have then predicted a decrease in economic migration of less skilled workers and an increase in economic migration of highly skilled workers after the first trade liberalization efforts. This result, however, depends on the assumptions of perfect competition in all markets and perfect information, which certainly do not hold for the Mexican case.

Economic integration can create more migration in the short run, when displacement is largest, but less migration in the medium and long term if the increases in wages and jobs it promotes are large enough to compensate the losses. According to Philip Martin, NAFTA would promote increasing migration (by 10 to 30 percent) in the first five to fifteen years to then decrease it, producing a migration hump.[18] This prediction seems to be crystallizing according to the latest data on Mexico-U.S. migration, because migration is now increasing at a lower rate. But the creation of opportunities in a recently liberalized economy can differ among groups of workers. It is then more accurate to expect changes in the composition of the migration flow when trade is liberalized.

Besides, other forces might be behind the number of Mexicans migrating to the United States. For example, if economic integration is not creating the number of good jobs the country requires, given the demographic pressures, while social networks are facilitating the insertion of Mexicans in good jobs in the United States, then we might not observe a permanent decrease in emigration despite increasing trade. According to the Mexican Institute of Social Security (IMSS), the number of formal private-sector jobs in Mexico in the year 2004 was around 12.5 million, while the Mexican labor force was around 41.1 million persons.[19]

Table 4.1.   Mexican Labor Force

Year	Total Labor Force	Permanent Formal Jobs*	Temporary Formal Jobs	Self-Employed	Other**
1998	38,344,658	10,047,624	1,213,372	6,932,714	20,150,948
1999	39,507,063	10,394,868	1,511,458	6,941,391	20,659,346
2000	38,242,174	10,913,044	1,693,709	6,663,699	18,971,722
2001	—	10,856,998	1,683,938	6,876,990	20,333,459
2002	39,633,842	10,725,207	1,710,458	7,015,190	20,182,987
2003	39,682,845	10,654,868	1,724,739	7,361,168	—
2004	41,085,736	10,778,692	1,760,651	7,798,073	20,748,320
Percentages					
1998	100.00	26.20	3.16	18.08	52.55
1999	100.00	26.31	3.83	17.57	52.29
2000	100.00	28.54	4.43	17.43	49.61
2001	100.00	27.31	4.24	17.30	51.15
2002	100.00	27.06	4.32	17.70	50.92
2003	100.00	26.85	4.35	18.55	50.25
2004	100.00	26.23	4.29	18.98	50.50

Source: IMSS, http:// www.imss.gob.mx, and INEGI, http://dgcnesyp.inegi.gob.mx/bdiesi/bdie.html, several
   years.
* Excludes formal public sector employment.
** Includes unemployed, agricultural, and informal workers.

An additional channel through which economic integration may shock
the relative demand for different kinds of workers is through its impact on
capital flows. Given that capital complements skilled labor, capital inflows
may increase the demand for skill, and this seems to have been the case in
Mexico.[20] The importance of capital inflows are reflected in the fact that
from 1980 to 1994 foreign direct investment (FDI) averaged 1.3 percent of
Mexico's GDP, while from 1995 to 2000 it averaged 2.8 percent of GDP.[21]
Some studies have indicated that FDI has caused important changes in Mexican labor markets,[22] and specifically that it has increased the relative demand for highly skilled workers. If this is the case, economic integration
should have then promoted more emigration of less qualified workers and
less emigration of highly skilled workers.

Another factor that might have affected the Mexico-U.S. migration patterns and that is correlated to economic integration is technological change.
Technology developed in advanced economies is transferred to developing
countries through FDI and capital imports. Technology is assumed to complement highly skilled labor and to substitute less skilled workers. If trade
liberalization has implied increases in the development and the adoption
of new technology, it might have promoted more migration of less skilled
workers.

Finally, trade theory predicts price-convergence among countries with economic integration, and if this were the case we could expect Mexico-U.S. migration to decrease in the long run. This is the reason why trade is considered a substitute of migration. Unfortunately this price convergence theory relies on a series of assumptions that hardly apply to the U.S.-Mexico case. For example, to expect convergence in factor prices, countries are supposed to share the same technology. Robertson analyzes wage convergence between Mexican and U.S. cities and finds that it exists mainly in the border area, but shows that the wages tend to return to the same gap after some shocks.[23] This wage gap among countries can be attributed to transportation costs, costs of job search, inherent language and skill differentials, non-monetary costs of relocation in the United States, and economic rents accruing to legal migrants and U.S. workers owing to labor market protection.[24] If factor prices do not converge between highly integrated countries, we could expect international wage gaps to remain despite the increases in trade flows, and therefore we should not expect migration to be deterred by trade, assuming migration responds to wage differentials among countries.

Wrapping up, economic integration might have different effects on migration in the short run relative to the long run, and it might affect economic conditions of different kind of workers differently. This means that we should expect the composition of the migration flow to be affected by trade, but the effect on the numbers of migrants is not very clear.

MIGRATION AND PRIVATIZATION

In the early 1980s the World Bank adopted privatization as a module of its structural adjustment programs for macroeconomic reform. Hemming and Unnithan define privatization as "an ideological principle that supports smaller governments, fewer taxes and less state involvement in society."[25] Privatization is supposed to increase economic efficiency, to bring new money to the economy via investors, and to reduce the need for government subsidies. Privatization forces firms to become more efficient in order to survive in a more competitive environment. This entails displacement of less productive and less skilled workers among industries and to unemployment and underemployment of these workers.

By the mid 1980s the Mexican government initiated a large privatization effort along with a reduction of the size of the government. The number of public firms went from more than 1,100 to less than 200 in a ten-year time span, and the number of public employees was dramatically reduced, inducing many of these individuals to search for economic opportunities in the informal sector while an opportunity in the formal urban sector opened up for them.

Private owners were able to update equipment and introduce new eco-friendly technology that was previously unavailable due to lack of government funding for such innovations and/or closed trade borders.[26] Therefore privatization, along with trade and financial liberalization, created new economic conditions in the country that privileged skilled labor relative to other kinds of workers because skills induce higher productivity. The increase in the relative demand for skill in the domestic formal sector may then have contributed to raise the probability of migration of unskilled workers, trapped in low quality jobs.

According to Massey et al., the penetration of markets and the privatization of industry within less affluent and underdeveloped nations provide the basis for an impoverished and migratory people.[27] Specifically in the case of Mexico, Massey et al. argue that economic reforms have increased the pressure for international migration from both rural and urban areas.[28] Not only did the displacement of workers from jobs in the government and public firms help promote more migration, but it also promoted the entire spectrum of conditions of the Mexican domestic labor markets. Privatization might have also caused increases in prices and may have raised the cost of living of precisely the population that faces more difficulties to get inserted in the modern economy. On the other side, the reduction in the size of the government might have implied the elimination of subsidies and the reduction of privileges certain groups enjoyed for political reasons.

A recent study by Cleveland et al., suggests that the privatization of public services in Mexico has increased the cost of living and has promoted more emigration in search of new sources of income.[29] These authors argue that the firms that have been privatized in Mexico are not only airlines, oil and sugar refineries, highways, construction firms, and others, but that the privatization policy has also implied the transfer of essential services such as water and electricity in rural and small urban areas to the private sector, and that this has made these services unaffordable for certain groups.

The privatization of the national banking system deserves special attention in this analysis because the financial sector is assumed to play a very important role in the migration decision, according to the new economics of migration. The return of the banking system to private hands initiated in 1992,[30] but regulation was not ready to face the new market conditions in the country. The new private banking institutions started providing credit to the private sector in large amounts that were not sustainable once the interest rates increased by late 1994. After the 1995 financial crisis, the credit granted by the financial sector dropped dramatically, and it did not recover to its previous levels. Additionally, the number of bankruptcies and debt defaults increased significantly, imposing large costs to the whole system. This situation may have promoted more volatility and insecurity in the domestic labor market and, therefore, more emigration to the United States.

EMPIRICAL ESTIMATION

Using data from two different sources, this section analyzes how labor conditions of individuals and families affect the migration decision in urban areas in Mexico. First I use a data set obtained in four different Mexican urban localities that comes from a sample survey aimed to establish a relationship between international migration and self-employment.[31] In this data set the unit of observation is the individual, and this characteristic allows me to test the validity of the neoclassical theory of migration in the sense that it analyzes the migration decision of individuals and not the decision of families to send a member abroad. I then use data from the 2002 National Urban Employment Survey (ENEU in Spanish), grouping individuals into households, to analyze the decision families make about migration.[32] These two estimations try to establish a relationship between the probabilities of migration and the labor conditions urban individuals and families face prior to the trip abroad. Both data sets include sociodemographic and economic information about each member of the household and about the migration decision of those individuals who stayed more than one month abroad during the last five years.

Economic theory predicts lower probability of migration among workers employed in the formal urban sector and among those with stable income sources. It also predicts higher probability of migration among workers inserted in low quality jobs and underemployed relative to those in more stable and well-paid occupations. The same results apply when the unit of analysis is a household instead of an individual. In this case we expect that urban households with more stable sources of income and those whose head holds a better quality job will send members abroad in lower proportions. These empirical results will shed some light about the supply forces behind the recent increase in the migration flow, and will allow us to define policy recommendations that might deter illegal emigration in the following years.

Estimation at an Individual Level

Table 4.2 presents the results of a probit regression run with the sample survey data at an individual level. In this estimation the dependent variable

Table 4.2. Probit Regression of Migration (dependent variable: individual is or was migrant)

Independent Variables	(1)	(2)	(3)	(4)
Self-employed	−0.5660 **	−0,6660 **	−1,1837 **	−1,3478 **
	(−3,55)	(−3,50)	(−4,90)	(−5,38)
Employee	1,0287 **	0,8831 **	0,7937 **	0,7116 **
	(6,81)	(5,05)	(4,32)	(3,76)
Unemployed	1,4927 **	1,1832 **	1,098 **	0,9953 **
	(7,12)	(4.81)	(4,22)	(3,71)
Family in USA	—	0.7303 **	0.7057 **	0.6673 **
		(5,37)	(5,07)	(4,66)
Sex	—	0.4806 **	0.4980 **	0.5093 **
	(3,51)	(3,49)	(3,48)	
Under 25 years old when migrating	—	−0.5319 **	−0.3793 *	−0.2271
		(−2.46)	(−1,70)	(−0,99)
Over 25 years old & under 40 when migrating	—	0.0725	0,1448	0,2295
		(0,45)	(0,87)	(1,32)
Children	—	−1.3091 **	−1,2320 **	−1,2705 **
		(−6.93)	(−6,28)	(−6,23)
Married	—	0.2134	0,2291	0,2963
		(1.21)	(1,25)	(1,57)
Schooling over High School	—	−0.0072	0,0314	0,0635
		(−0,05)	(0,22)	(0,44)
Retail Trade	—	—	0,6198 **	0,3646
			(2,63)	(1,42)
Services 1/	—	—	0,7329 **	0.3858
			(2.99)	(1,46)
Professional and Technical Services	—	—	0,9803 **	0.5809
			(2,71)	(1,54)
Manufacturing	—	—	0,1838	−0.0671
			(0,25)	(−0,09)
Working less than 10 hours	—	—	0,9680 *	0.9958 *
			(1,68)	(1.61)
Working more than 40 hours	—	—	−0,5607 **	−0.6666 **
			(−2,14)	(−2,46)
Altamira	—	—	—	−0.2561
				(−1,13)
Apaseo el grande	—	—	—	−0.8347
				(−3,54)
Comonfort	—	—	—	−0.7312
				(−3,54)
Constant	−1.1124 **	−0.6563 **	−0,3501	0.3365
	(−9,65)	(−3,02)	(−1,04)	(0,87)
Number of observations	793	793	793	793
Log-likelihood	−295.4758	−235.5308	−221.4889	−213.5944

Source: Own estimations using a data set obtained in four Mexican localities.
1/ Services other than professional and technical and retail trade
* Significant at 0.05
** Significant at 0.01

is a dummy equal to one when the individual declares to have migrated in the last five years at least once, and equal to zero when this condition does not hold. When the individual is still abroad but his/her family is not, the respondent provides the information about the migrant. The questionnaire inquires about the labor conditions faced by the migrant just prior to his/her trip. It also inquires about other sociodemographic characteristics that may have affected the migration decision and that have to be included in the regression as controls (to avoid omitted variable biases). I include four different versions of the probit estimation to test the robustness of the results regarding the role labor conditions play in the migration decision at an individual level. In the main text of this work I do not report the size of the coefficients or extract conclusions about elasticities, but I include an appendix with the transformed coefficients, to provide an interpretation of the results.[33] The first regression includes only three labor positions as independent variables. In the second regression I add some sociodemographic variables as controls. In the third regression I add more variables that reflect the kind of job the individual held when the migration decision took place, and in the fourth regression I include local fixed effects.

The first result worth mentioning in this estimation at an individual level is that people in different occupations and under different labor conditions seem to migrate in different proportions, even when additional controls are included in the regression. To analyze the relationship between the labor position of an individual and the migration decision, the whole sample was classified in four different labor brackets. These brackets are: employees, self-employed workers, unemployed, and people out of the labor force. The omitted group in the regressions is "out of the labor force." Self-employed workers may or may not have employees under their authority. The first column in table 4.2 includes only the labor brackets as regressors. The results of this first estimation suggest that the unemployed and the employees have significant higher probabilities of migration relative to the people out of the labor force, but that the self-employed migrate in lower proportions. These results have to be tested adding more controls to the regression. The controls try to take into account the variables that, according to different theories of migration, affect the migration decision at an individual level.

As migration is supposed to be highly dependent on social networks, a dummy variable equal to one when the individual declares to have family in the United States is included as an independent variable in versions 2, 3, and 4 of the estimation, along with other sociodemographic variables that take into account the different labor conditions individuals may face either in Mexico or in the United States. These sociodemographic variables are included to account for the income generating capacity of each individual in either country, given the difficulty to estimate individual wage differentials. Regarding these variables, some of the results are quite robust. First, as expected, individuals with family in the United States seem to migrate in higher proportions than individuals without these social networks. This result supports the cumulative causation theory of migration, which states that migration in a community creates more migration up to a certain point. Second, according to the estimation, individual migration in Mexico is still primarily a male phenomenon, at least in the four communities sampled. This is consistent with the idea that female migrants tend to take their families with them or join them, and to stay longer in the foreign country. Finally, in this estimation children seem to exert a significant deterring effect, meaning that individuals with nuclear families on their own tend to migrate in lower proportions relative to individuals without children.

In the third regression some other labor variables are included, such as the economic sector where the individual worked before departure and the number of hours worked in the last occupation. The economic sectors are classified in retail trade, professional, and technical services; other services; manufacturing; and other economic sectors. The omitted sector is the last one and includes activities in the agricultural sector, in construction and other industries. According to the results presented in Table 4.2, column 3, individuals working in the service sector tend to migrate in higher proportions relative to individuals in other economic sectors, while individuals in the manufacturing sector do not migrate in different proportions relative to those in other economic sectors. This is an interesting result because I separated occupations in the service sector according to the level of human capital required to perform the job. I assume retail trade and services in general do not require a high level of formal schooling or training, while professional and technical services do. I expected people in the professional and technical services to migrate in lower proportions, but this does not seem to be the case. In a recent work, Meza shows that the Mexican service sector is characterized by larger wage inequality relative to other economic sectors, and this could explain the higher probability of migration the workers in this sector present.[34] Regarding the number of hours worked, the results suggest that people who are underemployed, i.e., those who work less than ten hours per week, migrate in higher proportions relative to people working longer periods, while workers with more than forty hours per week in their jobs tend to migrate in lower proportions. This suggests that underemployment, inequality, and precarious labor conditions promote more emigration, while more stable and better jobs tend to exert a deterring effect.

The fourth estimation presented in Table 4.2 includes local fixed effects to test if our results are mainly driven by differences in the localities or not.

This regression suggests that the different labor positions indeed determine the migration decision, even when the differences in localities are taken into account. An interesting result is that different economic sectors do not seem to be correlated with the migration decision of individuals once the local fixed effects are included in the regression. This could be interpreted as the importance of the local migration culture.

The estimation carried out with the data set at an individual level has been useful to show that labor conditions may be highly correlated with the migration decision, but it also suggests that social networks and the migration culture in the localities are also significant determinants of the decision.

Now, to better understand the role labor conditions play in the migration decision it would be necessary to include some interactions to the estimation. Unfortunately, the number of observations in this sample limits the quantity of cells that can be created, and makes it necessary to use another data set to empirically estimate how different occupations determine migration.

To increase the number of observations and to achieve representation of the whole Mexican population, the following estimation uses data from the National Urban Employment Survey (ENEU). In this case the unit of observation is the household, and the labor data corresponds to the head of each household.[35] With this regression it is possible to empirically test the validity of some of the predictions of the "new economics of migration" theory because we can analyze the family characteristics that tend to promote more emigration among their members. I do not expect the above results to be replicated in this regression,[36] because of the change in the unit of observation. I do expect, however, to prove that precarious jobs and more volatile income sources for the family indeed promote more migration at a family level.

Estimation at a Household Level

Using data from the ENEU we can better characterize the different labor positions and the different economic sectors included in the last regression. Factor expansions are used in the calculations to make the results more representative of the Mexican population. These characterizations will be useful to better understand which labor conditions are more significant determinants of the migration decision. Table 4.3 presents some basic statistics about six different labor positions, and table 4.4 presents basic descriptive statistics of six different economic sectors.

According to table 4.3, the labor position that has the highest return is business owner with more than five employees. Among them, almost 65 percent receive fringe benefits of medical insurance services, but almost 95

Table 4.3. Descriptive Labor Statistics by Labor Position (means and percentages)

Income	Income	s.d. of Income	Hours Worked	s.d. of Hours Worked	% Fringe Ben.	% Retirement	No. Observations*/
Employees	3574.04	4360.77	42.56	13.3	34.03	32.42	214420
Unemployed	2094.34	3407.26	28.81	23.73	26.53	23.18	5163
Self-employed 1/	2508.33	3661.2	39.15	16.01	26.63	0.06	35568
Small firm owner 2/	3844.31	6099.54	44.6	14.45	45.67	0.07	19082
Business owner 3/	8042.18	10814.97	47.25	13.13	64.43	0.05	11009
Out of the labor force	146.92	1015.71	2.44	10.13	1.43	1.78	197939

Source: Own estimation based on NUES2002–04 from INEGI
1/ Self-employed without employees
2/ Business owner with less than 5 employees
3/ Business owner with more than 5 employees
*/ Number of observations in sample. Calculations are made using factor expansions in all cases.
Key: s.d. = standard deviation

Table 4.4. Descriptive Labor Statistics by Economic Sector

	Avg. Income	s.d. Income	Hrs. Worked	s.d. Hrs. Worked	% Informal	% Retirement	No. Obs. */
Agriculture	1,488.61	3,410.80	40.93	12.52	95.00	2.48	22,500
Manufacturing	3,499.87	4,453.76	43.07	11.48	43.58	54.09	44,550
Construction	3,826.80	3,414.59	45.38	8.87	77.97	18.48	18,201
Retail trade	3,343.17	4,166.66	45.16	15.25	78.57	27.49	49,488
Professional services	5,640.77	4,815.23	37.40	11.94	35.02	64.72	33,427
Non-professional services	3,562.66	3,952.57	42.25	14.64	72.21	27.52	77,077

Source: Own estimation based on NUES2002–04 from INEGI
*/ Number of observations in sample. Calculations are made using factor expansions in all cases.
Key: s.d. = standard deviation

percent do not have a retirement savings account. The following group with the highest income is small business owners, but the difference in income between these two groups is very significant.[37] A lower percentage of small business owners receive medical insurance (45.7 percent), but more than 90 percent of them do not have a retirement savings plan. The ones more protected in terms of medical insurance and retirement savings accounts are the employees, but their salary is much lower than the average income of the business owners. Among the unemployed we find a large percentage of people with retirement savings accounts (23.2 percent). This suggests almost one quarter of the unemployed were working as employees before the unemployment spell. This means that around 75 percent of these unemployed are new entrants to the labor market or were working in the informal sector before.

According to Table 4.4, the highest average salary among economic sectors corresponds to professional services. In this sector the average number of hours worked is also lower and the percentage of people working in formal establishments and saving for retirement is larger than in the rest of the sectors. The lowest average income in the sample corresponds to workers in the agricultural sector, and in this sector the proportion of formal establishments and the proportion of workers saving for retirement are also the lowest. In the rest of economic sectors labor conditions are more or less similar regarding salary and number of hours worked, and the most striking differences are in the percentage of formal establishments and the proportion of workers with retirement savings accounts.

Once the labor positions and the economic sectors that will be included in the regression have been summarized, I proceed to present the results of the migration decision regression, run with the ENEU data set. Table 4.5 shows the results of the different regression runs with ENEU data. In this case the dependent variable is a dummy equal to one when a member of the family worked or is working abroad. The question in the survey limits the time span of the migration decision to five years, but I only included in the sample those families who declared to have sent a member abroad during the year of the survey. Doing this I attempted to maintain the labor conditions of the family relatively constant between the migration decision and the time of the survey.

It is important to point out that I could not run a regression at an individual level in this case because I could not figure out what the migrant was doing before departure. I only had access to the information about the job he/she held in the foreign country, but this analysis was not what I wanted to achieve. In this case then, I took the head of household labor conditions as determinants of migration of a family member.

The first estimation carried out with this new data set is presented in Table 4.5, column 1. This regression includes as independent variables

Table 4.5. Probit Regression of Migration (dependent variable: is or was migrant)

Independent Variables	(1)	(2)	(3)	(4)
Employee	0.0707 **	0.0452 **	0.025 **	−0.2569 **
	(26.25)	(15.64)	(6.35)	(−12.58)
Unemployed	−0.1237 **	−0.0112 **	−0.1181 **	−0.9340 **
	(−10.73)	(−9.64)	(−9.66)	(−7.11)
Self-employed 1/	−0.0464 **	−0.0749 **	−0.0974 **	−3.8758 **
	(−13.52)	(−20.99)	(−21.50)	(−99.13)
Small business owner 2/	0.2149 **	0.1856 **	0.1613 **	−4.5342 **
	(52.98)	(43.93)	(31.62)	(−149.44)
Business owner 3/	−0.2584 **	−0.2596 **	−0.2573 **	−8.3930 **
	(−13.63)	(−13.74)	(−13.39)	(−340.16)
Sex	—	−0.5586 **	−0.5594 **	−0.5881 **
		(−218.13)	(−217.98)	(−219.47)
Under 25 years old when migrating	—	0.0332 **	0.0176 **	0.0185 **
		(8.02)	(4.13)	(4.16)
Over 25 years old & migrating	—	0.1080 **	0.0976 **	0.1107 **
		(33.50)	(29.77)	(32.24)
Children	—	0.0578 **	0.0491 **	0.0444 **
		(18.71)	(15.79)	(13.74)
Married	—	0.0240 **	0.0112 **	0.0092 **
		(7.55)	(3.46)	(2.72)
More than 9 years of ≈ formal education	—	−0.1851 **	−0.1873 **	−0.1877 **
		(−63.14)	(−63.42)	(−61.23)
Head of hh. working less than 10 hours	—	—	0.0556 **	0.0596 **
			(11.26)	(6.30)
Head of hh. working more than 40 hours	—	—	0.0596 **	0.0419 **
			(21.60)	(4.28)
Employee working less than 10 hours	—	—	—	−0.0387 **
				(−3.23)
Employee working more than 40 hours				−0.0428
				(−4.10)
Self-employed working less than 10 hours	—	—	—	−0.0991 **
				(−6.17)
Self-employed working more than 40 hours	—	—	—	0.0804 **
				(6.74
Small business owner working less than 10 hours	—	—	—	—
Small business owner working more than 40 hours				0.5076 **
				(30.03)
Business owner working less than 10 hours	—	—	—	—
Business owner working more than 40 hours	—	—	—	—
Employee in professional	—	—	—	0.1662 **
				(6.24)
Employee in non-professional services	—	—	—	0.4206 **
				(19.51)
Employee in manufacturing	—	—	—	0.2493 **
				(10.98)

Table 4.5. (*continued*)

Independent Variables	(1)	(2)	(3)	(4)
Employee in agricultural sector	—	—	—	−0.0162 (−0.41)
Employee in construction	—	—	—	0.1824 ** (7.03)
Employee in retail trade	—	—	—	0.4790 ** (20.84)
Self-employed in professional services	—	—	—	3.5566 ** (81.89)
Self-employed in non-professional services	—	—	—	3.7255 ** (95.63)
Self-employed in manufacturing	—	—	—	3.7036 ** (91.85)
Self-employed in agricultural sector	—	—	—	—
Self-employed in construction	—	—	—	3.8133 ** (91.23)
Self-employed in retail trade	—	—	—	3.9056 ** (98.08)
Small business owner in professional services	—	—	—	4.1328 ** (123.73)
Small business owner in non-professional services	—	—	—	4.2859 (156.27)
Small business owner in manufacturing	—	—	—	4.2001 ** (145.39)
Small business owner in the agricultural sector	—	—	—	4.4832 ** (110.34)
Small business owner in construction	—	—	—	—
Small business owner in retail trade	—	—	—	4.4445 ** (154.47)
Traditional	—	—	—	0.7380 ** (255.61)
North	—	—	—	0.2465 ** (75.03)
South	—	—	—	0.2676 ** (67.21)
Constant	−2.5906 ** (−1126.95)	−2.4100 ** (−606.38)	−2.4623 ** (−399.87)	−2.7463 ** (−272.96)
Number of observations	20914019	20914019	20914019	20751672
Log-likelihood	−703904.15	−674689.31	−673027.61	−631885.61

Source: Own estimations using the National Employment Survey 2002–4 and the Migration Module.
1/ Self-employed without employees
2/ Owner of a business with less than 5 employees
3/ Owner of a business with more than 5 employees
* Significant at 0.05
** Significant at 0.01

five different labor brackets. The whole sample was divided in six different labor groups: employees, unemployed, self-employed without employees, small business owner (with less than five employees), "large" firm owner (more than five employees), and out of the labor force. The omitted group is "out of the labor force." The first regression, without additional controls, suggests that a family whose head of household is an employee is more likely to send members abroad than a family whose head of household is out of the labor force. This result supports the evidence presented above and suggests that having a job in Mexico is not a sufficient condition to deter migration to the United States. It also suggests that poorer families cannot afford a migration decision, given the information presented in Table 4.3. It is very likely, however, that different kinds of jobs have different effects on the migration decision. This will be further analyzed by adding controls to this regression and by interacting some of the independent variables.

The second result of the first regression suggests that families with an unemployed head of household tend to send members abroad in lower proportions relative to families whose head is out of the labor force. As we found that unemployed heads of household declare to receive some income, from this result we assume that the migration decision of a family member is not taken in crisis situations but rather is a thoughtful response to a more structural labor situation. Somehow, however, this result supports the hypothesis that a certain labor income is needed to make the migration decision at a family level, and suggests that the income a head of household obtains from a job as an employee is partly used to finance the trip of the migrant member.

Now, the group of self-employed people was here disaggregated to better understand the kind of self-employment that promotes less migration. According to our results, when the head of the family is a self-employed worker and does not have employees, the family has a lower probability to send a member to work abroad. This could be interpreted in two different ways. First, it might be possible that families who provide themselves with a stable source of income have a lower tendency to send members abroad. If this was true, we would have observed the same negative relationship between migration and self-employment, despite the kind of self-employment. The second possibility is that workers who are self-employed and do not have employees receive very low incomes and it is not possible for them to finance a trip abroad for a member of the family. The data in Table 4.3 and the regression result regarding the owners of small firms supports the second hypothesis. In the first regression in Table 4.5 it is clear that small business owners send a family member abroad in higher proportions relative to those families whose head is out of the labor force. This suggests that the income obtained through the small business is partly used to finance the migration decision, and that the self-employed workers without employees have too low incomes to finance the trip of a family member.

Finally, the families whose head are owners of larger firms (with more than five employees) have lower probabilities of sending migrants compared to families whose heads are out of the labor force. This is to be expected given the information provided in Table 4.3 regarding income, fringe benefits, and retirement, which supports the predictions sketched above. Now, these results are not comparing similar families and this can be done by adding more variables to the regression. The variables added in column two take into account the income-generating capacity of the family member sent abroad. This means that the sociodemographic characteristics included in the regression refer to the migrant and not to the head of the household.[38] It is important to point out that this estimation does not include any variables about the part of the family which resides in the United States, because the data set was designed to have a perfect correlation between migration and a member of the family abroad. This means we are not considering family networks in the receiving country, and the results need to be taken with caution.

Column 2 in Table 4.5 shows that the results regarding the relationship between migration and labor conditions presented in column 1 are robust enough to maintain the sign and significance of the labor variables, despite the inclusion of important control regressors. The results suggest again that males migrate in higher proportions relative to females,[39] and that younger people tend to migrate in higher proportions relative to those older than forty-five. The size of the coefficient suggests that people between twenty-five and forty-five migrate more than the younger. An interesting result is that families with more children tend to send members abroad in higher proportions relative to families without children. This contradicts the evidence presented above, but the difference in the surveys' design may explain this difference. It is not strange that families with more dependents need additional sources of income and that they opt for migration as a means of getting it, but in this case it is not necessarily the parents of the children who migrate. In this regression we observe again that married people are more prone to become migrants relative to the unmarried. Finally, the regression suggests that migrants to the United States are more likely to have less than nine years of formal education, or that the average urban Mexican migrant to the United States has low human capital.[40]

Estimation 3, presented in the third column of Table 4.5, includes additional dummy variables as controls. These represent the economic sector where the head of household was working when the survey was carried out, and the number of hours he/she worked. I do not present in the table the results about the economic sector, but they suggest that agriculture, retail trade, and services other than professional and technical are positively correlated with family migration decisions. According to Table 4.4, these are precisely the sectors with lower average income and with the highest proportions of informality. It is interesting to point out that working in the construction sector seems to be negatively correlated with the migration decision.[41] According to the data, the average income obtained in this sector is higher than in other industries, but not by much. This might explain the sign of the correlation, but I do not think the wage differential is the only determinant of this result. The information about the standard deviation of income in construction does not denote higher volatility of income in this sector relative to the others, but what we find is that the number of hours worked in this sector is the largest of the sample. This could mean that finding a job in this sector is easier, and that this flexibility is negatively correlated with migration. The results about manufacturing and professional and technical services suggest households depending on a job in these sectors are equally prone to promote migration of a family member, and that these households have a lower propensity to send a member abroad relative to the extracting sector.[42] Regarding the number of hours worked, the regression suggests that head of households working less than ten hours a week and those working more than forty hours per week have almost equal propensities to send a member abroad. This says that the average worker who is underemployed is more prone to make decisions about family migration than other kinds of workers, but that he/she makes family migration decisions in similar proportions to those working more than forty hours a week. In the former case the reason could be the volatility of resources and the low quality of the job, while in the last case it could be that families have enough resources to finance the migration decision.

Now, to better understand the role labor conditions play in the family migration decisions I proceeded to add to the estimation some interactions with the position the head of the household holds in his/her job and the economic sectors and the number of hours he/she works. These interactions are possible because the sample is large enough to have some observations in every cell created. The results of this last estimation are presented in Table 4.5, column 4. This regression includes fixed effects by region that reflect the fact that families have different propensities to make migration decisions depending on the migration culture of their communities. Families in those states with a migration tradition are considerably more prone to send members abroad than families in the center of the country in states without a migration tradition. Families in the north and in the south seem to have higher probabilities of making a migration decision relative to those in the center, but the coefficients in these cases are not as large as the one corresponding to the traditional migration region.

When regressions include interacted variables it is important to understand that the interpretation of the coefficients greatly differ relative to estimations without them. In this case we need to add the coefficients of the relevant not interacted variables to the coefficient of the interacted variable. The appendix presents the whole regression with the corresponding coefficients and elasticities. Here I will only describe the main results. Regarding employees, the results suggest that those in professional and technical services, manufacturing, construction, and agriculture tend to send family members abroad in lower proportions relative to the omitted sector which in this case is the extractive industry. We have seen that jobs in the professional and technical services and in manufacturing provide better incomes than other sectors, and that income and labor conditions in the agricultural sector are characterized by precariousness. Once again, the result about the construction sector is striking but can be explained by the labor flexibility of the sector. In the two former cases the "better" labor conditions faced by the head of household seem to exert a significant migration-deterring effect. The employees in non-professional services and in retail trade seem to make family migration decisions in higher proportions relative to those employees in the extractive industry. In these two sectors income is more volatile than in other industries, and the average income is lower, which supports the idea that more volatile and lower-quality jobs promote more emigration. With respect to the number of hours worked by employees the regression suggests that those working less than ten hours tend to send family members to work abroad in similar proportions relative to those working more than forty hours. The sign of both coefficients is negative meaning that employees working between ten and forty hours are more prone to send a family member to work abroad relative to the other two categories. In the first case it could be possible that the average income is too low to finance the migration decision, while in the second case it could be possible that labor conditions are good enough to discourage migration.

Regarding self-employed workers without employees, calculations suggest that only those working in retail trade tend to send a family member abroad in higher proportions relative to the self-employed in the extractive sector. Self-employment in the other sectors has a significant migration deterring effect, and the reason behind this could be either the low income and the volatility observed in these occupations or the fact that families who provide themselves with a source of income are less prone to send working migrants. The results regarding business owners, either small or large, support the second hypothesis in the sense that all the self-employed workers included in the sample tend to send family members abroad in lower proportions relative to those self-employed in the extractive sector and, according to these results, even relative to other workers in different labor positions.

The results about the owners of larger firms are not included in the table because they predicted failure of migration perfectly and were dropped from the estimation by the computer. The negative sign of the dummy variable for this labor position alone strongly supports the idea that the owners of large firms have the lowest proclivity to send family members to work in a different country. These results reinforce the hypothesis that self-employment exerts an important migration-deterring effect, and they are robust enough to say that this seems to be true even when other characteristics of the family or the migrant are taken into account.

CONCLUDING REMARKS

Emigration to the United States is one of the main characteristics of the Mexican labor markets today. Almost one third of all Mexicans born in the United States arrived in this country during the 1990s, and the flow is close to half a million persons a year, despite the predictions in the opposite direction. This phenomenon is capturing the attention of policy makers and scholars, and research about it can contribute to ordering and legalizing the human movement across the largest border in the world. The greatest increase in Mexico-U.S. migration coincides in time with important changes in the Mexican economy and labor markets, and this paper has tried to link some of them to changing migration patterns.

Before 1980 workers in the agricultural sector and in low-skilled occupations were highly protected in Mexico for political reasons. The state was practically in charge of certain groups of the population, and labor conditions were highly dependent on the labor policy held by protected private and public firms as well as the government. This model was no longer sustainable by the mid 1970s, and the 1982 economic crisis forced the government to start the implementation of a series of liberal policies that eliminated the protection of the more vulnerable groups of the population. The dismantling of the old economic system was not accompanied by social policies that should have substituted the social protection institutions, and workers bore a large proportion of the costs of the change in the economic and political systems.

The increase in the informal sector can be considered one of the main supply-push factors behind the increasing Mexico-U.S. migration. This sector is theoretically considered a temporary staging post for internal migrants on their way to formal sector employments; but if formal sector jobs are not created in enough numbers, workers start looking for other options, and in the Mexican case this appears to be the U.S. labor market.

Economic integration, on the other hand, seems to have benefited highly skilled workers disproportionately, and this may have affected the migration composition, but we do not have theoretical elements to assert that it has increased migration. Economic integration tends to displace workers among sectors, and this effect appears to be larger in the short run than in the long run. In this sense this policy may have raised migration in the late 1990s, but it might decrease it in the long run if the tradable goods sector creates enough formal and high quality jobs that more than compensate the displacement of the early years. This, however, may not happen if the local labor market is under strong pressures for demographic and social reasons.

Finally, this paper analyzed the role privatization may have played in the increasing migration and concluded that it seems to have caused a large displacement of workers out of the public sector and into the informal and the unstructured economic sectors. It may have additionally increased the cost of living for a significant number of individuals, forcing them to look for additional sources of income in international migration. Additionally, privatization of the banking system caused an important drop in the credit available to Mexican families, and this may have contributed to migration, according to the new economics of migration theory.

The empirical estimation exercise showed that people and families that face more unstable and insecure labor conditions tend to migrate and to send family members abroad in higher proportions. It also suggested that people in better-quality jobs tend to migrate less, despite having social networks that facilitate their job search in the United States. Finally, a very robust result of the analysis is that self-employment exerts a significant migration-deterring effect because it provides better quality jobs that depend entirely on the families' or the worker's efforts. These results support the ideas about the role the changing labor conditions in the country have played as supply-push determinants of migration.

The main conclusion that emerges from this analysis is that if the Mexican economy creates formal and high-quality jobs in enough amounts, international migration might then start decreasing. But this is something that does not only depend on good intentions. The economy should grow at high rates for long periods of time, and this growth should be concentrated in sectors that offer opportunities for the group that tends to migrate more. Further analysis is certainly needed, but maybe the involvement of the U.S. government in the Mexican economic process (through grants like those that the EU offered to Spain or Greece) can help create the conditions for sustained and adequate job creation in the country.

APPENDIX

Table 4.2A.   Elasticities of the Probability of Migration

Independent Variables		
Self-employed	−0.2357	**
Employee	0.1245	**
Unemployed	0.1741	**
Family in USA	0.1167	**
Sex (male=1)	0.0891	**
Under 25 years old when migrating	−0.0397	
Over 25 years old & under 45 when migrating	0.0401	
Children	−0.2222	**
Married	0.0518	
Schooling over High School	0.0111	
Retail Trade	0.0637	
Services 1/	0.0674	
Professional and Technical Services	0.1016	
Manufacturing	−0.0117	
Working less than 10 hours	0.1742	
Working more than 40 hour	−0.1166	**

Source: Own estimations using a data set obtained in four Mexican localities.
1/ Services other than professional and technical and retail trade.
* Significant at 0.05
** Significant at 0.01

Table 4.5A.   Elasticities of Probability of Migration

Independent Variables		
Employee	−0.0022	**
Unemployed	−0.0008	**
Self-employed 1/	−0.0339	**
Small business owner 2/	−0.0396	**
Business owner 3/	−0.0734	**
Sex	−0.0051	**
Under 25 years old when migrating	0.0002	**
Over 25 years old and under 45 when migrating	0.0010	**
Children	0.0004	**
Married	0.0001	**
More than 9 years of formal education	−0.0016	**
Head of hh. working less than 10 hours	0.0005	**
Head of hh. working more than 40 hours	0.0004	**
Professional services	0.0010	**
Non-professional services	−0.0004	**
Manufacturing	0.0012	**
Agriculture	0.0003	
Construction	0.0002	**
Retail Trade	−0.0009	**
Employee working less than 10 hours	−0.0003	**

(*continued*)

Table 4.5A. (*continued*)

Independent Variables		
Employee working more than 40 hours	−0.0004	
Self-employed working less than 10 hours	−0.0009	**
Self-employed working more than 40 hours	0.0007	**
Small business owner working less than 10 hours	—	
Small business owner working more than 40 hours	0.0044	**
Business owner working less than 10 hours	—	
Business owner working more than 40 hours	—	
Employee in professional services	0.0015	**
Employee in non-professional services	0.0037	**
Employee in manufacturing	0.0021	**
Employee in agricultural sector	−0.0001	**
Employee in construction	0.0016	**
Employee in retail trade	0.0042	**
Self-employed in professional services	0.0311	**
Self-employed in non-professional services	0.0326	**
Self-employed in manufacturing	0.0324	**
Self-employed in agricultural sector	—	
Self-employed in construction	0.0333	**
Self-employed in retail trade	0.0341	**
Small business owner in professional services	0.0361	**
Small business owner in non-professional services	0.0375	**
Small business owner in manufacturing	0.0367	**
Small business owner in agricultural sector	0.0392	**
Small business owner in construction	—	**
Small business owner in retail trade	0.0389	**
Traditional	0.0064	**
North	0.0022	**
South	0.0023	**

Source: Own estimations using the National Employment Survey 2002–4 and the Migration Module.
1/ Self-employed without employees
2/ Owner of a business with less than 5 employees
3/ Owner of a business with more than 5 employees
* Significant at 0.05
** Significant at 0.01

NOTES

1. See chapter 1.
2. See chapter 1.
3. Susan M. Richter, Edward J. Taylor, and Antonio Yúñez-Naude, "Impacts of Policy Reforms on Labor Migration from Rural Mexico to the United States," NBER Working Paper No. W11428 (Cambridge, MA: National Bureau of Economic Research, 2005).
4. Export assembly plants.
5. Gonzalo Hernández Licona, "Oferta laboral familiar y desempleo en Mexico: los efectos de la pobreza," *El Trimestre Económico* LXIV(4), no. 258 (1997): 531–68.

6. Daniel Lederman, William Maloney, and Luis Servèn, *Lessons from NAFTA for Latin America and the Caribbean* (Washington, DC: The World Bank and Stanford University Press, 2005).

7. Douglas Massey et al., "Theories of International Migration: A Review and Appraisal," *Population and Development Review* 19, no. 3 (1993): 431–66.

8. Benjamin Davis, Guy Stecklov, and Paul Winters, "Domestic and international migration from rural Mexico: Disaggregating the effects of network structure and composition," *Population Studies* 56, no. 3 (November 2002): 291–309.

9. See Oded Stark, *Economic-Demographic Interactions in the Course of Agricultural Development: The Case of Rural-to-Urban Migration* (Rome: FAO, 1978); Oded Stark, Edward Taylor, and Shlomo Yitzhaki, "Remittances and inequality," *The Economic Journal* 96, no. 383 (September 1986): 722–40; and Taylor, J. Edward, "Undocumented Mexico-U.S. migration and the returns to households in rural Mexico," *American Journal of Agricultural Economics* 69 (1987): 626–38.

10. Guillermo Calvo, "Urban Unemployment and Wage Determination in LDC'S: Trade Unions in the Harris-Todaro Model," *International Economic Review* 19, no. 1 (1978): 65–81.

11. Philip Martin, "Economic Integration and Migration The Mexico-U.S. Case," World Institute for Development Economics Research Discussion Paper no. 2003/35, United Nations University, 2003.

12. Agriculture contributes less than 8 percent of Mexico's GDP, but almost ¼ of the population lives in rural communities.

13. Biswajit Banerjee, "The Role of the Informal Sector in the Migration Process: A test of Probabilistic Migration Models and Labour Market Segmentation for India," *Oxford Economic Papers* 35 (1983): 399–422.

14. In the underground economy literature, a main determinant of the informal sector is the excessive regulation of the market activities. Thomas, among others, argues that liberal economic policy is the best way to formalize economic activity. Elizabeth Thomas-Hope, "Emigration Dynamics in the Anglophone Caribbean," in *Emigration Dynamics in Developing Countries: Mexico, Central America and the Caribbean*, volume III, ed. Reginald Appleyard (Aldershot, U.K.: Ashgate Publishing Ltd., 1999), 232–84.

15. Zadia M. Feliciano, "Workers and Trade Liberalization: The Impact of Trade Reforms in Mexico on Wages and Employment," Working Paper (Harvard University, 1994).

16. Although maize is not a labor-intensive product, the great consumption of maize in the country makes it an important crop throughout the country. This means Mexico has a consumption or demand comparative advantage in the production of maize.

17. See Santiago Levy and Sweder van Wijnbergen, "Mexican Agriculture in the Free Trade Agreement: Transition Problems in Economic Reform," OECD Development Centre Working Paper no. 63 (Paris, 1992).

18. Martin, "Economic Integration and Migration."

19. See Table 4.1.

20. See Michael Ian Cragg and Mario Epelbaum, "Why has wage dispersion grown in Mexico? Is it the incidence of reforms or the growing demand for skills?" *Journal of Development Economics* 51 (1996): 99–116; and Liliana Meza González,

"Cambios en la Estructura Salarial de México en el periodo 1988-1993 y el aumento en el rendimiento de la educación superior," *El Trimestre Económico* LXVI (2), no. 262 (April–June 1999): 189–226.

21. Gordon Hanson, "What has happened to wages in Mexico since NAFTA? Implications for Hemispheric Free Trade," NBER Working Paper No. 9563 (Cambridge, MA: National Bureau of Economic Research, 2003).

22. See Robert C. Feenstra and Gordon Hanson, "Globalization, Outsourcing and Wage Inequality," NBER Working Paper No. 5424 (Cambridge, MA: National Bureau of Economic Research, 1996).

23. Raymond Robertson, "Wage Shocks and North American Labor Market Integration," *American Economic Review* 90, no. 4 (September 2000): 742–64.

24. Clark W. Reynolds and Robert K. McCleery, "Modeling U.S.-Mexico economic linkages," *The American Economic Review* 75, no. 2, Papers and Proceedings of the Ninety-Seventh Annual Meeting of the American Economic Association (May 1985): 217–22.

25. Ethan Hemming and N. Prabha Unnithan, "Determinants of Privatization Levels in Developing Countries," *Social Science Quarterly* 77, no. 2 (June 1996): 434–44.

26. Jon Sohn and Stephanie Hayes, "Making Privatization Work," *Friends of the Earth Review* (Unpublished Report, Washington, D.C., 1999).

27. Massey et al., "Theories of International Migration."

28. Massey et al., "Theories of International Migration."

29. Lisa Cleveland, John Gunnell, Salvatore Restifo, and Jason Russo, *Running for the Border: The Impact of Privatizing Essential Services in Mexico on Patterns of Mexican Migration* (Arizona State University West, 2001).

30. In 1982 President José López Portillo decided to transfer the private financial system to the government in an attempt to try to stop a massive outflow.

31. Sara Martínez Pellegrini, Carla Pederzini V., and Liliana Meza González, "Autoempleo como mecanismo de arraigo de la población en México: el caso de cuatro localidades," *Revista de Estudios Urbanos y Demográficos* 21, no. 3 (September–December 2006): 547–623.

32. In the fourth quarter of 2002 the NES included a migration module that inquired families about members abroad and the labor and economic conditions of the family members.

33. Appendix A contains information about this data set and a transformation of the regression coefficients to interpret them as the percentage change in the probability of migration when the independent variables change.

34. Liliana Meza, "Mercados laborales locales y desigualdad salarial en México," *El Trimestre Económico* LXXII, no. 285 (January–March 2005): 133–78.

35. I was not able to run migration regressions at an individual level using the ENEU data because the labor information refers to the week when the survey was conducted, and I would have needed labor characteristics prior to the migration decision.

36. The results presented in Table 4.2.

37. Business owners' average income is more than double the average income of small business owners.

38. The survey was not designed to know the number of natural-born children of each member of the household. Therefore, the variable "children" does not refer to the number of children of the migrant but to the number of people younger than twelve years old living in the household.

39. In this case the dummy variable equals one when the person is female.

40. The average schooling level of the whole Mexican population is around 7.3 years of formal education. This means that migrants are, on average, more educated than the average Mexican. This could be interpreted as an indicator of the positive selection of migrants in the country.

41. See appendix.

42. The sector omitted in the estimation.

5

Politics of U.S. Immigration Reform

Susan Martin, Georgetown University

BACKGROUND

Although there has long been migration between Mexico and the United States, the North American Free Trade Agreement (NAFTA) heralded a new era of cooperation and consultation on migration management. Until the 1990s, each government saw migration from its own perspective, doing little to understand the positions of the other or negotiate common approaches. The United States government pursued largely unilateral policies, particularly after the conclusion of the Bracero program. While there was recognition that policy changes might have a disproportionate effect on Mexican migrants, there was no interest in designing Mexico-specific policy responses. Rather, such legislation as the Immigration Reform and Control Act of 1986 provided legal status to Mexican undocumented aliens on the same basis as those who came from other countries.

The Mexican government, for its part, chose to "have a policy of no policy" on migration to the United States until the late 1980s. During the 1990s, however, that position changed and the Mexican government became more visibly engaged. As the 1997 *Binational Study of Migration Between Mexico and the United States* concluded:

> Mexican authorities now lobby in the United States on political and economic matters, which they did not do prior to the NAFTA negotiating process. The Mexican government no longer operates solely via its Secretariat for Foreign Relations [SRE] communicating with the U.S. Department of State, but rather fans out across the spectrum of U.S. private interest groups, public agencies, and the Congress. The increased closeness of the economic relationship and its

salience for Mexican economic recovery and growth also means that it is important to handle other problems in a way that avoids prejudice to economic cooperation.

NAFTA itself included a number of immigration-related provisions that would ease movements of managers and executives of multinational corporations and highly skilled professionals in some seventy occupations. During the first ten years after ratification of NAFTA, numerical limits and labor market tests would continue to be applied to Mexicans, but beginning in January 2004, these restrictions would be removed and personnel movements from Mexico would be treated equally with those from Canada.

Also during the 1990s, the Binational Commission Working Group on migration and consular affairs provided tangible opportunities for enhanced cooperation between the two countries. As described in the 1997 *Binational Study*:[1]

> In May 1997, when President Clinton visited Mexico, the Working Group discussion dealt with the exchange of information on migration policies and legislation, consular protection, and increased cooperation at the border. The Joint Statement on Migration adopted by the two Presidents signals a commitment to enhance bilateral cooperation in the management of migration.
>
> The bilateral engagement has led to a number of unilateral and cooperative actions. Fast lanes were set up to facilitate crossing into the United States. The wait to cross at San Ysidro was reduced from two hours to twenty minutes. Cooperation to prevent drug smuggling was increased at the border. Grupo Beta is a Mexican effort to make the border safer. Mexicans participate in the Citizens' Advisory Panel on the U.S. side. There is a joint Border Liaison Mechanism. Both sides took steps to reduce smuggling of immigrants.

Of course, the enhanced consultation did not always yield positive results, and migration remained a tense issue in the bilateral relationship. The economic situation in both countries—an economic boom in the United States' very slow recovery from the 1994 bust in Mexico—led to record numbers of Mexicans entering the United States during the second half of the decade. A much-publicized increase in border enforcement did little to stem the tide, but the higher cost and greater risk of crossing the border encouraged unauthorized migrants to remain for longer periods in the United States. At the same time, repeated efforts to achieve a new binational approach or comprehensive U.S. reforms that would include legalization and temporary worker programs, along with enhanced enforcement, have failed. As of the writing of this chapter, the most recent efforts by the U.S. Senate to enact comprehensive legislation failed to produce results, with opposition from the Republican right and, to a lesser degree, the Democratic left preventing the leadership from bringing the bill to a vote.

This chapter reviews the reform efforts in the Congress, analyzing the bases of opposition and the potential for future reform. For a more detailed discussion of efforts at the presidential level, see chapter 6.

CONGRESSIONAL GRIDLOCK

Several legislative proposals have been introduced but not enacted during the 108th through 110th Congresses.[2] Part of the reason for the repeated failure to achieve comprehensive immigration reform is the controversial nature of the immigration issue in American politics, which sparks intense debate from both sides of the political spectrum. Different groups are equally committed to ensuring that unauthorized migrants, on the one hand, are kept out of the country and do not receive amnesty if they have entered illegally, or on the other that those who provide needed work gain the fullest access possible to employment opportunities, benefits, and citizenship.

Among the plethora of issues under debate in Congress concerning immigration reform and temporary worker proposals, some of the recurring questions are the following:

- Whether to create a separate guest worker program for agricultural workers and another for nonagricultural workers, or whether to include both groups in the same program
- Whether to limit eligible participants to aliens currently within the United States, aliens outside the country, or both groups
- Whether to include a legalization or earned adjustment program that would lead to legal permanent residency in the United States
- Whether to include multiyear work requirements in the criteria for legalization, or whether to leave out such conditions for fear they could lead to exploitation of workers that fear being fired or could exclude many short-term agricultural workers
- Whether to offer derivative status to family members under a new guest worker program, or whether such measures should be eliminated to encourage eventual return to the country of origin
- Whether current procedures for labor certification should be retained to protect job opportunities for U.S. workers, or whether a more streamlined process should be created, for example, replicating the labor market attestation process currently in place for H-1B specialty workers or developing a certification process specific to an employment sector or region of the country
- Whether numerical limits should be placed on the number of individuals able to participate in the guest worker program, and whether such limits should be phased out over time

- Whether to enforce return to the participant's country of origin—for example, through deportation—at the end of the guest worker program, or whether to provide financial incentives for return home
- How to protect homeland security through the operation of the guest worker program, and how to ensure that individuals that pose a security threat are not allowed to enter the country under the guest worker program.[3]

For the most part, the debate does not envision a separate or special migration agreement with Mexico. Rather, the reforms enacted would apply universally. Nevertheless, there is recognition that Mexicans constitute the largest source of both unauthorized and legal immigration into the United States. Hence, the changes would have disproportionate impact on Mexico—for better or worse.

A number of competing and sometimes complementary bills reflect the various approaches taken to immigration reform. Reviewing the legislative history is useful to understanding the nature of the debate over three sessions of Congress.

Recurrent Legislative Proposals

Two bills have been repeatedly introduced and incorporated into the more comprehensive legislation that has been introduced: AgJOBS and the Dream Act.

AgJOBS, introduced by Senator Larry Craig, was the principal legislative effort to reform the system for admitting temporary agricultural workers (for a more detailed discussion of the provisions of AgJOBS, see chapter 6).

In addition to gaining bipartisan support in Congress, the AgJOBS bill also benefited from the backing of many non-governmental organizations, activists, and academic researchers. For example, Demetrios Papademitriou of MPI called AgJOBS a "well thought out piece of bipartisan legislation." He argued it would stabilize the agricultural workforce in perishable crops, enhance work-related benefits and legal protections for all the sector's workers, and strengthen cooperation with the Mexican government. This collaboration in turn could decrease smuggling activity and overall crime in the border region.[4] La Raza similarly offered its support for AgJOBS, although the organization stressed the bill represented only a first step toward comprehensive immigration reform. La Raza particularly welcomed the fact that the bill would provide H-2A guest workers the right to go to federal court to enforce their rights under the H-2A program. It also commended the bill for streamlining the H-2A hiring process, while protecting and enhancing key labor protections for the guest workers.[5]

Despite these promising beginnings, AgJOBS was left to languish in committee in late July 2004. Senate majority leader Bill Frist, at the urging of the White House, convinced Senator Craig not to offer the bill up for a vote. Both the Bush administration and the Senate leadership reportedly feared the bill would provoke an extreme reaction from the more conservative wing of the Republican Party.[6] Because of this combined assault, Senator Craig chose not to submit the bill for a vote, but he reintroduced the bill in the 109th Congress. Its forty-eight cosponsors in the Senate and the forty-six cosponsors of the companion bill in the House represented a bipartisan coalition. As with the other legislation discussed herein, AgJOBS was soon superseded by efforts to enact comprehensive reform.

Originally sponsored by Senator Orrin Hatch of Utah, the DREAM Act (Development, Relief, and Education for Alien Minors Act—S. 1545) obtained forty-seven cosponsors before an amended version of the bill was approved by the Senate Committee on the Judiciary on October 23, 2003. The bill was reintroduced in the 109th Congress by a bipartisan group, but without the sponsorship of Senator Hatch. It has reappeared in the legislation introduced by a bipartisan group of Senators in the 110th Congress. In October 2007, Senate proponents failed to obtain the sixty votes needed to bring the bill to a vote as a stand-alone bill although a majority supported it.

The DREAM Act seeks to facilitate the entry into institutions of higher education of those illegal immigrant minors that have obtained a high school diploma. The DREAM Act further would create a two-stage process whereby eligible unauthorized aliens could acquire legal permanent residency. According to Senator Hatch, the DREAM Act would assist the approximately 50,000 undocumented immigrants that graduate from high school each year. Currently, these students are barred legally from seeking employment and are constrained from pursuing additional education because of the high costs of out-of-state tuition. The DREAM Act would amend the Illegal Immigration and Immigrant Responsibility Act of 1996 to authorize *states* to determine state residency for higher education purposes, regardless of an individual's immigration status. It thereby would facilitate these individuals' pursuit of higher education and at the same time raise their earning potential as adults.

In addition to the provision regarding in-state tuition for higher education, the DREAM Act would address several immigration-related issues. First, it would authorize the Secretary of Homeland Security to cancel removal of, and adjust the status of an alien admitted for permanent residence for, any illegal alien that has been admitted to an institution of higher education. Second, the bill would permit the student to apply for permanent residency after a six-year wait, provided that he or she has completed at least two years in a degree program or in the U.S. military. While

Senator Hatch argued it is critical to enforce immigration law and enhance border security, he argued in introducing the legislation that the DREAM Act responds to a persistent reality and promotes the overall national interest. Bringing undocumented minors out of the shadows and providing them an opportunity to increase their skills and earning potential would help integrate these individuals into American society and reduce the need for costly welfare programs to support them in the future.[7] As mentioned, despite the broad support for the DREAM Act, its sponsors have been unable to move the legislation forward, either in the context of comprehensive reform or as a stand-alone bill. Opponents argue that it is an amnesty for lawbreakers, that the numbers of beneficiaries could be very large, and that it was unfair for unauthorized children to jump the queue of legal immigration given the large numbers of family members of legal permanent residents who were caught in the backlog of visa applications for admission.

Reform in the 109th Congress

In the 109th Congress, the Senate and the House of Representatives took very different approaches to immigration reform. The House focused primarily on enhanced enforcement while the Senate tried for comprehensive reform.

The "Border Protection, Antiterrorism, and Illegal Immigration Control Act of 2005" (H.R. 4437) was introduced by James Sensenbrenner, the Chair of the Judiciary Committee. It passed the House in December 2005, but was stopped in the Senate. The bill addressed a number of enforcement issues, but it was roundly criticized because it included what were widely seen in immigration circles as draconian measures and did not include any legal alternatives to unauthorized migration. The bill's border security provisions included increased staffing and training for the Border Patrol, technology to be deployed along the border, and physical infrastructure to deter unauthorized crossings. The bill also required development of a national strategy for border security, and it expanded the scope and enhanced penalties for smuggling and trafficking offenses.

In a particularly criticized provision, the bill increased the penalties for "harboring" an unauthorized migrant in a manner that would risk imprisonment of staff of religious and social services organizations that assist immigrants. As described by the American Immigration Lawyers Association, "This incredibly overbroad definition of smuggling would criminalize the work of social service organizations, refugee agencies, churches, attorneys, and other groups that counsel immigrants, treating them the same as smuggling organizations. In addition, family members and employers could be fined and imprisoned for "harboring," "shielding," or "transporting" undocumented family members or employees, filling our prisons with people who have done nothing more than try to reunite their families, or help a worker, friend or client."[8]

In an equally criticized provision, the bill created a new felony offense— unlawful presence in the United States. Traditionally, simple violations of immigration law have been treated as civil offenses, not criminal ones. Other provisions enhanced the use of mandatory detention, expanded the definition of aggravated felonies that would result in mandatory removal, put into place new definitions of terrorist-related reasons for inadmissibility and removal, and eliminated or reduced access to the courts to hear certain immigration-related cases. It also made changes in the burden of proof for an asylum seeker, requiring him or her to establish that "his or her life or freedom would be threatened in the country in question, and that race, religion, nationality, membership in a particular social group, or political opinion would be at least *one central reason* for such threat."[9] A number of these provisions overturned federal court rulings.

The bill also addressed the work magnet for unauthorized migration. It required the Secretary of Homeland Security to implement an employment eligibility verification system, building on the Basic Pilot Program already in use in verifying work authorization. The system would become mandatory for employers. Employers would need to verify not only new hires but also their existing workforce.

The House-passed legislation created uproar among immigrant advocacy organizations, businesses and civil rights and civil liberties groups. Opponents argued that enforcement-only approaches would not solve the immigration problem, just further criminalize individuals whose main purpose in violating immigration law was to work. Demonstrations across the country showed the depth of concern within ethnic communities with large immigrant populations. These demonstrations, along with the concerns of business that immigration reform must address their legitimate need for foreign workers, paved the way for a radically different approach in the Senate.

The Secure America and Orderly Immigration Act of 2005 (S. 1033, H.R. 2330) was introduced by Senators McCain and Kennedy and Representatives Kolbe, Flake, and Gutierrez. The bill addressed a wide range of issues ranging from earned regularization and temporary work programs to increased border security and new employment verification provisions. It attempted to provide answers to three aspects of reform: (1) what to do about the existing unauthorized migrants; (2) how to meet the legitimate needs of employers for foreign labor and families for reunification; and (3) how to deter future unauthorized migration.

For the existing unauthorized population, the bill provided for earned regularization. The legislation established an H-5B program for persons who were present in the United States without authorization before the date of the Act's introduction; and were employed in the United States before the date of the Act's introduction as full time, part time, seasonal, or self-employed workers; and have been employed in the United States since that date. The applicant would pay a fine of $1,000 in addition to an application fee. Family reunification was permitted under the H-5B visa. The H-5B visa conveyed work authorization and the individual could travel outside of the country.

After completing a period of authorized stay of six years, the H-5B worker would be eligible to adjust to permanent resident status if he or she paid an additional $1,000 fine as well as the application fee; was admissible under immigration laws; underwent a medical examination; showed proof of payment of taxes; demonstrated the requisite knowledge of English and U.S. civics; successfully underwent criminal and security background checks; and registered for military selective service, if applicable. The children and spouse of the H-5B worker would also be eligible to apply for adjustment. The adjustments were exempt from regular visa ceilings.

To address future demand for workers, the legislation created the H-5A temporary worker program, referred to as the Essential Worker Program. The original formulation of the bill provided for 400,000 visas for workers not covered under the H-1B, H-2A, L, O, P, and R visas (respectively, for professionals, agricultural workers, intracompany transfers, the exceptionally qualified, performers, and religious workers). The ceiling on visas could be increased if market forces demonstrate that there is additional demand for the workers, as evidenced by the number of applications per quarter. Visas would be granted for three years, renewable for a further three years. Workers could apply for adjustment to permanent residence, either via an employer petition or, after four years as an H-5A, via a self-petition.

The worker would need to demonstrate he/she is capable of performing the labor or services required for an H-5A occupation and would provide the consular officer with evidence of employment in the United States. Employers seeking to hire H-5A workers would need to attest that they have posted the employment opportunity in a new Job Registry for at least 30 days in an attempt to recruit U.S. workers. Employers must maintain a record of such recruitment efforts for one year and must demonstrate why U.S. workers who applied were not hired. The legislation also included new provisions to regulate labor contractors who recruit H-5A workers on behalf of employers.

The legislation also included provisions to reduce the backlogs in the current system for admitting permanent residents to the United States. The unrestricted number of visas for immediate relatives of US citizens would no longer count against the overall ceiling on family admissions, increasing the number available for the restricted categories including the spouses and minor children of legal permanent residents. The number of employment-based visas would increase from 140,000 to 290,000.

To help ensure that employers utilize the new temporary work program, rather than continue to hire unauthorized workers, the legislation phased in a new employment verification program. The Employment Eligibility Confirmation System would have to be used by all employers of H-1A workers to verify their authorization for work, and over time, would replace the current verification system for all new hires. The legislation also increased the number of officers available for worksite enforcement. It further required the Secretary of Homeland Security to develop a strategic plan for border enforcement.

Comprehensive Enforcement and Immigration Reform Act of 2005 (S. 1438) was introduced by Senators Cornyn and Kyl in the 109th Congress. It too provided a mechanism for regularization of unauthorized migrants in the United States, but it was far more restrictive than the McCain-Kennedy approach. The bill created a new Deferred Mandatory Departure (DMD) status for eligible migrants present in the U.S. on the date of the bill's introduction. Unauthorized migrants would have to apply within six months of enactment of the law. The migrants would be eligible to remain in the country for up to five years but would be required to return home within that period or forfeit eligibility to return to the United States. If migrants leave immediately, there will be no fine if they re-enter legally. The longer they remain before departure, the higher the reentry fines would be.

The bill provided no mechanism by which the regularized migrants could adjust to permanent resident status. The bill did include a new temporary work program to which the migrants may apply along with others interested in entering the United States for work purposes. The "W" visa would be valid for two years. The worker would have to remain outside of the U.S. for one year and then could re-enter for two more years, up to a total of six years of employment. Workers would be required to maintain a foreign residence and return home for short visits each year. Spouses and minor children could visit the worker for a maximum of thirty days. Workers would be paid at least the greater of the hourly wage prescribed under the Fair Labor Standards Act or the applicable state minimum wage.

There were no numerical restrictions on the number of W visas, but the legislation established a taskforce to examine its usage, which could then be used as a basis for setting annual numbers. There was no mechanism for adjustment to permanent residence. No worker could participate in the program unless there was a bilateral agreement between the United States and his or her country of origin that committed the home country to accept back its nationals and cooperate in reducing unauthorized migration.

The legislation also introduced new worksite enforcement mechanisms. It required the issuance within one year of secure, machine-readable, tamper-resistant Social Security cards and established minimum standards for state-issued birth certificates. It also required within one year that all new hires participate in a Social Security-based electronic employment eligibility verification system.

The legislation explicitly addressed the source countries of immigration in an unusual manner. It required countries to enter into bilateral agreement with U.S. government before the nationals of the country are allowed to participate in a temporary worker visa program or the new Deferred Mandatory Departure status. Participating countries must cooperate in efforts to control illegal immigration; immediately accept return of nationals who are ordered removed from the United States ; work with the United States to reduce gang violence, human trafficking and smuggling; and provide access to databases and information on criminal aliens and terrorists.

A compromise negotiated by Senators Hagel and Martinez paved the way for passage of legislation building on the McCain-Kennedy bill. The guest-worker and earned regularization programs were scaled back. The Hagel-Martinez legislation permitted admission of 200,000 temporary workers, and eliminated the market-based increase in numbers contained in the original bill. The compromise also offered a tiered approach to earned regularization. Migrants unlawfully in the country for five years or longer would be granted work authorization, legal status, and a path to permanent residence and citizenship. Those unlawfully in the country for more than two years, but less than five years, would be granted Deferred Mandatory Departure; they would be expected to leave the country and reenter as temporary workers, with the possibility of eventual adjustment to permanent residence. Those unlawfully in the country for less than two years would be ineligible for regularization but could apply for the temporary work program.

Reform in the 110th Congress

As of the writing of this chapter, it appears unlikely that comprehensive reform will pass the 110th Congress. The result of discussions between senators from both parties and the administration, S.1348, a bill "to provide for comprehensive immigration reform," reached the floor of the Senate but failed to muster sufficient votes to be brought to a final vote. The bill represented a compromise that lifted elements from each of the previous legislative attempts and introduced new policies not previously encompassed in any of the legislative packages. The bill was comprehensive in scope and radical in many of its strategies for curbing unauthorized migration and reforming legal admissions.

The legislation included an earned regularization program (Z visa) that is at the same time more generous and more restrictive than previous versions. It is more generous in its scope, providing a route to legal status for all unauthorized migrants in the country as of January 2007. Eliminating the three-tiered system of the previous legislation, the provision would treat all unauthorized migrants similarly. They would regularize into a new non-immigrant visa that could be renewed every four years, with new fees and English and civics testing requirements applied at the renewals. While eligible for eventual permanent residence and citizenship, the Senate bill put new restrictions on access to these benefits. The regularized would be at the back of a long waiting list, estimated to take about eight years to clear. Moreover, the Senate bill would require what is referred to as a "touch back" requirement that the heads of all regularized families would have to return home to reenter as permanent residents. They would also have to meet the requirements of a point system. While unauthorized migrants would immediately find relief from deportation, the full regularization program would only go into effect when certain benchmarks are met in the enforcement of immigration laws.

The Senate bill also introduced a new temporary worker program (Y visa) that would introduce a rotational requirement. Workers would be granted an initial two-year visa, renewable twice more. What makes the Senate version of a temporary worker program a radical departure is the requirement that workers return home for one year between each renewal. After three rotations, they would not be eligible to reenter. A ceiling of 200,000 Y workers was approved by amendment on the floor of the Senate, but a mechanism to permit increases in the ceiling if demand is high remained.

The Senate legislative initiative included major changes in the program for permanent admission. After clearing the backlogs of current applicants, the legislation would eliminate the extended family, employer-petitioned, and diversity visa categories for admission. While immediate family (spouses, minor children, and parents) of U.S. citizens and permanent residents would still be eligible, all other immigrants would be admitted on the basis of a point system that would reward education, English language ability, and qualifications in shortage occupations. A small number of points would be awarded for family ties if the applicants amass a minimum number of points in these other areas.

Most of the enforcement provisions were lifted in their entirety from previous bills or represent a variation on the themes of already negotiated provisions. The legislation emphasized both border security and interior enforcement. With regard to worksite enforcement, the bill included provisions for mandatory electronic employment verification, as well as increased penalties for illegal hiring of unauthorized workers.

Despite initially broad bipartisan support for the legislation, there has been sustained opposition from both conservative Republicans and liberal Democrats. On the right, the concerns are about earned regularization, referred to as amnesty throughout the debate. Fueled by grassroots opposition to "rewarding illegality," the opponents have argued for an enforcement only approach that more closely mirrors the House legislation in the 109th Congress. The compromise legislation has unsuccessfully attempted to bridge the divide with an "enforcement first" approach, tougher border and worksite enforcement policies, and increased budget for enforcement. To date, these provisions have not swayed opponents to earned regularization but they have made supporters more cautious in their endorsement of the bill.

On the left, the opposition takes two forms. First is opposition to the expansive temporary worker programs, which, they argue, would weaken labor standards protection and reduce wages for already resident workers. Second is opposition to the changes proposed in admission of permanent residents, particularly the elimination of certain categories of family admissions. At the same time, business groups have expressed concern about the introduction of a point system, fearing that they would have increased difficulties obtaining green cards for valued employees who might not qualify under the point system.

During 2007, the House held extensive hearings on immigration reform proposals but the leadership deferred action to see how reform fared in the Senate. Representatives Flake and Gutierrez introduced the bipartisan Security through Regularized Immigration and a Vibrant Economy Act of 2007 (STRIVE Act), which incorporates some of the concepts in the Senate bill, including triggers for implementation of the regularization and temporary worker programs and mandatory electronic employment verification. The new temporary worker program would provide a route, however, to permanent residence on the basis of either an employer petition or self-petition. The regularization process involves two steps, with unauthorized migrants first qualifying for a six-year grant of conditional nonimmigrant status and then an opportunity to adjust to permanent residence. As with the Senate bill, there is a touch back requirement in the STRIVE Act. The legislation also includes increases in the number of permanent admission visas, but unlike the Senate bill, it makes no major changes in the categories or priorities for family or employment-based admissions.

As of this writing, the Senate failed to close debate on the comprehensive immigration reform, allowing it to die without a vote. With the presidential campaign heating up, most political observers declared the bill dead for this legislative season.

WHY HAS IMMIGRATION REFORM FAILED?

Comprehensive immigration reform is the exception, not the rule, in American politics. Until 1875, there were few laws regulating immigration to the

United States. From then until 1921, the Congress put into effect a series of rules that excluded immigrants from certain countries/races (primarily through the Chinese, Japanese, and other Asian exclusion acts) and restricted others on the basis of their health, morals, likelihood to become public charges, and other similar factors. During the last decades of the nineteenth century and early into the twentieth century, debate on immigration heated up as the numbers of southern and eastern European immigrants increased dramatically. As would be the case in later reform efforts, the Congress established the Dillingham Commission to assess the impact of immigration and make recommendations included in its 1911 report. At first the debate focused on a literacy test that proponents thought would restrict immigration to those with higher levels of education. After passage of the literacy requirements in 1917 failed to shift immigration origins and numbers as expected, opponents of mass migration turned to a more comprehensive approach that resulted in the National Origins quota system passed in 1921 and was refined into its definitive form in the Johnson-Reed National Origins Act of 1924.

The National Origins Act placed overall numerical restrictions on immigration from the Eastern Hemisphere and set per country quotas based on the percentage of Americans in the 1890 Census who originated from specific countries. As the 1890 Census preceded the mass migration from southern and eastern Europe, higher quotas went to the United Kingdom and northwestern Europe. The quotas for Italy, Poland, and Greece were 4,000, 6,000, and 100, respectively; by contrast, more than 285,000 Italians entered the United States in 1907 alone.

The National Origins laws stayed in place until 1965 despite great criticism in the period after World War II and a series of bills that enabled admission of refugees and displaced persons outside of the quotas. The Congress, over President Truman's veto, renewed the National Origins quotas in the 1952 McCarran-Walter Act, otherwise known as the Immigration and Nationalities Act. The Act also established a system of preferences for skilled workers and the relatives of U.S. citizens and permanent residents. In the context of the emerging Cold War, the legislation tightened security as well, barring admission on a number of ideological grounds.

In September 1952, Truman established a commission which issued a report in January 1953 entitled "Whom We Shall Welcome" that recommended elimination of national origins and establishment of criteria based on broader U.S. interests. The Commission held that U.S. immigration laws "flout fundamental American traditions and ideals, display a lack of faith in America's future, damage American prestige and position among other nations, ignore the lessons of the American way of life."

It was not until 1965 that a comprehensive overhaul of U.S. immigration policy took place. Introduced in the context of the broader civil rights movement, the 1965 amendments eliminated national origins quotas, replacing them with a per country limit of 20,000 visas per country and an overall ceiling of 160,000 for the Eastern Hemisphere. The legislation also established the first ceiling on Western Hemisphere migration, set at 120,000 visas per year. Immediate family (spouses, minor children, and parents) of U.S. citizens would be admitted outside of the numerical limits. Within the numerically limited categories, a seven-preference system was established that permitted admission of relatives, foreign workers, and refugees. Subsequent legislation established a global ceiling of 290,000, eliminating the separate ceilings for the Eastern and Western hemispheres.

Legislation for admission of refugees underwent a similar lengthy process until reform was achieved. During the 1930s and early 1940s, many refugees had been rejected for admission to the United States. The most extreme case was the *St. Louis*, the ship of Jewish refugees, which was turned back by the United States (and other countries) and forced to return to Europe where many passengers died in the Holocaust. After the war, the United States admitted thousands of displaced persons via a series of Presidential rulings and ad hoc laws that, in effect, mortgaged the national origins quotas. In 1951, the UN Convention Relating to the Status of Refugees was adopted, but the United States did not ratify the Convention despite its participation in its drafting. Only in 1969 did the United States ratify the 1967 Protocol to the Refugee Convention. It was not until 1980, however, that the country passed legislation that adopted the UN refugee definition[10] and put in place a permanent system for refugee resettlement and asylum proceedings. Previously, refugees from Hungary, Cuba, Indochina, and the Soviet Union were admitted through the parole authority of the Attorney General because those emergency programs exceeded the 17,000 refugee visas included in the regular immigration legislation.

When unauthorized migration grew in the 1970s, Congress considered legislation but failed to reach consensus. Instead, it formed the bipartisan Select Commission on Immigration and Refugee Policy (SCIRP), a time-honored way, as we have seen, to navigate the complexities and emotions in immigration policy. SCIRP included four cabinet officers, four senators, four representatives, and four public members. The final report issued in 1981 recommended a three-legged stool that included enhanced enforcement, particularly in the form of sanctions against employers who hired illegal workers; legalization for the estimated 3 to 6 million unauthorized migrants already in the country; and reforms in legal admissions programs that would increase dramatically the number of immigrants to be admitted on the basis of their skills. The basics of the SCIRP proposals were taken up by successive Congresses. The employer sanctions/legalization recommendations were finally enacted in the 1986 Immigration Reform and Control Act by a narrow vote in the lame duck Congress. The legal admission reforms were not enacted until the 1990 Immigration Act. As unauthorized migration grew again after implementation of IRCA, the Congress asked still another Commission to advise it on immigration reforms. While some of the Commission on Immigration Reform's recommendations were adopted by administrative action and in the 1996 immigration legislation, its recommendations for an electronic employment verification system—the heart of its 1994 report to Congress—and clearance of the family backlogs—the heart of its 1995 report—were never fully implemented.

In the context of these historic trends, the current Congress' failure to enact comprehensive reform despite strong bipartisan agreement on many points is not surprising. Major changes in immigration policy generally require years of preparation and negotiation. Even the imprimaturs of blue ribbon commissions help but do not ensure quick passage of new approaches.

The nature of the political coalitions that form around immigration explains some of these difficulties in gaining consensus. In previous writings, I have described four groups, characterized by attitudes about immigration levels on the one hand and immigrant rights on the other.[11]

The first group, Advocates, is favorable to high levels of immigration as measured by numbers of admissions and a commitment to the protection of the rights of immigrants; their preference is for permanent admissions that provide access to citizenship. The second group, Free Marketers, also supports high levels of immigration, but its members are willing to restrict the rights of those admitted; their preference is for large-scale temporary worker programs, limitations on access to public welfare programs, and measures that permit quick removal of any migrants that commit criminal or other offenses. The third group, Restrictionists, also supports limits on the rights of migrants, but in the context of limitations on the numbers to be admitted. The fourth group, Integrationists, sees rights as paramount and is comfortable with numerical limits on admissions, especially on categories that inherently limit the capacity of migrants to exercise their rights (e.g., temporary worker programs and unauthorized migration).

In debates over immigration reform, these groups often form coalitions in support of specific provisions. For example, the supporters of high levels of immigration (Advocates and Free Marketers) will often join together to defeat efforts to restrict movements. Nevertheless, they break apart when issues regarding rights of immigrants come up for votes, when the Free Marketers will often join with the Restrictionists. The shifting interests end up creating strange bedfellows who find it difficult to gain consensus on comprehensive reforms, even if they are able to agree on many elements of policy.

Making the process of reform even more difficult is a basic ambivalence within the American public regarding immigration. Most Americans speak fondly and nostalgically about their own immigrant forebears who, in their mind, created this nation of immigrants. At the same time, they are fearful that today's immigrants are somehow different and less likely to contribute and assimilate—become true Americans. This ambivalence is by no means new. Benjamin Franklin worried that the Germans immigrating to Pennsylvania in the eighteenth century would never learn English. The result of this ambivalence is the absence of any strong consensus among the public about changes in immigration policy. A small group that knows what it opposes can often pre-empt action (as witnessed in both the immigrant rallies that derailed the House Republican enforcement measures and the talk radio shows that derailed the Senate regularization measures) but pressure for positive changes is too often lacking. The safe decision for politicians is no decision—at least until there is no choice but to act.

THE WAY FORWARD

NAFTA introduced an era of enhanced cooperation and economic integration of Mexico, the United States, and Canada. In the long term, when economic progress reduces income disparities among the three countries, freer movement of people will likely follow the already recognized benefits of freer movement of goods, services, and capital. At present, however, such integration of the labor markets is unlikely to occur, given the large differences in wages. The United States will continue to be a magnet for Mexicans seeking higher wages and more stable employment. Parts of Mexico will continue to rely heavily on remittances from workers in the United States to support families and contribute to economic development.

The United States and Mexico share the goal of improving management of migration between the two countries. It is in neither country's interest that hundreds of thousands of people risk their lives each year to cross illegally into the United States. Nor is the continued presence of millions of unauthorized migrants, living and working in the shadows, of benefit to either country. Immigration reform is needed that will deter future illegal migration while regularizing the status of those already living in the United States.

Migration from Mexico to the United States remains a major issue that continues to need senior-level policy attention in both countries. Efforts at top-down reform failed in 2001, partly because of the terrorist attacks, but more fundamentally because they sought to achieve too much too quickly. Similarly, the efforts in the U.S. Congress failed because of opposition from the left to an enforcement-only approach and opposition from the right to what appeared to be an amnesty.

What the United States needs now is comprehensive reform achieved incrementally to ensure the effectiveness and test the impact of new approaches. Such an approach has a better chance of convincing the skeptics on both sides.

As a first step, the Congress must address the work magnet that stimulates illegal migration. The highest priority is a more secure method of verifying the authorization of would-be employees to work in the United States. The Basic Pilot employment verification program, mandated in the 1996 Immigration Act, is still in testing mode, hampered by false negatives that question the right of authorized workers and false positives that allow unauthorized workers to assume the identities of those who are legally authorized to work. Congress should invest considerable resources now to improving the data used to verify work authorization and testing the use of biometrics and other mechanisms to reduce abuse—both of which are needed precursors for universal implementation of the program.

Second, Congress should establish targeted employment programs for foreign workers in business sectors that are now highly dependent on unauthorized workers. There is no need now for the type of large-scale, open-ended temporary worker program that was included in the Senate bill. New programs should be tailored to the specific situation of those sectors of the economy that can demonstrate current shortages of domestic workers even when reasonable wages and working conditions are offered. Employers participating in foreign-worker programs should be required to participate in Basic Pilot.

If the labor is seasonal or short-term, as in agriculture, temporary worker programs may be appropriate. AgJOBS, carefully negotiated between growers and worker advocates, is a good model that should not be held hostage to comprehensive reform. If the work is of indefinite duration, however, the programs should allow for transition to permanent residence. The Senate bill's rotational scheme has been tested in other countries and failed. The United States should not follow suit. Current employees, regardless of their legal status, should be given the opportunity to apply for the new worker programs and receive their work permits inside the United States. Otherwise, there is little chance that these programs will serve as effective substitutes for unauthorized migration. Employers will not want to lose tested and valuable employees, and now unauthorized migrants will not risk leaving the country to reenter as legal workers.

In addressing the need for new admission programs for lesser skilled workers, Congress should test mechanisms to help reduce future dependence on foreign workers. In too many cases, access to cheap labor impedes investment in a higher skilled workforce or mechanization that may improve productivity. Fees paid by employers who hire foreign workers could usefully be targeted at exploring alternatives. The residual demand for foreign workers is likely to be lower than current levels and could be handled by new programs.

One program could test a method for reducing the dependence of U.S. agriculture on Mexican migrants and spur development in migrant communities of origin. The AgJOBS proposal would grant temporary legal status to unauthorized migrants who did U.S. farmwork, allow them to earn an immigrant status with continued farmwork, and simplify procedures for farmers to obtain additional guest workers. If this is all that is done, individuals will have their status legalized, but U.S. agriculture will remain dependent on foreign workers.

An agricultural pilot guest worker program could test methods to use the payroll taxes collected from guest workers and U.S. employers to encourage worker returns as well as promote the mechanization made increasingly necessary because of increased global competition in labor-intensive commodities, especially from China. Farm employers who hire migrants are usually well organized in associations that already collect fees (assessments) to support research and marketing of particular commodities. A pilot program could allow employers to have guest workers admitted more easily in exchange for fees that would be used to subsidize mechanization and encourage worker returns.

A second program could test removing the "temporary job" requirement of the H-2B program, which would enable meatpackers and other industries that hire large numbers of unauthorized Mexicans to obtain legal guest workers. Employers who agree to participate in the Basic Pilot verification program for all new hires could be allowed to hire guest workers under a pilot H-2B program even if the jobs were year-round, which would test the concept of rotating guest workers through year-round jobs. Guest worker returns could be encouraged by isolating and refunding worker and employer payments made on behalf of guest workers for Social Security and unemployment insurance benefits, or crediting the guest workers for these contributions in the Mexican social security system. For example, if the priority for new workers still in Mexico were given to members of families participating in the antipoverty program *Oportunidades* (formerly *Progresa*) or the farm payment program *Procampo*, payments could be adjusted or health check up dates set to help to ensure compliance with return rules.

Meat and poultry processing is a high-turnover industry; so far more than 500,000 individuals, the average employment in the industry, work on "disassembly" lines sometime during a typical year. Many meatpackers already participate in the Basic Pilot verification program, under which I-9 employment verification is subpoenaed from employers and checked for discrepancies such as invalid A (immigrant) or Social Security numbers. However, they avoid fines for hiring unauthorized workers by refusing to continue to employ workers after being informed that there are problems with employee names/numbers or by hiring workers via third parties, such as employee leasing firms.

A third program could test an expansion of the L-1 intracompany transfer program. The L-1 visa allows multinationals to transfer "key employees" including executives, managers, and workers with "specialized knowledge" from the company's operations abroad to a U.S. branch, parent/subsidiary, or affiliated entity. The pilot could permit multinational firms with operations in both Mexico and the U.S. to use L-1 visas to bring unskilled Mexican workers to the U.S. for employment and training, with the expectation that the Mexican worker would return to Mexico and be employed in the firm's Mexican operation after one to three years of U.S. employment. Such a program involving hotels, medical care providers, and other services would provide continuity in employee seniority with one firm, and make the multinational firm a partner in ensuring that program rules are followed.

Third, Congress should fix the most egregious problems in the permanent admissions program—the long backlogs that separate family members for years. Of most concern are the delays for immediate relatives of permanent residents. Spouses and minor children of legal immigrants from Mexico, for example, must wait five years or longer to enter the United States. Few U.S. natives would tolerate such long separations. Not surprisingly, many family members instead wait for their visas in the United States. The stock of unauthorized migrants could be significantly reduced by clearing these backlogs within the next year. Eliminating numerical quotas on these close family members would help reduce the flow of future unauthorized migrants who are only seeking to be with their spouses and parents.

Fourth, the administrative capacities of the immigration bureaus within the Department of Homeland Security, State Department, and Labor Department should be beefed up and professionalized. The Senate bill would have placed tremendous pressures on these agencies. As has already been seen in the passport crisis, it is not enough to tell agencies to implement massive new requirements. They must be given the time and resources to build their capacity to take on new challenges.

Once these steps are implemented, Congress should revisit immigration reform to determine the residual unauthorized population and assess the extent to which the new, targeted programs have achieved their aims. Once the inflow of unauthorized migrants has been reduced significantly and the impacts of new targeted admission programs are known, a broader legalization and further reforms in legal admissions may well be needed. By that time, however, the public may indeed have greater confidence in the ability of the government to manage immigration.

NOTES

1. CIR/SRE (Commission for Immigration Reform, Secretaría de Relaciones Exteriores), *First Binational Study of México-U.S. Migration* (Washington, Mexico City, 1997).

2. Unless otherwise noted, all information related to legislation was found through Thomas, U.S. Library of Congress, available at: thomas.loc.gov.

3. "Immigration: Policy Considerations Related to Guest Worker Programs," CRS Report for Congress, June 8, 2004, 17–23, price.house.gov/UploadedFiles/Immigration.pdf.

4. Demetrios G. Papademetriou, Testimony before the Senate Foreign Relations Committee, March 23, 2004.

5. "Immigration Farmworker Legislation (AgJOBS)," National Council of La Raza. Available at www.nclr.org/content/policy/detail/1354.

6. "Congress May Reject Immigration Reforms," *Los Angeles Times*, November 6, 2004, A4.

7. "S. 1545: The DREAM Act," Statement of Senator Orrin Hatch before the Senate Committee on the Judiciary, October 16, 2003, hatch.senate.gov.

8. American Immigration Lawyers Association, *The Border Protection, Antiterrorism, and Illegal Immigration Control Act of 2005 (H.R. 4437), as Amended and Passed by the House on 12/16/05, Section-by-Section Analysis,* 5.

9. American Immigration Lawyers Association, 23.

10. Until 1980, U.S. law limited recognition of refugees to those who escaped Communist countries and countries in the Middle East.

11. For a fuller discussion, see Susan Martin, "Politics and Policy Responses to Illegal Migration in the U.S.," Conference on Managing Migration in the 21st Century, June 21–23, 1998, Hamburg, Germany, available at http://isim.georgetown.edu/Publications/SusanPubs/SMartin_PoliticsAndPolicy.pdf, and Susan Martin, "The Politics of U.S. Immigration Reform," in Sarah Spencer, ed., *The Politics of Migration: Managing Opportunity, Conflict and Change* (Malden, Mass.: Blackwell Publishing, 2003). Daniel Tichenor uses a similar typology in *Dividing Lines: the Politics of Immigration Control in America* (Princeton N.J.: Princeton University Press, 2002).

6

Immigration Reform in the United States

Rafael Fernández de Castro, ITAM
Roberta Clariond Rangel, ITAM

This chapter examines the unsuccessful attempts at immigration reform in the United States between 2001 and 2007, the first seven years of the presidency of George W. Bush. In the early months of 2001, Mexico played an important role in denouncing the troubled U.S.-Mexico immigration status quo. In its attempts to negotiate a comprehensive immigration agreement, the Fox administration argued that the tacit agreement between Mexico and the United States to leave the American border "half-open" to Mexican undocumented immigrants was riddled with problems and was increasing costs—as seen, for example, in the rising number of Mexican immigrants who died while crossing the Arizona desert. This tacit agreement had been in place from the end of the Bracero programs in 1965 until the mid-1990s, when the Clinton administration decided to increase obstacles to undocumented immigration.

At the time of this writing, the summer of 2007, there is pervasive consensus that immigration reform has failed, and that a new window of opportunity will only present itself with the election of a new Congress, the 111th Legislature, and a new president, both of which will come to power in January 2009. From Mexico's perspective, the failed immigration reform has created a highly undesirable scenario. Mexican immigration is currently subject to the "stick" of immigration reform—strengthened enforcement provisions and the hardening of the border, while the "carrots" of the reform are yet to come—regularization of the approximately six million Mexican nationals without proper documentation and a guest worker program.

We argue in this chapter that there is a consensus in the United States about the necessity of immigration reform. Both Democrats and Republicans agree that it is necessary to create a more orderly and legal immigration flow, but there are strong disagreements about how to convert the current immigration system, which is fairly unregulated, into a more regulated one. Meanwhile, with Congress paralyzed by the lack of agreement about how to improve the current system, there have been numerous attempts by the executive, the state legislatures, and more surprisingly, local authorities to curb immigration. The consequence is that the prospect of a new immigration system currently appears far away, and the prevalent immigration atmosphere, which is highly influenced by talk shows heralding an invasion from the south, has worsened conditions for Mexican immigrants already living in the United States and those who are yet to come.

LEVERAGING THE HONEYMOON PERIOD INTO AN IMMIGRATION AGREEMENT

Vicente Fox was elected president of Mexico in December 2000, enjoying ample international and domestic support, as well as a "democratic bonus" for being the first president to oust the longstanding PRI regime. His inauguration coincided with that of George W. Bush in the United States, and from the beginning, the relationship between the two presidents was unique. This uniqueness stemmed from the fact that Mexico was the only foreign country with which Bush was very familiar and, consequently, it was his main foreign policy interest. He solidified his commitment to Mexico by choosing it as his first international visit as president. Bush was considered by many to be highly knowledgeable about Mexico and border issues. As a major U.S. newspaper declared during the 2000 presidential campaign: "As governor of a state that exported $41 billion worth of goods to Mexico last year across 1,200 miles of shared border, Bush may be the most Mexico-savvy politician ever to run for president."[1]

Bush's interest in Mexico coincided with Fox's substantive change in the Mexican government's approach to a crucial border issue: immigration. For President Fox and Foreign Affairs Minister Jorge Castañeda, positioning immigration on the bilateral agenda became a priority. Mexico became conscious for the first time that the status quo was unsustainable. New U.S. immigration policies, designed in the 1980s and 1990s, had created a dysfunctional immigration system that not only had been unsuccessful in deterring immigration, but also had generated negative consequences for both immigrants and the United States. The U.S. Border Patrol was strengthened both in budget and numbers, walls and fences were erected at the border, new technology was implemented to detect undocumented immigrants, and the hiring of illegal immigrants became punishable by law.

These enhanced controls at the border translated into higher risks and costs of migrating and generated unintended negative consequences, including: (1) the strengthening of criminal transnational organizations that smuggled humans and drugs; (2) the consolidation of a black market for fraudulent documents; (3) the increase in the number of deaths at the border; and (4) the alteration of traditional migratory patterns by decreasing the circularity of the flow and increasing the rate of permanent settlement. Although immigrants kept entering the United States in record numbers, they were forced to cross through more remote and isolated areas, increasing their risks of dying and paying higher fees to illegal people-smugglers known as *coyotes*. These worsened conditions served as decisive factors in leading immigrants to choose to settle permanently. As sociologist Douglas Massey has stated: "We've got more monetary power and more equipment than at any other time in our history, [but] it's all been counterproductive. You don't deter them from coming in, you deter them from going home."[2] The result of increases in the budget and controls translated into longer sojourns in the United States, because going back and forth to Mexico became riskier and more costly.

NEGOTIATING AN IMMIGRATION AGREEMENT

Despite the fact that approximately 10 percent of the Mexican population lives in the United States, Mexico still does not view itself as a country of emigrants. This lack of national consciousness has its origins in a century-long tradition of going to the United States to work and a "policy of no policy" by the Mexican government toward migration and migrants.[3] With the exception of its collaboration with the U.S. government on the Bracero program, Mexico has mostly ignored the migratory phenomenon and settled for defending its nationals' rights in the United States through its embassy and numerous consulates.

This neglect by the Mexican government of its nationals in the United States took its toll during the Mexican presidential elections of 1988, when large sectors of the Mexican diaspora questioned the regime's credibility and the triumph of the PRI's candidate, Carlos Salinas de Gortari. When President Salinas decided to push for a North American Free Trade Agreement (NAFTA), he could not afford to see Mexican communities opposing his project. Thus, the Mexican government was forced to acknowledge its diaspora and establish certain programs, with the aim of using Mexican nationals in the United States as a platform to lobby in favor of NAFTA. Some of these programs, like the *Programa Paisano*, which facilitated the return of immigrants to their hometowns, and the Mexican Communities Abroad Program (now the *Instituto de los Mexicanos en el Exterior*, IME), which promotes contact between the immigrant communities and their communities of origin, made progress in improving the attention, services, and protections offered to Mexican nationals.[4] However, after NAFTA was approved, Mexican communities were half-forgotten, until President Fox vindicated their struggle and called them "national heroes." Most importantly, Fox's government devised an aggressive policy toward immigration and planned ambitious negotiations aimed at reaching an immigration agreement with the United States.

Between Bush's February 2001 visit to Guanajuato, Fox's home state, and the terrorist attacks of September 11, there appeared to be momentum for the signing of an immigration agreement between Mexico and the United States. Fox determined the bilateral agenda, which entailed deepening and ameliorating the terms of regional integration, with a comprehensive immigration agreement as the first step. In the spring of 2001, President Fox and Foreign Minister Castañeda initiated immigration negotiations with their counterparts in the United States, putting immigration on Bush's agenda. For the first time, Mexico came forward with an immigration proposal, which defined the problem as a shared responsibility of both countries. This represented an important change from previous Mexican administrations, which had ignored the phenomenon and acquiesced to the United States' unilateral decisions. The negotiations centered on the following issues: (1) the establishment of a guest worker program; (2) an earned regularization for undocumented immigrants who complied with certain criteria; (3) socioeconomic development projects in Mexico's traditional sending regions; (4) cooperation on the administration and security of the border region; and (5) favorable conditions for family reunification.

However, the terrorist attacks in the United States on September 11, 2001, brought these negotiations to an immediate stop. The urgent reform of the U.S. immigration system came to an abrupt halt, and any possibility of a bilateral immigration agreement with Mexico vanished. The special relationship was transformed into one characterized by mistrust. President Fox became paralyzed, and his reaction to the terrorist attacks on U.S. soil was influenced by domestic pressures. This paralysis reflected a turn in Mexican foreign policy toward the U.S. from a proactive attitude to one that was reactive and nationalistic. This new attitude eliminated any possibility for a deep change in Mexico-U.S. relations during Fox's presidency.[5]

Following Mexico's lukewarm reaction to the 2001 attacks, the two presidents did not meet again until the Monterrey Summit in March 2002. Fox's team arrived with high expectations that a new dialogue on immigration would ensue, but the United States ignored Fox's initiative and imposed its own security agenda. The only substantial exchange was the signing of the Smart Border Agreement, which centered on the need to implement intelligent borders that favored efficient legal crossings, while detaining potential terrorists and smugglers.

It was difficult for the Mexican government to understand that Washington was now primarily concerned with waging a war against terrorism and that, as a result, the attention given to bilateral issues would never return to their pre-9/11 level. Mexico felt betrayed by U.S. disinterest and the bilateral relationship remained distant. Relations worsened in the first months of 2003 when Mexico refused to align with the United States in the UN Security Council on the issue of going to war with Iraq.

After months of strained relations, many Mexican politicians, including President Fox, were deeply surprised when Bush announced his principles for immigration reform in January 2004. This was seen by many as an electoral move designed to attract the Latino vote in the 2004 U.S. presidential elections. However, after being comfortably reelected, Bush stressed in his 2005 State of the Union address the necessity of reforming an "immigration system [that is] outdated—unsuited to the needs of our economy and to the values of our country."[6]

BUSH'S DESIRE FOR REFORM

President Bush's interest in reforming the immigration system may have had various motivations, but it is clear that one of the major factors was his conviction that the current system was obsolete and in true need of reform. He stated in January 2004: "We see millions of hard-working men and women condemned to fear and insecurity in a massive, undocumented economy. Illegal entry across our borders makes more difficult the urgent task of securing the homeland. The system is not working. Our nation needs an immigration system that serves the American economy and reflects the American Dream."[7] Bush continuously repeated the idea that the system was dysfunctional and not beneficial to the U.S. economy. In addition to the humanitarian issues involved, it is clear that he believed that a reform of the immigration system would bring substantive economic benefits, especially with regard to labor shortages.

Bush was also interested in attracting Latino voters to the Republican Party. Hispanics had become by that time the largest minority group in the United States, amounting to almost 40 million—approximately 14 percent of the American population. More than 15 million of these Hispanics were Mexican Americans and an additional 10.5 million were born in Mexico, which meant that the community of people of Mexican origin represented 65 percent of the total number of Latinos in the United States.[8] The Latino community was therefore an important electoral constituency, and was particularly important in the five key states of Florida, Nevada, New Mexico, Arizona, and Colorado.

These numbers offer an indication of the growing political importance of the Latino, and particularly the Mexican, community in the United States. Traditionally, these groups have favored Democrats in elections, but in the 2004 presidential election, President Bush enjoyed greater support from Latino voters than in 2000. Although no consensus exists, some sources such as CNN indicated an increase from 32 percent to 44 percent of total Latino voters favoring Bush between his first and second elections. The reasons for this increase are not completely understood, but the lack of attention that John Kerry, the 2004 Democratic presidential candidate, paid to immigrant communities likely played a role. In addition, Bush's position on "moral values," especially his opposition to abortion and gay marriage, probably attracted many votes in a community that is more socially conservative than mainstream U.S. society. A reform of the immigration system was seen as a potential political tool for maintaining and increasing Latino support for Bush and the Republican Party.

A final motive for Bush was his legacy, as an immigration policy reform was considered to be his last chance to leave a major mark on U.S. relations with Mexico and the rest of Latin America. The Bush administration generally did not push a strong agenda in Latin America, and once the Free Trade Area of the Americas (FTAA) came to appear infeasible, immigration reform was seen as the only way of leaving a clear impact on the region.

Another factor that may have been important in compelling Bush to advance an agenda with Mexico was Tony Garza, the U.S. Ambassador to Mexico. As a close friend of the Bush family, he likely encouraged Bush to leave a positive mark on Latin America while in office.

President Bush's Proposal

According to Alexander Aleinikoff of the Georgetown University Law Center, U.S. immigration policy since 1986 has been constructed around a control paradigm.[9] Strongly based on the principle of national sovereignty, the main focus of immigration policy has been to deter illegal immigration and supervise the legal immigration system. Consequently, discussions have centered on controlling the border, while at the same time promoting humanitarian policies for those already in the country. Aleinikoff argues that Bush's 2004 proposal for immigration reform signaled a change of this control paradigm. For the first time, Bush's reform principles did not center around controlling illegal immigration, but rather on establishing a legal channel for this flow that responded to an international labor market.

The Immigration Reform and Control Act of 1986 was a clear example of the control/law enforcement paradigm. The Border Patrol was strengthened and employer sanctions for hiring illegal immigrants were implemented; at the same time, however, amnesty was extended to all immigrants who had entered the country before 1982. In accordance with the control paradigm, border and interior controls were increased, but access to regularization of status was also granted to those who had entered the country illegally. Regularization under this paradigm became the second-best solution. This "humane" policy was devised because it was not viable to deport all illegal immigrants already in the country, but the real aim of the policy was to control the undocumented flow.

Bush's proposal, on the other hand, had at its core the issue of labor markets. It consisted of four major elements: (1) the creation of a new guest worker program that would allow foreign nationals to work legally in the U.S. for a specific amount of time and then return home; (2) an annual increase in the numbers of legal immigrant visas, which would permit a portion of these temporary workers to remain in the United States; (3) economic incentives for temporary workers to return home; and (4) workplace and immigration law enforcement.

Through this program, foreign nationals, as well as undocumented immigrants already in the United States, would have access to temporary work visas for a period of three years, which would be renewable for an additional three years. Bush insisted that he was not granting amnesty and that those undocumented immigrants who wished to participate in the program would have to be employed, pay a one-time registration fee, and at the expiration of their visas, return home. If any worker wished to remain in the United States and become a citizen, he or she would have to follow the regular application process; therefore, participation in the program would not grant any advantages in the regularization of status.

If Bush's program had been accepted, there would now be a new hemispheric labor market paradigm, given that a broad temporary guest worker program, which extended to undocumented workers already residing in the United States, is not consistent with the control paradigm. The new policy centered on the existence of an international labor market operating across borders, with the notion that workers from Mexico can and should compete for jobs in the U.S. as its central premise. Although Bush did not describe his program as a paradigm shift, he did go beyond the usual rhetoric of border control, calling for a transnational "matching of willing workers with willing employers."[10]

Bush not only recognized that the existing system continuously malfunctioned, but also that the U.S. economy was highly dependent on immigrant workers and that, as such, any reform would have to take into account the reality that "some of the jobs being generated in America's growing economy are jobs American citizens are not filling."[11] As a result, much emphasis was given to the economic benefits of the program. Bush also stressed the importance of helping to prevent the exploitation of immigrant workers by granting them the right to change jobs, earn fair wages, and enjoy the same working conditions that the law requires for American workers, protecting the wages of all workers in the process. This last point went hand in hand with another crucial element of the proposal: increased law enforcement at the workplace. This language, as Aleinikoff concludes, is not the language of national sovereignty and humanitarian policies, but of labor markets.

A key novelty introduced in this proposal was the creation of economic incentives for immigrants to return home. Bush offered to work with foreign governments on a plan to allow temporary workers to contribute a portion of their earnings to tax-preferred savings accounts, which they could collect upon returning home, and to give credit to returning immigrants in their own countries' social security systems for time worked in the United States. These financial incentives were seen as a way to restore circularity in the migration flow, especially the flow from Mexico. This circularity had been affected by the reforms of the 1990s, which, instead of reducing illegal immigration, had the negative effect of "locking people in" and making it harder to go back and forth between Mexico and the United States based on employment seasons.

Critics of the Concept of Temporary Workers Program

By announcing his principles for reform and calling on Congress to work out the details, Bush initiated a process that had the potential to lead to a new immigration system. The questions were when and what form the reforms would take. Bush faced three main obstacles: (1) a generally negative attitude to the concept of a guest worker program; (2) an anti-immigration political climate in the United States; and (3) a Congress, whether controlled by Republicans (who had the majority when Bush made his first reform proposal) or Democrats, that was divided on immigration. Republicans and Democrats, as well as some immigrant advocacy groups, such as the National Immigration Forum, and anti-immigrant think tanks, like the Center for Immigration Studies, made a number of positive and negative arguments concerning comprehensive immigration reform.

The most contentious component of Bush's proposal was the temporary worker program. The memory of the Bracero program, and its association with worker exploitation and the increase of undocumented immigration, led some interest groups and politicians to denounce the proposal for a new guest worker program. Major concerns regarding these programs have tended to center, on the one hand, on their economic impact on wages, the federal budget, and native workers and, on the other hand, on their political effects, increased immigration, and exploitation.

Regarding the economic aspects, opponents argue that temporary worker programs have four negative consequences. First, they increase mutual economic dependency in the countries involved. Employers become dependent on cheap labor and sending countries become dependent on immigration as a means of alleviating unemployment pressures. As Phil L. Martin and Michael S. Teitelbaum argue: "Guest worker programs are virtual recipes for mutual dependence between employers and the migrants who work for them. Employers naturally grow to depend on the supply of low-wage and compliant labor, relaxing their domestic recruitment efforts and adjusting their production methods to take advantage of the cheap labor."[12] Second, there is a concern about the economic costs to an already exhausted and underfunded immigration system in order to meet the challenge of administering thousands of new applications for temporary visas and an extension of the number of permanent visas. Any attempt to increase the number of permanent and/or temporary legal immigrant visas would require an overhaul of financial, human, and technological resources.[13] Third, opponents fear that a program of this magnitude would adversely affect the wages and conditions of American workers. They point out that the agricultural sector is already plagued by unemployment and low wages and that a guest worker program would discourage mechanization, thereby keeping wages depressed.[14] Finally, critics argue that Bush's main argument about "filling jobs that Americans do not want" is weak. They affirm that any shortage of workers would disappear if wages were increased enough to attract American workers.[15]

Concerning the political aspects of the program, critics insist that lessons from past temporary worker programs between Mexico and the U.S. be considered.[16] First, they claim that guest worker programs contribute to the expansion and consolidation of immigrants' social networks, which in turn sustain, and even increase, immigration flows. They argue that guest workers often become permanent residents, bringing their families with them and stimulating further undocumented entries through chain immigration. According to Doris Meissner, former commissioner of the U.S. Immigration and Naturalization Service (INS): "The lasting effect of the Bracero Program has been that it spawned and institutionalized networks and labor market relationships between Mexico and the United States. These ties continued and became the foundation for today's illegal migration from Mexico."[17] Second, right-wing and anti-immigrant groups such as the Federation for American Immigration Reform (FAIR) view these programs as a form of amnesty because they permit undocumented immigrants to work legally in the U.S. for a specific period of time. These organizations oppose guest worker programs based on the idea that they are a reward for illegal immigration, arguing that "granting amnesty, regardless of its disguise as a guest worker program for illegal aliens, is simply wrong and misguided, especially in our post 9/11 security conscious age."[18] Third, human rights groups and liberal politicians express concerns about workers' rights and the likelihood of exploitation. The most liberal sectors of U.S. politics and society, including unions such as AFL-CIO, have argued in favor of allowing the portability of the temporary visa to give the workers more negotiation leverage. Fourth, there is skepticism about whether undocumented workers already in the United States will register in a program that will only grant them temporary legal status.[19] Finally, given the enormous difficulty of creating economic incentives for temporary workers to return home, many believe that participants will want to stay after their visas expire. In response, several groups and individuals, especially Democratic congressmen, have emphasized the need to deal with this population by creating a path toward earned legalization that will allow them to leave the shadows in which they live and work.

Advocates of Guest Worker Programs

It is mainly the business community that advocates the expansion of guest worker visas, especially sectors that depend on seasonal temporary workers, arguing that in order to have a stable and orderly labor pool, immigration reform is necessary. Some states like Maryland face labor shortages, especially during the spring and summer seasons, and have pressured their representatives in Congress to increase legal paths for accessing temporary workers. This pressure is reflected in the "Save Our Small and Seasonal Businesses Act of 2005," which seeks to expand the cap on the H-2B visas for workers that perform nonagricultural, seasonal, and temporary work in areas such as tourism, swimming pool management, the timber industry in Maine, the catfish and timber industries in Louisiana, crab processing in North Carolina, and the shrimp industry in the Southeast.[20]

Some of the states that are negatively affected by labor shortages have demanded that Congress increase the pool of available workers. They argue that there are thousands of jobs not being filled by U.S. workers, which forces many small and seasonal businesses to limit services or close permanently. They successfully managed to have provisions lifting the H-2B visas' restrictive cap of 66,000 workers for FY 2006 included in immigration control legislation attached to an emergency Iraq-Afghanistan spending bill, which was ratified by the Senate. However, such advances have tended to be nothing more than short-term solutions that continue to leave the issue of labor shortages unresolved for many seasonal businesses.

The U.S. Chamber of Commerce proclaimed in an official statement that "by not creating adequate legal avenues for hiring foreign workers and not addressing the status of workers already here, Congress and this administration are not fully safeguarding the economy for the future. While there are fluctuations in employment rates, the long-term threat of a shrinking labor pool lingers in the United States."[21] Accordingly, the business community has consistently agreed with Bush about the need to reform the immigration system in order to guarantee a stable and orderly pool of workers and avoid present and future labor shortages.

NATIONAL ANTI-IMMIGRATION CLIMATE

At the national level, the immigration debate has been represented, on the one hand, by the pro-immigration and immigrants' rights coalition and, on the other hand, the anti-immigration coalition. The first coalition includes a range of different groups, including unions, such as the AFL-CIO; Latino organizations, like the Mexican American Legal Defense Fund (MALDEF) and the National Council of La Raza (NCLR); the business community; activists, such as the National Immigration Forum; groups within the Catholic Church; and some think tanks, like the Migration Policy Institute (MPI).

The anti-immigration coalition is also composed of a range of groups, including think tanks, such as the Center for Immigration Studies (CIS); activist organizations like FAIR; and conservative Protestant groups. The latter are especially prevalent in southeastern states like Georgia, North Carolina, and South Carolina, which have seen the numbers of immigrants increase tenfold in recent years. Additionally, local governments and groups have played an increasingly large role in this debate by promoting the passage of state laws that seek to limit immigrants' access to public services. These measures have had an impact at the national level because they influence public opinion and members of Congress. One notable example of this is the Minuteman Project in Arizona, which, although limited in numbers and in its impact on border control, was widely covered by national and international media.[22] This helped to spur a debate about the U.S. government's lack of control of the southern border and provoked similar reactions in other border states and more general calls for a closed border.

Academics have become increasingly involved in this debate. The most notorious example is the case of Harvard professor Samuel Huntington, whose book *Who Are We? The Challenges to America's National Identity* claimed that Mexican immigration was a grave threat to U.S. national identity due to the supposed failure of immigrants to assimilate and learn English.[23] His thesis has been proven wrong by the vast majority of second- and third-generation Mexican immigrants who are fluent in English and not in Spanish. Nonetheless, having a distinguished professor endorse this position has increased the ammunition of radical anti-immigrant groups that pursue closed border and deportation strategies.

THE ROLE OF THE STATES

Although the U.S. federal government has jurisdiction over immigration law, several states have passed anti-immigrant legislation in response to what was seen as an absence of federal action on the issue. Many groups within these states, especially in border states like Arizona and California, have advocated increasing border controls and denying state public services to illegal immigrants. These state governments argue that they suffer from the cost of granting services to a growing undocumented population. What some states do not realize is that barring immigrants from many of these services, especially health and higher education, will only prolong their position as an underclass, thereby transforming them into a dormant social problem that could explode in the medium term.

One of the most notorious of these cases was the easy passage of Proposition 200, "Save Arizona Now," which was submitted to voters in the form of a referendum during the 2004 presidential elections. The legislation denied undocumented immigrants access to state and local public services and stipulated that state public employees had to check the identity and immigration status of any person requesting services. If they failed to do so, they could be charged with a U.S. $750 fine and up to four months in prison. Additionally, it demanded proof of citizenship before registering to vote in any election. The bill was vague and did not offer a clear definition of state public services. In theory, therefore, it could be used to deny illegal immigrants access to public parks and libraries, as well as to bar them from receiving police or nonemergency medical services.

As if Proposition 200 had not been enough, Arizona's House Appropriations Committee voted to deny a new host of state services and privileges to undocumented people, including higher education. This legislation greatly expanded what voters approved in Proposition 200. Under this bill a person would have to prove citizenship or legal residency in order to become an adoptive parent, participate in the Family Literacy program, enroll in adult education services, and obtain housing assistance. It also required both the Department of Economic Security and Department of Health Services to verify the legal status of applicants for any state-funded programs with the exception of emergency services. Additionally, undocumented individuals would be banned from state universities or community colleges, even if they paid the higher tuition charged to nonresidents.

Beyond the potential damage to the immigrant community in Arizona, it is also crucial to consider the political message conveyed by this law. Having the majority of Arizona's population approve Proposition 200 sent strong anti-immigrant signals to Congress and the White House. In addition, it encouraged many local anti-immigration groups to try and pass similar legislations in their own states.

New civil groups have formed, further inspired by this type of immigration control legislation, such as in the case of "The Minuteman Project," a group of civilians in Arizona that in April 2005 announced their recruitment of 2,000 individuals from across the country in order to form an immigrants watch group. Their goal was to "help" the Border Patrol stop illegal immigrants from entering the country through Arizona's border with Mexico. The intention of this "immigrant hunters" group, as it has been called, was supposedly only to spot undocumented immigrants crossing the border and report them to the Border Patrol. However, many of them were carrying arms, risking potential confrontations with immigrants that they encountered. This led numerous immigrants' rights groups to accuse them of risking immigrants' lives and safety and helped to radicalize the immigration debate in the United States.

The impact of this project on decreasing the flow of undocumented immigrants was insignificant. The publicity generated was enough to persuade undocumented immigrants and their smugglers to use other crossing points. Additionally, less than 200 volunteers actually showed up, and many abandoned their posts days and even weeks before April 30, the last day of the project. However, their goal of escalating the immigration debate was successful. Although President Bush and even the Border Patrol denounced their activities, arguing that control of the border was the responsibility of the federal government and that civilians should not interfere in this process, other groups and politicians, such as California's governor Arnold Schwarzenegger, applauded their actions and stated that the U.S. government is not fulfilling its responsibility of controlling the border. In the end, their main goal was to send a clear message to Washington and the American public about tightening control of the border. As Minuteman organizer Jim Gilchrist admitted to the *L.A. Times*: "This thing was a dog-and-pony show designed to bring in the media and get the message out, and it worked."[24] Despite the criticism that this project encountered, organizers made plans to hold similar events in other border states like California and Texas.

Such controversies have not occurred only in border states. In Colorado, a House legislative committee defeated a bill that sought to deny state services to illegal immigrants. Its sponsor, Republican Rep. David Schultheis, said that he would submit the same proposal in the form of a concurrent resolution, which, if passed, would put the proposal before the voters in the form of a ballot referendum. Democrats argued that the bill could create an anti-immigrant climate and feed discrimination and hatred. A representative from the American Civil Liberties Union who testified against the bill stated that the measure could require residents of Colorado to carry identification before accessing state services like hiking trails. Nevertheless, the bill's proponents argued that it was justified because providing services to illegal immigrants was draining the state budget and preventing funds from being used on legal residents.

Another state that faced the passage of anti-immigration legislation was Virginia. Bills were approved by the state House and Senate requiring a valid ID in order to prove legal residence for Medicaid applicants, with an exception made for children younger than nineteen years of age. Other bills seeking to bar undocumented students from attending state-funded colleges and universities were defeated in the Senate. In practical terms, these bills were redundant, given that most applicants for benefits in Virginia already had to prove legal residence. This meant that the bills' main effects were to force all Virginians to carry more documentation and go through more paperwork. Nevertheless, the political message of such bills and their contribution to an anti-immigration climate at the national and local levels was worrisome.

In California, some groups have fought to put Proposition 187 back on the ballot in light of the success that other states have had in passing similar legislation. Other states have followed their lead, with the result that at the state and local levels, anti-immigration coalitions have gathered strength and become a major obstacle to the passage of a comprehensive immigration reform bill in Congress.

Meanwhile, pro-immigrant groups have lobbied in favor of immigrants' rights, trying to visit numerous states in an effort to educate people on the benefits that immigrants bring to the U.S. economy. They have not been alone in their efforts, since there are some states whose position regarding immigrants is more liberal, such as Illinois and Wisconsin. Governor Jim Doyle of Wisconsin has favored legislation that would allow illegal immigrants who graduate from Wisconsin high schools to pay in-state tuition at the University of Wisconsin system. In the traditional system, they have been expected to pay out-of-state tuition, leaving many of them without the possibility of continuing their education, despite the fact that they have lived in the state for most of their lives.[25] In California, even with all of the recent anti-immigrant rhetoric of its governor and certain groups, Los Angeles voters elected Antonio Villaraigosa as the city's Hispanic mayor in 2005.

CONGRESS' POSITION TOWARD BUSH'S PROPOSAL

Although the U.S. president is capable of proposing reforms on immigration, such legislation is ultimately the domain of Congress and must therefore be enacted by this body. The result is that there has been heated debate on the issue within Congress.

In general, temporary programs have tended to be a highly divisive and controversial political issue. Conservative Republicans, such as James Sensenbrenner (R-WI), John Culberson (R-TX), John Hostettler (R-IN), Nathan Deal (R-GA), Dana Rohrabacher (R-CA), and Tom Tancredo (R-CO) tend to view Bush's proposals for immigration reform as too generous to immigrants who entered the U.S. illegally. The possibility of giving them access to a regularization of their status for three to six years has been seen as amnesty and a form of rewarding illegal workers. Rep. Elton Gallegly (R-CA), who headed the Subcommittee on International Terrorism, Nonproliferation and Human Rights, urged the Bush administration to drop its proposed temporary guest worker program and not "reward Mexican nationals living and working illegally in the United States" with legal status.[26]

Liberals, on the other hand, many of them Democrats like Senators Edward Kennedy (D-MA), Christopher Dodd (D-CT), and Rep. Luis Gutierrez (D-IL), have considered Bush's reform proposal as not generous enough to the undocumented population and demanded a path to legalization for illegal workers in the U.S. who meet certain criteria. Without such a path to legalization, they have argued that these communities will not be able to improve their economic and working conditions and that their way of life and access to opportunities will be negatively affected. In addition, they have criticized the absence of reforms to ameliorate the tremendous backlogs for family-based visas that have kept U.S. citizens apart from their immediate families for many years, leading some to use illegal channels as a way to bring their spouses and children into the United States. Finally, they have expressed concern for labor protection of potential temporary workers, arguing that they were unclear and that they would weaken workers' bargaining power in the workplace, given that in order to obtain a three-year temporary visa, a worker would have to be sponsored by his/her employer, after which the work visa would only be renewed if the worker still had a job. This situation could create a sort of "labor tutelage" that, as observed in other guest worker programs, could effectively translate into exploitation. They have therefore demanded that any guest worker program grant workers independence from their employers and full labor rights in order to counteract this sort of labor vulnerability.

Congress on Broader Immigration Reform

Within both political parties there are individuals and groups who have tended to favor either more comprehensive immigration reform or an increase in border controls. On the one hand, there are individuals like Senator Edward Kennedy (D-MA), who has played a key role in immigration issues since the mid-1960s and whose bills have always presented broad proposals. On the other hand, there are those like Congressman Tom Tancredo (R-CO), who has advocated closed borders.

President Bush has not been the only one to present an immigration proposal. A number of congressmen and senators have submitted their own proposals in recent congressional sessions, generally without success. In the 108th congressional session, many bills were either defeated or, in the case of the AgJOBS[27] bill, not presented by Congress because the Republican leadership of the time acquiesced to the White House's desire not to have Senate pass such a highly controversial bill immediately before the presidential election. However, the 109th session of Congress was more active regarding immigration legislation. In addition, Bush reiterated his interest in reforming the immigration system on various occasions, announcing that immigration reform was a high priority for his administration and that he was willing to spend political capital to see it through.

Previous Legislation

During the 108th Congress (2003–2004), most immigration reform proposals dealt with two major issues: (1) temporary work visas, and (2) the regularization of status for undocumented workers already in the United States. In the case of work visas, differences in the legislation had to do with the duration of temporary work visas, extent of labor protections, and access of the undocumented population to these visas. In the case of regularization, the main debate was about whether or not there should be a path to legalization. The bills differed on the conditions and criteria necessary to achieve regularization and the length of time involved in these procedures. Some proposals went further and demanded a solution for the backlogs pending in the current immigration system, especially those for immediate family-based visas. Others also responded to pressures for a reinforcement of immigration law.

Legislation in the 109th Congress

Bills introduced in the 108th congressional session expired in January 2005, when the 109th Congress took over. From the 109th session, three immigration bills are worth mentioning: (1) the reintroduction of the AgJOBS bill; (2) the Real ID Act, ratified by Congress and introduced by Rep. James Sensenbrenner (R-WI); and (3) the Secure America and Orderly Immigration Act of 2005, introduced by Senator McCain and Senator Kennedy.

AgJOBS

The only bill from the previous congressional session that was reintroduced for consideration was the Agricultural Jobs, Opportunities and Benefits Act of 2005 (AgJOBS, S. 359 / H.R. 884). The fundamentals of the bill remained in place, with only nominal changes. This piece of legislation was the result of years of negotiations between workers' advocates and employers, and it was the only bill that enjoyed wide bipartisan support, with 63 sponsors in the Senate and 126 in the House. It focuses on reform of the H-2A visa category and proposed two basic reforms. First, it would grant legal permanent residence, on a one-time-only basis, to unauthorized migrants that had worked in the agricultural sector for the equivalent of 100 workdays, during any 12 consecutive months, of the 18-month period ending on

Table 6.1. Key Immigration Proposals during the 108th Congress, 2003–2004

Immigration Proposals	Guest Worker Visas, Non-Sector Specific	Guest Agricultural Worker Visas	Reform Employment-Based Visa System	Regularization	Labor Protection	Law Enforcement	Reform Family-Based Visa System
Immigration Reform Act, Hagel (R-NE), Daschle (D-SD)	X		Only a temporary fix	X	Not enough	X	X
SOLVE Act, Kennedy (D-MA), Gutierrez (D-IL)	X		X		X		X
Border Security and Immigration Reform Act, Cornyn (R-TX)	Signing of guest worker accords with foreign countries			Limited and long process			
Land Border Security and Immigration Improvement Act, McCain (R-AZ), Flake (R-AZ), Kolbe (R-AZ)	X			Long process			
Aglobs, Kennedy (R-MA), Craig (R-ID), Cannon (R-UT), Berman (D-CA)		X		Just for farm	Limited		

(continued)

Table 6.1. (continued)

Immigration Proposals	Guest Worker Visas, Non-Sector Specific	Guest Agricultural Worker Visas	Reform Employment-Based Visa System	Regularization	Labor Protection	Law Enforcement	Reform Family-Based Visa System
DREAM ACT, Hatch (R-UT), Durbin (R-IL), Cannon (R-UT), Berman (D-CA), Roybal-Allard (D-CA)				Only for undocumented students			
CLEAR ACT, Norwood (R-GA), Hart (R-PA), Boyd (D-FL), Deal (R-GA)						Authorizes police to enforce federal immigration law	

August 31, 2004. This would apply to approximately 500,000 foreign farm-workers currently in the U.S., in addition to their spouses and minor children. Adjustment to permanent residency (green card) would be possible, although not automatic. It would require performing an additional 360 days of agricultural work over the next six years. Second, AgJOBS would streamline the H-2A temporary, nonimmigrant guest worker program. It would make the hiring process more similar to the expedited hiring for H-1B high-tech workers. The H-1B process only requires an "attestation" that the employer has been unable to fill the position with an American worker, as opposed to the much lengthier certification process involving the Department of Labor that is required to obtain an H-2A visa.[28]

The bill was designed to create an earned adjustment program for undocumented farmworkers and streamline the existing agricultural guest worker program through simplified procedures and paperwork, less delays and less government oversight. The bill was introduced in the Senate to see if it could be approved, but although it enjoyed the support of the majority with 54 votes, it did not garner the 60 votes necessary to stop the filibuster. Thus, although the bill had the possibility of getting approved, it was nevertheless seen as a victory for the anti-immigrant coalition.

Real ID Act

The Real ID Act (H.R. 418) had three major components: (1) to limit the granting of asylum by raising the necessary burden of proof; (2) to impose federal standards on driver's licenses, prohibiting states from issuing them to undocumented immigrants; and (3) to waive laws (environmental, labor, immigration, health, etc.) in order to expedite the Department of Homeland Security expansion of a portion of the wall on the San Diego-Tijuana border. Although pro-immigrant groups fought the bill, it was finally introduced and approved in the Senate as part of a supplemental appropriations package for funding troops in Iraq and Afghanistan and financing tsunami relief efforts in Asia.

The bill's sponsor, Rep. Sensenbrenner (R-WI), applauded this ratification, arguing that it would enhance border security. He affirmed that "by targeting terrorists' travel, the Real ID Act will assist in our war on terror efforts to disrupt terrorist operations and help secure our borders."[29] This sort of national security rhetoric was employed by supporters of the Real ID Act in order to introduce immigration legislation.

In the 108th Congress, legislation was passed in order to implement the advice of the 9/11 Commission on how to reform the intelligence system. Some of those favoring restrictions of immigration added anti-immigration provisions that were eliminated from the final version. However, proponents were determined to see them through in this new Congress. The Real

ID Act incorporated the main content of these provisions and sought to present itself not as an immigration bill, but as national security legislation.

The Real ID bill had a number of effects: it made it harder for refugees in the U.S. to obtain asylum; it endangered the wetlands between Baja California and California, which were until then protected by environmental law, by extending the wall on the San Diego-Tijuana border; and it required Americans to prove their citizenship before obtaining a federally approved electronic driver's license consistent with Department of Homeland Security standards. Additionally, undocumented immigrants would not be able to get a driver's license, which would bar them from accessing insurance. Given that driving is essential for the jobs of many immigrants, the bill would make U.S. roads more dangerous by increasing the number of uninsured drivers. Furthermore, these immigrants would not be able to board a plane, open a bank account, or enter any federal building without this new federal identification. These restrictionist measures were similar to others enacted in the 1990s, which ultimately proved to be ineffective at curbing immigration, but which did make immigrant communities more vulnerable.

President Bush, who had remained silent on the Real ID Act, eventually endorsed it in late April and asked Congress to include it in the final bill. This led some analysts in Washington to conclude that some kind of compromise had been reached with Sensenbrenner in order to eventually bring about the greater good of comprehensive immigration reform. According to one of his advisors, Sensenbrenner had insisted that he would not consider broader immigration reform until his bill passed the Senate. As Chairman of the Committee on the Judiciary, which has jurisdiction over matters relating to the administration of justice in federal courts, administrative bodies, and law enforcement agencies, Sensenbrenner had the clout to stop comprehensive reform, as the scope of the Committee included immigration through its Subcommittee on Immigration, Border Security, and Claims. As such, Sensenbrenner represented an obstacle to the passage of any type of comprehensive reform; simply put, the committee he presided over would not even contemplate comprehensive reform until his bill was approved.

Secure America and Orderly Immigration Act

Senators John McCain (R-AZ) and Edward Kennedy (D-MA) introduced the Secure America and Orderly Immigration Act of 2005 (S.1033 / H.R. 2330), a bipartisan comprehensive immigration reform bill that reiterated the main points of Bush's proposal, such as a temporary visas program, but which also incorporated a path to regularization for undocumented immigrants in the United States and workers applying for a visa from abroad as well as new strategies for enforcement of immigration law (see a more detailed account in chapter 5).

The much anticipated McCain-Kennedy legislation was introduced in May both in the House and the Senate. It consisted of five major points: (1) the creation of a new three-year guest worker visa (H-5A) to allow unskilled foreign workers to fill available jobs in the United States, renewable once and with an initial cap of 400,000; (2) access for undocumented immigrants in the U.S. to the guest worker program; (3) tougher law enforcement through the creation of a new electronic work authorization system; (4) the creation of a public-private foundation to promote citizenship and fund civics and English lessons for immigrants; and (5) economic incentives for temporary workers to return home by requiring foreign governments to enter into immigration agreements with the U.S. In particular, the legislation sought to work with the Mexican government in order to advance economic opportunities, reduce pressures to emigrate, and to provide access to health care in Mexico for Mexican immigrants.[30]

Supporters like Tamar Jacoby, a senior fellow at the Manhattan Institute, argued that this bill would fix a broken system that had allowed the undocumented population in the United States to swell over the last decade.[31] The National Restaurant Association also expressed support for the McCain-Kennedy initiative, calling it a "realistic and balanced approach to addressing the security and economic shortcomings of our immigration system."[32] Meanwhile, opponents of the bill, like Dan Stein, the executive director of FAIR, argued that it destroyed working opportunities for Americans because "there is no such thing as cheap labor, just cheap employers who will not pay decent wages and benefits for a day's work."[33] Senator Dianne Feinstein (D-CA) also expressed her disagreement to the McCain-Kennedy proposal, arguing that "any guest worker program, even one requiring employees to eventually return to their home country—would be a magnet for illegal immigration."[34]

The bill's sponsors dismissed the idea that it would only encourage more illegal immigration, insisting that in contrast to past legislation like IRCA, it would provide legal channels for future temporary workers and also implement better law enforcement procedures. They also argued that their bill did not provide amnesty, given that it required recognition of wrongdoing, and also that undocumented immigrants would not get a free pass to regularize their status, but rather would have to go to the end of the line. Finally, they pointed out that in order to have an impact on the U.S. immigration system, any comprehensive reform would have to address the more than ten million undocumented immigrants in the country, not only for humanitarian reasons, but also for security concerns. The legislation was designed to grant legality to immigrants and make it easier to know who was actually in the United States.

The 109th legislature experienced a bitter and wide-ranging debate over immigration reform, but ultimately stalemated. On December 16, 2005, the House of Representatives approved the Border Protection, Anti-Terrorism, and Illegal Immigration Control Act (H.R. 4437), sponsored by the Chairman of the House Judiciary Committee of the time, James Sensenbrenner. The bill contained tougher sanctions against illegal immigrants by making it a felony to be undocumented in the United States. Being undocumented represented a violation of immigration laws, thus making illegal immigrants subject to deportation. By making it a felony, law enforcement officials would be able to chase down immigrants and detain them. The bill also required employers to verify workers' legal status, facing fines if they did not comply.

After the bill was passed, several groups protested against its tough measures. In April and May 2006, millions of immigrants took part in rallies across the United States, boycotting work and school activities for a day. These protests were aimed at pressuring Congress to abandon the tough measures passed in December 2005. The largest demonstrations took place in Los Angeles and Chicago, where as many as 400,000 protesters took their demands to the streets. These highly visible rallies led to a renewed effort in Congress to fix the broken immigration system by drafting a more comprehensive bill.

On April 2006, Senators Chuck Hagel (R-NE) and Mel Martinez (R-FL) drafted the Comprehensive Immigration Reform Act of 2006. It increased border security measures, including construction of border fences in Arizona and the hiring of 12,000 new border patrol agents. It also created an electronic employment verification system for employers to evaluate the authorization of newly hired workers. Besides these security measures, the bill aimed at creating a temporary worker program, capped at 325,000 workers. Undocumented immigrants who had resided in the U.S. for at least five years prior to April 5, 2006, would be eligible for eventual permanent legal status. This provision was heavily criticized by several groups, who declared that it amounted to amnesty for as many as 8 million people, and was the main obstacle to its passage in the House. Although the bill was passed in the Senate, the House disagreed with its provisions, and the immigration debate came to an end without effective legislation being enacted. For the rest of 2006, attention was focused on the November midterm elections, and the prospects of a new bill were postponed until the next year and the new Congress.

The 110th Congress and Immigration Reform: Early Collapse

Immigration reform was heavily debated during the midterm congressional election of November 2006. This may partially explain why the Republicans lost both houses of Congress. The main electoral problems for the Republicans were the war in Iraq and the low popularity of President Bush.

The 110th Congress opened in January 2007 with a slim Democratic majority in both houses, which led to some renewed hopes about the passage of a comprehensive immigration reform bill. Some optimistic observers claimed that Bush wished to leave an improved immigration system as his main domestic legacy. In addition, Karl Rove, his main political adviser of the time, was also apparently committed to passing comprehensive immigration reform.

The new congressional leaders, Nancy Pelosi (D-CA), Speaker of the House of Representatives, and Harry Reid, (D-NV) Senate Majority Leader, both embraced comprehensive immigration reform from the beginning of the 110th Congress. But the reform camp soon lost one of its staunchest allies, Senator John McCain (R-AZ), who, as a candidate for the Republican presidential nomination, realized that immigration reform was one of the least popular issues among the conservative base of the Republican Party. It was therefore necessary to find a new Republican sponsor in the Senate, but there were few who had the same appeal to Democrats as McCain.

During the 110th Congress, coalitions acquired significant importance, since the Senate required 60 percent of votes in order to offset the practice known as filibustering. This meant that Democrats would need nine Republican votes in order to break the legislative gridlock. In May, a group of Senators led by the majority leader Harry Reid introduced the Comprehensive Immigration Reform Act of 2007. It was drafted by both Democrats and Republicans, notably Senators Jon Kyl (R-AZ) and Lindsey Graham (R-SC), which appeared to signal a new momentum for the immigration reform debate.

The bill incorporated aspects of the old Kennedy-McCain initiative. On the one hand, it included tougher provisions aimed at strengthening border security, increasing the number of border patrol agents from 13,000 to 18,000, and extending or replacing fencing along the U.S.-Mexico border. It also proposed tougher sanctions for employers who hired illegal immigrants, with a fine of $5,000 for a first offense and up to $75,000 for subsequent offenses. These provisions were directed at those senators who believed that not enough was being done to secure the nation's borders. On the other hand, it offered generous provisions for the regularization of undocumented migrants. It specified that up to 12 million immigrants who had arrived prior to 2007 would be eligible to apply for a "Z" visa, giving them the right to remain in the country, provided that they paid a fine and renewed their visa every two years. It also created a "Y" visa as part of a temporary worker program. This visa would be renewable twice and would allow 200,000 workers per year into the country.

In addition to its provisions for strengthening the border and regularizing undocumented immigrants, the bill proposed the establishment of a new, highly controversial "point" system for determining potential immigrants. This merit-based system would favor skills over family ties, thereby changing the structure and dynamics of the immigrant population. People with higher education, job skills, English proficiency, and who met market needs would be given preference over immigrants' relatives when applying for a green card. By deemphasizing family reunification, the bill was criticized by several liberal groups, which created an obstacle for the reform's final passage.

Senator Reid tried to push the bill for a floor vote and invoke cloture, which would have ended debate on the measure and put it to a simple "yes" or "no" vote. However, even though the group who had drafted the bill tried hard to convince their colleagues to end debate, the attempt fell short of the sixty votes needed, with a final tally of forty-six to fifty-three in June. One of the fiercest critics of the bill was Senator Jeff Sessions (R-AL), who claimed that it amounted to amnesty and did nothing to protect the country from potential terrorists. Ultimately, heavy pressure from constituents and conservative groups, including the media, was responsible for the failure of this latest attempt at immigration reform. In the summer of 2007, with the 2008 presidential race heating up, there was widespread consensus that the next serious attempt at comprehensive immigration reform would have to wait until a new Congress came into being in 2009.

What Can Mexico Do?

In the United States, immigration is viewed as a domestic issue, not a foreign policy one. It is now clear that the Fox administration had almost no chance of conducting a successful bilateral negotiation over immigration. In the face of the prolonged U.S. legislative debate over immigration reform, what can Mexico do? Should it simply watch and wait for the U.S. Congress to announce a reform, or should it take a more active role and try to at least influence the process? There is a split view in Washington on the role of Mexico. On the one hand, there are those like Congressman Sensenbrenner and other conservative Republicans who consider any involvement of Mexico in the immigration legislative debate to be a transgression of U.S. sovereignty. On the other hand, there are those like Senator Kennedy who demand that Mexico cooperate in finding solutions to some of the major problems between the two countries. They consider Mexico a demanding country that does not reciprocate and think that it is time for it to engage in real commitments at the border and accept its responsibility in this process.

A common question in Washington is what measures the Mexican government should take in order to diminish domestic pressures to emigrate.

Critics argue that Mexico is not focusing on policies and reforms that could ameliorate economic conditions in certain areas, instead appearing to view migration as a solution, not a problem. As an example, they point to the *Guía del Migrante* (Migrant's Guide), published by the Mexican government and distributed in high migratory regions, which gave advice to migrants about how and where to cross the border, how to act and carry themselves in order to avoid getting caught, etc. Many in the United States were enraged by what they saw as the Mexican government promoting illegal immigration.

For those who call on Mexico to cooperate more fully, there are three central demands: (1) increased control of its southern border, a key crossing point for thousands of undocumented Central Americans; (2) a full frontal attack on criminal transnational organizations that smuggle humans and drugs and operate on both sides of the border; and (3) the implementation of economic policies and infrastructure that promote development in certain areas and states in Mexico, especially those with a long tradition of sending immigrants to the United States.

There are also some major questions that proponents of comprehensive reform must face. Could Mexico help to control the flow of undocumented immigrants once a guest worker program was in place? What economic incentives could be introduced in order to encourage Mexican immigrants to return home? Would Mexico cooperate with the United States in establishing these mechanisms? One crucial challenge for comprehensive reform is to restore the circularity of the migration flow, and in this respect the Mexican government could provide help in finding common solutions.

Some in the United States have made unrealistic demands on Mexico, such as that it take responsibility for OTMs (Other Than Mexicans) apprehended at the U.S. border. The United States argues that due to lack of resources, it cannot detain these individuals. Instead, they are usually set free in U.S. territory while waiting for a court appointment to review their case. Obviously, the majority of these individuals never appear in court. Due to these loopholes in U.S. immigration law, the fear that terrorist organizations may one day use them as an infiltration route is understandable. However, Mexico also lacks the economic and human resources to take care of these people.

In light of these considerations, Mexico must take a realistic approach to cooperation. The days in which a bilateral immigration agreement seemed possible are definitely over; any reform that occurs will be taken unilaterally by the United States. However, Mexico has leverage in the form of its numerous immigrants in the U.S. who may in time be able to change the status quo.

Although it is now clear that any kind of immigration reform in the United States will be unilateral, there remains a question about what role

Mexico, whose nationals represent about one-half of undocumented and one-third of legal immigrants in the United States, could play in the process. Should the Mexican government endorse a temporary worker program, knowing that it will not meet the needs of its undocumented population in the United States? Or should it openly advocate a comprehensive reform, even though this may spark the anger of many Americans? Additionally, what should be Mexico's response to U.S. demands that it play a tougher role in attacking criminal organizations at the border and controlling illegal immigration? Mexico will have to decide the level of commitment it is willing to make, especially given the new post-9/11 security framework.

Priorities and Recommendations

1. The Deepening of North American Integration

Mexico should insist on advancing toward a North American economic community, with NAFTA deepened and widened. Mexico's position toward immigration and other bilateral topics should take into account that the region will be more economically integrated in the future. In order to advance toward this economic community, it will be necessary to overcome certain bottlenecks, such as the Mexican trucks entering into U.S. territory. All three North American countries will benefit from increased economic integration, making the region more competitive and prosperous.

The North American countries are interdependent not only economically, but also in security matters, such as in the cases of terrorism, drug trafficking, and international organized crime. It is essential to face these threats and challenges as a region. In 2004, the borders between Mexico, the United States, and Canada were crossed more than 400 million times. In March 2005, the three countries signed the Security and Prosperity Partnership of North America (SPP). President Bush described the reach of the SPP as a common commitment "to markets, democracy, liberty, trade, mutual prosperity and mutual security." Nevertheless, the last trilateral summit in Montebello, Canada, in the summer of 2007 made little headway in the SPP process. North Americans should look at the European example, which reveals that both leadership and institutions are necessary in order to advance toward greater integration.

Given these common challenges and opportunities in the North American region, it is arguable that Mexico and Canada should receive special treatment from Washington. As such, the three NAFTA countries should eventually establish a common labor market.

2. Shared Responsibility

The new immigration status quo should be based on a sense of shared responsibility between the receiving country—the United States—and the countries with high rates of emigration—Mexico, El Salvador, Guatemala, Honduras, and Nicaragua.

The limited dialogue and cooperation that currently takes place between Mexico and the United States on immigration is shocking when one considers the high levels of cooperation in other areas. In economic and trade issues, Mexico and the United States are highly integrated and sophisticated partners. This level of cooperation and communication should be extended to immigration. A good example of this lack of cooperation on issues of immigration is the lack of management of the H-2A (visas for agricultural workers) and H-2B (visas for service workers). Last year, the United States granted 28,683 agricultural visas and 31,774 service visas to Mexican workers. Unfortunately, there was practically no involvement of the Mexican and U.S. governments on allocating these visas.

It is urgent to improve the way that Mexico and the United States manage immigration. Traditionally, U.S. immigration policy has been considered a domestic matter and, consequently, the authorities there have unilaterally managed immigration issues. Mexico, meanwhile, maintained for many years a policy of not having a policy. During the Fox and Bush administrations, small steps were taken toward increased dialogue and cooperation, but much more needs to be done.

Mexico and the United States must increase their level of dialogue and cooperation in both managing the flow of migrants and creating a more secure and efficient border. There is a pressing need to decrease regulations at the U.S.-Mexico border. The U.S.-Canada border is a model to follow. It is also necessary to assess the U.S.-Mexico institutional framework for dealing with the border and immigration. After 9/11, the United States dramatically transformed its governmental structures through the creation of the Department of Homeland Security. These changes implied important bureaucratic disruptions in the United States, while Mexico kept most of its governmental structures intact. Such differences create obvious institutional and practical problems for bilateral coordination. In the aftermath of 9/11, it is essential to establish efficient bilateral coordination on security and border issues.

3. Comprehensive Reform

There is a new consensus in the United States on immigration: the current system is broken. As such, it should be subjected to comprehensive reform. It will not be enough to merely address the challenges and problems posed by the high levels of immigration from Mexico and Central America to the United States; it is necessary to deal with the needs of both the sending and receiving countries.

At the beginning of his presidency, Vicente Fox initiated a dialogue with George W. Bush on the possibility of a comprehensive immigration agreement. The window of opportunity for that agreement closed on September 11, 2001. Nevertheless, the Fox proposal helped to create a new consensus among Mexican analysts, businesspeople and policy makers about the need for a broad change in the U.S.-Mexico immigration status quo. This explains why the Kennedy-McCain initiative, the "Secure America and Orderly Immigration Act," was welcomed in Mexico and in some Central American countries, such as El Salvador.

Any future comprehensive immigration reform should address the five major elements contemplated in the original Kennedy-McCain bill: regularization, a guest worker program, greater enforcement at the border and within the United States, reduction of current backlogs for naturalization, and encouragement of development in Mexico and Central America.

Mexican analysts and advocacy groups, such as the National Migration Institute Citizen Council, have urged both the Mexican government and Congress to engage in advocacy in favor of comprehensive reform. Since migration has become a high priority for every political force and party in Mexico, there is a generally positive attitude in Mexico about a U.S.-based comprehensive approach to migration reform.

4. The Creation of an Efficient and Secure Mexican Southern Border

Mexico's border with Guatemala and Belize is not simply porous—it is open. Historically, there has been much economic interdependence between southern Mexico and northern Guatemala. This resembles the case of the U.S.-Mexico border. For example, the city of Tapachula, Chiapas, is highly dependent on Guatemalan agricultural and service workers, as well as trade with Guatemala. For many decades, an open Mexican southern border did not represent a major problem. However, this is no longer the case in the post-9/11 security-oriented atmosphere.

In 2002, Mexican immigration officials deported 138,000 Central American nationals, mostly from Guatemala, El Salvador, and Honduras. In 2004, the number of Central American deportations increased to 215,000. This can be explained by two factors: the economic depression in Central America caused by the natural disasters of the late 1990s, such as Hurricane Mitch in 1998, and post-9/11 security requirements. Mexican officials have increased their efforts to stop undocumented migrants not only from Central America, but also from many other countries, including some considered by Washington to be high terrorist risks.

Mexico must not replicate the California experience of the late 1990s, in which the construction of walls and fences, as well as an increase in the number of border patrol agents, were imposed in an attempt to stem the flow of immigrants. A decade after the implementation of this policy, it is clear that it has only produced negative consequences.

In addition to entering into a dialogue with Central American and U.S. authorities, the Mexican government should make a major effort to strengthen the National Migration Institute and reorganize the police forces and the military operating on the southern border. In addition, corruption among Mexican officers must be put to a stop, both for ethical and security reasons.

5. Formalize a Subregional Dialogue on Migration Issues

The migration patterns of the last two decades have formed a new hemispheric subregion composed of Mexico, the United States, and four Central American countries: Nicaragua, El Salvador, Honduras, and Guatemala. Mexico and these four Central American countries account for more than three-quarters of total immigration to the United States. In the past two decades, and especially in the most recent one, the immigration rate from these countries to the United States has accelerated. In the chart below, Jeffrey Passel from the Pew Hispanic Center indicates the growing numbers of Mexican-born immigrants.

The chart below provides estimates of the unauthorized immigrant population as of March 2005, divided by the country/region of birth. It shows that in that year there were approximately 6.2 million (56 percent) illegal

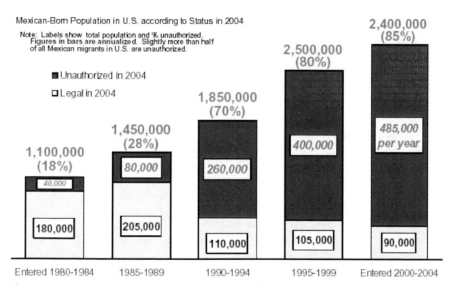

Figure 6.1. Mexican-Born Migrants in the United States by Legal Status and Date of Arrival as of March 2004

Source: Jeffrey S. Passel, "Unauthorized Migrants: Numbers and Characteristics," *Pew Hispanic Center Report*, March 2005, http://pewhispanic.org/files/reports/46.pdf.

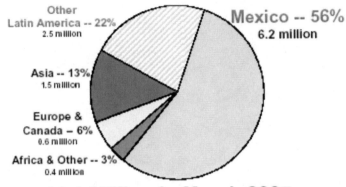

Other
Latin America -- 22%
2.5 million

Asia -- 13%
1.5 million

Europe &
Canada - 6%
0.6 million

Africa & Other -- 3%
0.4 million

Mexico -- 56%
6.2 million

11.1 Million in March 2005

Figure 6.2.   Country or Region of Birth for the Undocumented Migrant Population as of March 2005

Source: Jeffrey S. Passel, "The Size and Characteristics of the Unauthorized Population in the U.S." (Pew Hispanic Center, March 2006), http://pewhispanic.org/files/reports/61.pdf.

immigrants from Mexico. The other Latin Americans were mainly from Central America and amounted to about 2.5 million (22 percent). In total, therefore, Latin Americans accounted for more than three-quarters (78 percent) of undocumented immigrants in the United States.

These accelerated rates of migration explain some new dynamics specific to the subregion. One example is the emergence of transnational youth gangs, such as the *Mara Salvatrucha* and the *Barrio 18*. These gangs represent a threat to the security of all countries in which they operate and have been surprisingly resistant to national efforts to cope with them. When the government of the former president of El Salvador, Francisco Flores, implemented a "firm hand" (*mano dura*) policy for dealing with these gangs, the *Mara Salvatrucha* spread to Honduras, Guatemala, and Mexico, and some of its leaders returned to the United States. In this case and in many others, it is necessary to develop subregional approaches in order to cope effectively with the specific challenges.

6. Areas in Which Mexico Should Focus in Order to Increase the Possibility of a Successful Immigration Reform in the United States

- *Return to a circular pattern of migration.* The Mexican government, as well as the business community, should attempt to create the economic conditions and implement the incentives necessary for motivating immigrants to return to Mexico. The willingness of Mexican workers to return is the core of a successful temporary worker program.

Mexican financial officials should seek the cooperation of their U.S. counterparts in order to create savings accounts with tax preferential rates and a retirement system tailored for immigrants (See *Pension Totalization* in chapter 7).

- *Improve the health and education coverage of Mexican nationals, including those who migrate to the United States.* One of the most controversial aspects of the immigration debate in the U.S. centers on the costs to the taxpayer of providing immigrants with education and health care. Mexico should seek to strengthen health coverage programs such as the *Seguro Popular*, a public health program for low-income families not covered by traditional private or public programs. In addition, Mexico should seek to develop a binational health insurance plan—an idea about which firms in both countries have already expressed interest. As far as education is concerned, there is much that Mexico can do, including improving English as a second language education; utilizing new technology in classrooms, especially the internet; and collaborating with U.S. school districts that have a high concentration of Spanish-speaking immigrants.
- *Improve security.* In the Security and Prosperity Partnership of North America, which was created by the leaders of the three North American countries in 2005, a series of measures are outlined for how to strengthen the security of the region. In some instances, such as the Mexican southern border, Central America should also be included in regional security measures.
- *Border safety.* Finally, the Mexican government should engage in some activities to prevent the numerous accidents at the U.S.-Mexico border. For example, it could prevent the entrance of Mexican nationals into dangerous zones, such as some areas on the Arizona-Sonora border (see also chapter 7). In addition, Mexican authorities should strengthen cooperation with their U.S. counterparts in cases of deportation of those known as OTMs (Other Than Mexicans). The two countries could also cooperate in the expansion and institutionalization of the program for voluntary repatriation to the interior of Mexico.

NOTES

1. Esther Schrader, "Bush's Mexico connection signals key policy initiative," Latimes.com, June 22, 2000.

2. Cited in Scott Johnson, "The Border War at the Texas Summit," *Newsweek International*, March 27, 2005.

3. Jorge Durand, "From Traitors to Heroes: 100 Years of Mexican Migration Policies," *Migration Information Source*, March 2004, http://www.migrationinformation.org/Feature/display.cfm?ID=203.

4. Ibid.

5. Rafael Fernández de Castro and Andrés Rozenthal, "El amor, la decepción y cómo aprovechar la realidad," in *México en el Mundo: En la Frontera del Imperio*, ed. Rafael Fernández de Castro (Mexico City: Planeta, 2003), 107-19.

6. State of the Union Address, Office of the Press Secretary, White House, February 2, 2005, www.whitehouse.gov/news/releases/2005/02/20050202-11.html

7. Remarks by the President on Immigration Policy, Office of the Press Secretary, White House, January 7, 2004, www.whitehouse.gov/news/releases/2004/01/20040107-3.html.

8. Jorge Santibáñez and Rodolfo Corona, "El voto de los ciudadanos mexicanos en el extranjero: aspectos cuantitativos," report, El Colegio de la Frontera Norte, 2004.

9. T. Alexander Aleinikoff, "No Illusions: Paradigm Shifting on Mexican Migration to the United States in the Post-9/11 World," *U.S. Mexico Policy Bulletin*, no. 5, Wilson Center (June 2005), http://www.wilsoncenter.org/topics/pubs/Mexico PolicyBulletin.Aleinikoff.Immig.May.pdf.

10. Remarks by the President on Immigration Policy, Office of the Press Secretary, White House, January 7, 2004, www.whitehouse.gov/news/releases/2004/01/20040107-3.html.

11. Remarks by the President on Immigration Policy.

12. Phil L. Martin and Michael S. Teitelbaum, "The Mirage of Mexican Guest Workers," *Foreign Affairs* 80, no. 6 (November/December 2001): 117-31.

13. Maia Jachimowicz, "Bush Proposes New Temporary Worker Program," *Migration Information Source*, February 1, 2004, http://www.migrationinformation.org/Feature/display.cfm?ID=202.

14. Robert S. Leiken, "Enchilada Lite: A Post-9/11 Mexican Migration Agreement," report, Center for Immigration Studies, Washington, D.C., March 2002, http://www.cis.org/articles/2002/leiken.pdf.

15. Aleinikoff, "No Illusions: Paradigm Shifting."

16. The first Bracero program with Mexico lasted from 1917 until 1921 and ended amid Mexican government complaints of mistreatment of its citizens. The second Bracero program lasted from 1942 until 1964 and ended as a result of pressures from civil rights groups.

17. Doris Meissner, "U.S. Temporary Worker Programs: Lessons Learned," *Migration Information Source*, March 1, 2004, http://www.migrationinformation.org/Feature/display.cfm?ID=205.

18. Federation for American Immigrant Reform, "S. 1387, Border Security and Immigration Reform Act," November 20, 2003, http://www.fairus.org/site/Page Server?pagename=leg_legislation73e3.

19. One survey of the PEW Hispanic Center on the immediacies of several Mexican consulates found that more than 70 percent of the immigrants surveyed would participate in a temporary workers program such as Bush's. However, one has to consider that almost half of those who participated were recent immigrants (less than five years in the U.S.) and that a clear majority responded that they intended to stay in the U.S. for as long as they could, or for the rest of their lives. Thus, it is hard to know whether once enrolled in a temporary program, they would willingly return to Mexico after the expiration of their visas or simply disappear again into the shadows.

20. American Immigration Lawyers Association, "H-2B Emergency Relief: Save Our Small and Seasonal Businesses Act of 2005," American Immigration Lawyers Association, February 10, 2005.

21. U.S. Chamber of Commerce, "Essential workers," www.uschamber.com/issues/index/immigration/essentialwork.htm.

22. Group of volunteers recruited to "patrol" a portion of the Arizona-Mexico border with the intention of stopping undocumented crossings during the month of April 2005.

23. Samuel Huntington, *Who Are We? The Challenges to America's National Identity* (New York: Simon & Schuster, 2004).

24. Marc Cooper, "The 15-Second Me," *Los Angeles Times*, May 1, 2005.

25. J. R. Ross, "Doyle Agrees to Exchange Program Between UW System, Mexican School," *St. Paul Pioneer Press*, March 12, 2005.

26. Jerry Seper, "Congressmen urge Bush to drop guest-worker plan," *The Washington Times*, November 17, 2004.

27. *The Agricultural Jobs, Opportunity, Benefits and Security Act*, S. 1645 / H.R. 3142.

28. "AgJOBS Legislation," Issue Briefing, Senator Larry Craig, craig.senate.gov.

29. Declan McCullagh, "Senate Approves Electronic ID Card Bill," *The New York Times*, May 11, 2005.

30. National Immigration Forum, www.immigrationforum.org.

31. Tyche Hendrix, "Immigrant labor bill creates 3-year visas for guest workers," SFGate.com, May 13, 2005.

32. Johanna Neuman, "Joint Bill Would Revamp Immigrant Worker Rules," *Los Angeles Times*, May 13, 2005.

33. Federation for American Immigration Reform, www.fairus.org.

34. Dena Bunis, "Feinstein targets agricultural workers," *Orange County Register*, May 18, 2005.

7

Mexican Policy and Mexico-U.S. Migration

Agustín Escobar Latapí,[1] *CIESAS Occidente*

INTRODUCTION

Mexico-U.S. migration has gradually become one of the largest such flows in the world today. It is characterized by its extremely long history and persistence regardless of numerous policy changes in the United States, especially IRCA, new border enforcement strategies and acts of Congress, such as the immigration, welfare and anti-terrorism bills of 1996, massive growth in the U.S. Border Patrol staff and budget, or the Real ID act of 2005. This study emphasizes that, while U.S. policy could develop a much better approach to regulate this flow, reforms are likely to fail unless Mexico plays a role in two respects: Firstly, to contribute to the regular character of the flow, which would impact Mexican migrants in a very positive sense; and secondly, to enhance the internal developmental impact of emigration. I agree with Philip Martin (this volume) in the sense that development, not the export of labor, is and should be, to a much greater extent than today, Mexico's overriding goal and policy objective. To quote a well-known Mexican economist, Mexico urgently needs a development policy to guide, and make sense of, economic, social and decentralization efforts.[2] This chapter concentrates on Mexican policies relating to migration: their current nature, quality, and impacts, and their potential within a broad, articulated Mexican stance toward emigration.

Mexico has developed a number of policies that could contribute significantly to the regulation of migration. These policies and programs must be considerably strengthened and expanded, and some components must be added or perfected. These policies and programs, however, will not be of much consequence without three additional elements. The first is a Mexican

179

vision of the role migration can play in Mexican development. This vision should serve to articulate the various components of this comprehensive policy, and the subsequent implementation of specific incentives for specific kinds of migration, together with appropriate disincentives for those deemed undesirable. The second is an economic policy leading to sustained economic and employment growth. The third is U.S. collaboration. The current two-sided U.S. policy, which favors some barriers to illegal entry and places increasing restrictions on social services and means of identification but, at the same time, fosters the employment of undocumented immigrants, will thwart any Mexican efforts to collaborate in the promotion of legal migration. Legal avenues for migration must be made available to migrants who know employers wish to hire them, and their cost/benefit assessments must unequivocally favor legal migration. At the same time, employers must be able to take advantage of these new and enhanced avenues for the employment of immigrants, and they must conclude that the employment of unauthorized workers is not worthwhile.

There are three main areas in which we believe Mexican policy should be developed to achieve the twin goals of regulation and enhanced development. The first is development. The second has to do with social policies that should reduce poverty and inequality in Mexico, and improve access to basic lifetime assets. The third, finally, consists of the development of migration management policies and programs, including those relating to the Mexican diaspora.

MEXICAN DEVELOPMENT

This study has stressed that NAFTA did alter the dynamics of North American integration, and that it had a major impact on Mexico. This impact, however, is not leading to the social and economic convergence of Mexico with its trading partners (Alba, this volume), although some studies show that there has been a modest level of internal intermunicipal convergence in per capita incomes.[3] Newer initiatives, such as the SPP (Security and Prosperity Partnership), on the other hand, have so far had a negligible impact on trade and the creation and development of enterprises in Mexico. SPP, admittedly, must be studied closely in coming years. The processes of integration triggered by GATT (now the WTO) in 1986, and by NAFTA in 1994, however, are moving ahead.

Mexico-U.S. migration is itself the most significant proof that the Mexican and U.S. labor markets are complementary and can benefit each other. During the last five years, approximately 500,000 Mexicans have moved every year from Mexico to the United States, and two-thirds of them have found jobs there that benefit themselves, their families, and their employers.[4] North American integration has proceeded rapidly not just in terms of trade and investment, but in labor markets also. This "third dimension" of integration, however, contrasts with trade and investment in at least two senses. First, it lacks a North American (or Mexico-U.S.) institutional framework for its regulation, and is to a large extent taking place illegally. Second, NAFTA envisioned a future in which labor complementarities would be developed by North American and other enterprises in Mexico, and not via the export of labor.

Between 1994 and 2000 (with the significant exception of a critical 1995), it seemed the Mexican government had developed a "NAFTA path" for North American integration that provided abundant new jobs for Mexicans in Mexico.[5] Mexico created an unprecedented number of new formal jobs from 1996 to 2000 in all areas of the economy, and its exports swelled.[6]

This path, however, failed to become a viable form of development for three reasons. Firstly, Mexican in-bond export industries developed new and highly competitive labor organization patterns and made modest but significant advances toward research and technological development, but they failed to create the domestic provider networks that could have provided the thrust for sustained economic growth.[7] In stark contrast to what happened in China, they remained a "thin" and enclave-style layer of industry scarcely articulated to the rest of the economy. There are significant exceptions, mostly in the automobile and I.T. industries, but they account for a minority share of total exports. Second, the advent of China as a major competitor with a very low-paid labor force that in addition did possess industrial and technological policies assuring that exports provided up-stream growth was not foreseen, nor did it become the object of policies that could make Mexico equally competitive. As a result, Mexican exports have grown more slowly, and they are being consistently lost to Asia. Finally, U.S. employment growth significantly outpaced the growth of its own population of working age, which created unprecedented demand for immigrant workers. Mexico possessed the labor force reserve, as a result of sluggish economic growth in the 1980s and early 1990s and a restructuring of its agriculture undertaken since 1989, and this sparked very significant increases in migration flows. Demand became a significant driver of migration.

Mexico is not stagnant. Export growth is lower than China's, but still considerable. From 1994 to 2004, China's manufacturing exports to the U.S. grew by an average of 19.2 percent per year, and Mexico's by 12.7 percent.[8] There is growth in a number of export and domestic industries. But this growth is taking place slowly, and it is not pervading the Mexican economy. In the medium and long terms, Mexico-U.S. migration will become manageable only if Mexico develops the policies yielding economic and employment growth. The Mexican executive and many observers have stressed that Mexican development is blocked by poor fiscal, energy, and other structures that need urgent reform. Mexico needs these reforms, but the experience of the 1980s and early 1990s shows that they can be ill-managed, and political support for them has waned. A fiscal reform reducing private expenditure will not spur growth unless heretofore inexistent economic policies do so. Reforming the energy, transportation and other sectors can equally backfire unless they provide a truly competitive environment. When they were privatized, Mexico's largest airlines failed. Privatized banks ran into trouble during the crisis of 1995, and the bail-out implemented at the time doubled Mexico's governmental debt. The benefits of the privatization and globalization of Mexican banks in terms of the provision of formal credit to Mexican households and small- and medium-sized enterprises have been small.[9] The privatization of Mexico's airports increased, rather than decreased, the cost of flying. Private Mexican roads also had to be bailed out by the government. Although some Mexicans are leery of reforms for ideological reasons, many fear them on the basis of these ill-fated experiences.

Any additional reforms must therefore lead to economic and employment growth, a truly competitive economic environment, and fairer conditions for ordinary citizens. Significant reasons for migrating include the defenselessness of ordinary and poor citizens in Mexico, a cumbersome regulatory environment, and what they perceive as the unfair advantage of a well-connected few.[10]

Finally, one potent factor underlying current migration patterns is the breakdown of the links that tied small rural producers to the market. These producers have fewer resources to produce, fewer price incentives, and very little access to credit. Whether the agrarian sector is restructured to motivate large, capitalist enterprise, small producers, or both, it is imperative that this population renew its connection to production. Otherwise, rural emigration to Mexican cities and abroad will continue, with downward effects on urban labor markets, and a large labor flow to the United States.

But these reforms are not themselves sufficient. Growth must be sought. While this is the job of the Mexican government, it is an area in which collaboration can be particularly fruitful.

The following areas hold particular promise:

1. Growth of maturing sectors and their suppliers: motor vehicles, IT and computer manufacturing. Mexico has performed reasonably well in these areas since NAFTA was signed, but massive government support is needed to keep them competitive. What has been gained can easily be lost.
2. Growth of U.S. immigration—dependent industries in Mexico: Meatpacking, general assembly, furniture manufacturing, suppliers to U.S.

construction. The underlying idea is to provide a context within which industries that rely on an immigrant workforce can further their competitiveness by employing those workers in Mexico.

3. Agriculture. Mexico-U.S. collaboration for the production of staples and export fruit and horticulture has increased, but it still pales by comparison to the recent growth of comparable agricultural production in the U.S. Mexican emigration is far more frequent in rural areas, which account for roughly half the total flow and are currently losing about 1 percent of the total workforce in Mexico every year. Serious agricultural development is likely therefore to have a major impact on migration pressure *and eventually* on migration flows, provided demand in the United States comes under (labor and immigration) regulation. Large U.S. and other firms are set to compete still more intensely against Mexican agriculture, cattle, and poultry in the near future. Similarly to the car parts, IT and computer industries, those gains that can be observed in Mexican agriculture cannot be taken for granted in the near future.

4. Personal services, health care, and retirement communities. The expatriate and retirement communities in Jalisco, Guanajuato, Baja Sur, and the Mexican Caribbean are token to what can be achieved, if granted substantial support. A number of recent initiatives did not bear fruit. This support should include easing regulations for settlement, the provision of urban and personal services, agreements that guarantee that medical care can be provided in place, and the facilitation of legal immigration in Mexico. Importing clients for personal services is one of the strategies that can easily yield the largest employment multipliers. Schemes operating in India, by which European patients are flown in for non-emergency surgery, are but one example of what could be done. In this last case, the service personnel delivering the services could earn far above the average local wage, but still provide the service at a lower cost than in the United States.

5. As our chapter on demography clearly shows, Mexico has become a significant exporter of skilled labor, with a large part of the total number of Mexicans holding M.A.s and Ph.D.s residing in the United States. Facilitating the reincorporation and employment of postgraduate Mexicans in Mexico is likely to provide the necessary synergy for a much more rapid increase in productivity throughout the economy. But currently, *Hacienda* (Revenue and Expenditure Secretariat) regulations make new hiring in the public (academic and research) sector virtually impossible, and provide no significant incentives for private enterprises to do so. Policies that support education, research, and the employment of highly skilled Mexicans in Mexico can have a large impact on overall international competitiveness. Mexico still devotes a

far smaller portion of its GDP to science and higher education than many comparable countries in Asia and Latin America. Special sectors (such as the above) could be specifically targeted.

In summary, Mexico must rebuild a vision to guide its own development in the near future, and implement it. This is the first, necessary condition for the gradual improvement in the legality and manageability of migration flows. Clearly, migration can serve this purpose, by targeting certain sectors and skills in which to train and attract Mexicans abroad. But the vision, the programs and the funding come first. Inaction may, in fact, worsen current conditions and increase emigration.

SOCIAL POLICY

Most analysts and public officials agree that poverty is one of the major factors underlying emigration, together with labor demand in the United States, geographical proximity, and the operation of transnational networks. The connection, however, is neither clear nor simple. The emigration rate among poor families is lower than among the non-poor. People who increase their incomes in Mexico often use them to finance their trip to the United States. But there is an increasing connection between poverty and emigration. During the past twenty years, emigration has risen particularly rapidly in states with high poverty and marginality rates, and especially in the South (Oaxaca, Veracruz, Puebla, Campeche). Even when these states do not send migrants abroad, they send them to other, more dynamic Mexican states, thus crowding labor markets and triggering international migration. It is reasonable to expect that a substantial reduction in poverty should, eventually, increase purchasing power and help develop markets and opportunities wherever there are poor Mexicans today, thus lessening emigration (supply-side) pressure.

Mexico's social policy has shifted and evolved significantly over the past ten years. There has been a paradigm shift, but in addition there have also been significant technical and political changes. The paradigmatic shift consisted in the abandonment of a vision which relied on a highly regulated economy as the main instrument against poverty. State intervention in the pricing and distribution systems was meant to ensure that the poor drew particular benefits from state subsidies. Under this system and through prices, the federal government provided substantial subsidies to producers of staples, was in charge of mass distribution, and provided additional subsidies to consumers in the cities. Similar mechanisms were in place in the case of fuel, electricity, mass transit systems, and others. Under this system, specific government actions targeted at the poor were few. A progressive tax-

and pricing system was supposed to embody most of the prosocial action of the state. This has led some analysts to view this period as a "prehistory" of Mexican social policy.[11] The system was complex, highly segmented along corporate and political lines, and provided various "tiers" of quality and attention.[12] The health care and social security administrations, for example, were aimed almost exclusively at the workers of large enterprises and the public sector. The Health Ministry, which was in charge of health services to the population otherwise lacking them, had a much smaller per capita budget and was at pains to provide anything other than basic care. Rural anthropologists and sociologists unveiled the usual situation among poor Mexicans in the seventies. In the countryside, it was close to impossible for poor individuals to access subsidized pricing schemes. A large part of the price subsidies benefited those with privileged connections and/or bribing government officials.

Mexico has a long tradition of successful nutrition programs aimed at the poor. These programs effectively reduced malnutrition. But recent analyses have shown that, until the early 1990s, the chances of poor, rural, and indigenous children of benefiting from these programs were approximately one-tenth those of children in the capital city.[13] These programs needed much better targeting.

The price-subsidy system provided significant support for the livelihood of the poor from 1950 to the mid 1980s, but it had significant shortcomings. From 1957 to 1977, the share of total household income captured by the lowest income decile fell from 2.3 percent to 1.1 percent.[14] Poverty did not rise because GDP grew at such a pace that even this falling participation entailed stable or rising incomes, but one should not mistake the impact of growth and the impact of these policies. They were not as effective as once thought.

The system was abandoned in two phases during the 1980s. First, government intervention in wages and prices was abandoned. Second, its participation in the distribution system was ended, and import taxes and barriers were dismantled, which allowed low-price cereals and other staples in the Mexican market, but also led to rapidly rising prices for staples in Mexican cities, since the subsidized government distribution mechanism no longer operated. The new free-market system, therefore, hurt both poor producers and consumers.

Starting at that time, social policy was recreated along new lines. But a number of elements of the new approach had been tried since the 1970s. In 1978, the government launched COPLAMAR, a federal commission aimed at special government intervention in poor rural areas. This system established the determination of state and municipal marginality indexes, which became the basis for targeted programs. At the same time, in urban centers the food distribution commission, or CONASUPO, launched a subsidiary (LICONSA) nutrition program aimed at poor urban children. COPLAMAR and CONASUPO were dismantled soon after, but LICONSA exists to this day. It is significant because it provides nonsubsidized, half-price enriched milk to poor households. LICONSA was and remains virtually self-financing. In 1988–1989 President Salinas launched a much more ambitious program called *Solidaridad*, which benefited from the restructuring of Mexico's foreign debt; carried out large, significant, and diverse[15] actions throughout Mexico; and channeled a large part of federal expenditure. This program was intended to embody "social liberalism," a philosophy pushing for market-based reform together with specific actions for the reduction of poverty. In addition to *Solidaridad*, the Salinas government (1988–1994) devised two cash-subsidy programs for farmers. One provides small subsidies to rainfed-agriculture poor farmers who no longer had access to the agricultural bank, because of its restructuring. It was called "credit on your word."[16] The other is called PROCAMPO,[17] and is intended to serve all farmers, large and small. Both programs subsist today.[18] The few published analyses of *Solidaridad*, however, stress that it was biased toward states that were at risk of being lost to the official party while missing poorer states, and that within states it privileged metropolitan and large urban areas, to the exclusion of the poorest municipalities and communities. In addition to extremely poor or biased targeting, many analysts showed that the program was corrupt. It allowed officials to pocket significant shares of the budget, and funds recovered from productive investments were allowed to remain in the hands of local political bosses. There is no indication that *Solidaridad*, in general, had an impact on the reduction of poverty. Its only component that successfully reduced income poverty was a program which granted scholarships to poor children.

The above experiences, nevertheless, were assessed when the government of Zedillo came to power in December 1994. The object was to design a program that was free from political biases, which reached Mexico's poorest, and could be shown to reduce poverty. The result was *Progresa*, a program providing cash transfers; educational, nutrition, and health services; and nutrition supplements to poor rural families throughout (initially) rural Mexico, on the basis of "coresponsibility":[19] families and individuals have to attend school, comply with a health supervision program, and participate in health talks and community improvement efforts. Children receive scholarships to attend school, according to their sex and the grade they attend, and households receive an amount called "food support" to enable them to improve the quality of their meals. By the year 2000, the program included 2.6 million households, or close to 12 million people, and it reached its planned target coverage in 2005, with 5 million households.[20] Targeting was extremely careful. Communities were chosen on the basis of their marginality levels, and households were selected after a community census showed who qualified on the basis of their weak asset base and other variables. *Progresa* was also original because it included, as part of its design, a quasiexperimental impact evaluation from its inception.

Progresa was transformed into *Oportunidades* in 2002. Scholarships, which were initially restricted to grades 3-9, now extend to grade 12. Recruitment methods have changed. Now families can apply for inclusion in the program, which lessens the risk of going undetected by interviewers. Since 2001, on the other hand, it has expanded gradually to larger settlements, and it now operates in every Mexican city. Since the program requires beneficiaries to attend schools and clinics, it provides no coverage for the poor living in extremely isolated locations, who have no reasonable access to these institutions. A newer program (PAL, or *Programa de Apoyo Alimenticio*) serves this isolated population.

Progresa-Oportunidades can show, on the basis of evaluations performed by the International Food Policy Research Institute, the (Mexican) National Institute of Health, CIESAS, and other institutions, that it has reduced poverty levels among beneficiaries, increased their schooling levels, and improved their health, as measured by days lost to illness per year. It cannot yet show that it has improved the occupational status of "graduates" of the program, basically because the cohorts benefiting from the program since the third grade have not entered the labor market, and because job generation in Mexico has been unsatisfactory recently, which is bound to diminish their success.

Progresa-Oportunidades is significant for various reasons. First, a program that significantly reduces poverty should, in the medium term, have an impact on emigration. Research on the micro-level effects of *Progresa-Oportunidades* on emigration have found several impacts. Our 2000 evaluation found small changes in opposite directions: First, low cash transfer amounts tended to increase the propensity of one or more household members to migrate. It seems this resulted from the provision of a secure basic (but insufficient) income, which frees the household to undertake risk. Higher cash transfer levels, which produce a more marked improvement in total income, tend to reduce emigration levels.[21]

Angelucci[22] has found that participation in the program tends to lessen the migration of the young, because the program provides incentives for them to stay in school longer, but at the same time may increase the emigration of the adults, for the same reason stated above, i.e., program transfers enable the household to take risks. Stecklov et al.,[23] on the other hand, point out that outmigration from poor and indigenous communities was generally increasing at the time the *Progresa* database was collected (1997–1999). Nevertheless, they find that the odds of international migration fell by roughly 58 percent among program beneficiary households. Domestic migration did not seem to be affected by the program. Because in the sample higher education levels are associated with emigration and the program provides incentives for permanence in school, however, they suggest that, in the longer term, emigration might increase as a result of the program. Badillo Bautista[24] uses actual remittance, transfers, and occupational data for living migrants to estimate migration effects. She finds that "control" samples are affected by the program, because of anticipation and spillover, and concludes that *Progresa–Oportunidades* significantly reduces emigration. It would appear that families enrolled in the program do in fact emigrate less frequently to the United States. However, as Stecklov et al. warn, long-term impacts may be different, particularly if occupations requiring higher schooling levels do not increase in these rural areas.

Escobar[25] has pointed out that the emigration patterns of the poor tend to reflect less planning and less contacts, possibly as a result of higher vulnerability to catastrophic events and lower social capital levels, and that participation in *Oportunidades* tends to improve these two aspects of the migration process, possibly because it reduces catastrophic events thanks to the low but secure income provided through cash transfers. This could lead to more regular migration provided there were new opportunities to do so.

Extreme poverty has fallen significantly from 2000 to 2006, from 24 percent to 13.8 percent, as diagnosed by an independent group of experts (*Comité Técnico de Medición de la Pobreza*) and by the National Evaluation Council (CONEVAL). This reduction has been most significant in rural areas. More than half of all rural families benefit from *Oportunidades*, and their social policy transfers have increased markedly during this period. In rural communities, extreme poverty levels have fallen from 42.4 percent in 2000 to 24.5 percent during the same period. In very small rural settlements (those with less than 2,500 inhabitants and the highest Oportunidades coverage) levels have fallen even more rapidly, from 52.9 percent to 27.3 percent. Two main changes seem to underlie falling poverty levels: increasing real wages and government transfers.[26] Also, however, remittances have increased, which to some extent also explains falling rural poverty (although the largest remittance amounts go to non-poor households). This position is supported by Unger[27] who shows that per capita income has risen faster than average in high emigration municipalities. The rise in rural wages is as yet unexplained but widely observed, and the lack of recent national farm production censuses is a major obstacle to explain it satisfactorily. But there are at least three factors, although their relative weight is unknown. One is diminishing labor supply due to emigration; the second is increasing labor demand by commercial producers. Finally, a fall in supply due to social policy transfers is also possible, particularly among teenagers, who receive scholarships to stay in school (up to $70 dollars a month).

Thus, development of a successful social policy program can impact migration, provided jobs are created. But there may be additional connections between social policy and migration policy, particularly in the area of temporary worker programs. *Progresa–Oportunidades*, on the basis of its own databases and with the collaboration of the Education and Health Ministries and Mexican Banks and Telegraph services:[28]

Controls a nationwide network of offices that can certify a person's presence in their community (coresponsibilities are certified every two months, to guarantee beneficiaries access to their cash transfers).

Channels personalized payment amounts to 5 million families and 7 million children and youths in schools in that network.

Routinely processes information on participants. This includes their compliance with rules, their migration experience, and poverty levels.

The program performs the above functions efficiently and without corruption.[29]

For these reasons, Escobar suggested that the *Progresa* program infrastructure could be extremely useful for the management of a large-scale temporary migrant program.[30] Today it is even more aptly suited to that task, because it has expanded from a coverage of high and very high marginality communities to include almost the entire country, and from a payroll of 2.6 million households to 5 million, in both rural and urban settings.

The program can be articulated with the Mexican task of managing a large temporary migration program because:

It already possesses information regarding the migration experience of individuals. This would allow program administrators to select regions, communities, and households which have migration experience, to avoid creating new flows, on the basis of their poverty levels, thus ensuring a high poverty-alleviation impact of the migration program.

It possesses the service infrastructure which would allow it to refund taxes, program fees, and other payments to migrants when they return home, on the basis of their certified presence in their hometowns, in order to provide significant incentives for return and a practical means of refunding them these payments.[31] This infrastructure would also allow the program to assess the health of migrant workers before and after their stay in the United States.

Its database is large and comprehensive enough to allow the turnover of migrant workers, to maximize the distributional impact of remittances and savings. Currently, it is estimated that 73 percent of Mexico's poor families participate in the program, and the payroll is constantly being expanded, recertified (to check for households that are no longer poor), and perfected.

The program is gradually increasing its agreements with state governments for the inclusion of participant families in the *Seguro Popular*, or Popular Health Insurance, which guarantees the coverage of medical treatment for members.[32] The *Seguro Popular* "borrows" targeting from *Oportunidades*, enrolling them free of charge. Other families pay a subsidized fee.

This relatively new development could respond to a much-stressed demand by migrant workers, who fear health emergencies will hurt their immediate relatives when they are away.

A question that must be addressed is the performance of recruiters. U.S. guest worker programs have relied extensively on private recruiters. Although recruiters are efficient in the sense that they provide the labor required by employers and do so at low cost, their recent performance in Mexico can be held responsible for:[33]

- Opening new flows. Recruiters have an incentive to operate where the labor supply is ample, i.e., where emigration is not widespread. In so doing, they create new flows.
- Increasing the cost of legal temporary migration. Once supply has been created, recruiters increase total *net* program entry fees, mainly through the employment of sub- or pre-recruiters, who charge illegal pre-recruitment fees.
- Leading workers to abscond their legal temporary U.S. employment. Because undocumented workers have become increasingly easy to employ, H-2 programs tend to serve only those employers who cannot find these workers, and who provide extremely poor pay and difficult work conditions. Once legally recruited workers arrive on site, experience the real work and pay conditions, and realize they may not be able to reach their saving or remittance targets, many abandon those jobs for better, if illegal, opportunities with other producers or in U.S. cities.

The Mexican government has the instruments to regulate the operation of recruiters, both from its extensive databases on population, poverty, and migration, and its extensive network of health clinics that may serve to certify workers' return, to reimburse them various costs and taxes, and to gather information on the quality of the work of recruiters. Underperforming and overcharging recruiters should be effectively banned, with the collaboration of the U.S. consulate general, and if necessary a system benefiting from social policy experience (that may include private recruitment firms) can be put into place.

Oportunidades is not the only social policy program that can achieve this. In poor urban areas, *Hábitat*, a new program developed in 2002, also has comprehensive databases including migration information, and also controls community centers that can fulfill the same role as rural health clinics. Its operation is intensive (it concentrates large investments in critical urban poverty areas) and limited to a few hundred urban areas, however, and would need to be expanded if a temporary work program for *non*-agricultural workers is put into place.

Microrregiones, finally, is a program which provides infrastructure and basic services to hundreds of carefully selected "Strategic Microrregional Centers." It covers, and has substantial information on, 1,300 poor *municipios*, more than half of the total in Mexico. Its analyses can also be used to make sure that temporary migration programs are targeted to the right regions, and that they will have a developmental impact.

In summary, and in contrast to Mexican economic policy, social policy has advanced since the late 1990s, and is far more effective than previously. But while social policy may be seen as a long-term investment and a basic government responsibility, it calls for a substantial portion of the government's budget. It is unlikely that social policy will be able to do much more unless (1) state and federal authorities start working together to coordinate their policies, which are currently developed mostly independently of each other, and (2) sound economic and fiscal policies provide additional resources to social programs. The future of social policy therefore depends on better economic policy.

Social policy can work in coordination with migration policy. In the U.S. Congress, bills requiring sending country collaboration to participate in temporary worker programs have not been sufficiently specific on the role these governments should play. Collaboration must be more clearly defined, to allow migration policy to succeed in managing migration, and to help it become a key component of poverty reduction and development. Whether through the program itself or through a parallel institutional arrangement benefiting from *Oportunidades* infrastructure, and information, this kind of collaboration is much more likely to succeed than one based exclusively on collaborative enforcement of returns.

POLICIES SPECIFICALLY AIMED AT MIGRATION

Remittances

The 1997 *Binational Study of Mexico-U.S. Migration* concluded, in parallel with a number of studies and governmental pronouncements, such as the Regional Conference on Migration or *Puebla* Process, that migration is, in general, positive for the migrants as well for sending and receiving governments. The Binational Study, the *Puebla* Process, the Global Commission on International Migration, however, have also stated that policies are necessary to regulate the flow in order to enhance its humanitarian, social, and economic benefits. The main area of study in this regard is remittances. Although this author agrees with the above pronouncements, it is clear that, in the case of the impact of migration on Mexico, they must be backed up by recent findings regarding specific regions, periods, and groups if they are to be regarded as serious scientific statements.

Experts agree that remittances have increased rapidly in Mexico to about 3.5 percent of GDP in 2005, although they differ on the total size of the flow.

Remittances have recently been hailed as a remarkably positive phenomenon that reduces poverty, softens crises in sending regions, and may unleash regional development. Recent studies, however, suggest that Mexico benefits much less than other countries from remittances, when the size of its diaspora and its per capita GDP are taken into account. Each Haitian, Brazilian, and Bolivian migrant in the United States sent home remittances more than three times their countries' per capita GDP in 2003. Honduran, Colombian, Guatemalan, Ecuadorian, Peruvian, and Salvadoran migrants sent home, on average, slightly less than the above, but their per capita remittances were still larger than their countries' per capita GDP. Mexican migrants in the United States, on the other hand, remitted an average of less than one quarter of Mexico's per capita GDP.[34] Mexico's share of its working population in the U.S. is quite large: 17 to 18 percent, but remittances are equivalent to only 3.5 percent of Mexico's GDP.

It also seems that the impact of remittances on poverty alleviation may be smaller—in spite of their huge volume—than previously considered. When total household income (including remittances) is analyzed, the distribution of remittances is only modestly less unequal than total income distribution. Further, although poor households show the largest dependence on remittances (the proportion of poor households receiving remittances is larger than among other income groups and the degree of dependence of poor receiver households is greater), the total amounts received by non-poor income strata, and especially the highest, are greater. Thus, poor households receive *relatively* greater remittances in terms of their own income, but *absolutely* smaller amounts than the top groups.[35]

If households are stratified on the basis of their Mexican (nonremittance) income, the absolute amounts added to their Mexican income are largest for the top strata, second largest for the poorest, and smallest for the middle strata.[36] The lowest income quintile is most dependent on remittances, with 19 percent of its total Mexican income supplemented by them,[37] and the highest proportion of households receiving remittances (6.4 percent in 2000). This contrasts with the highest quintile, in which only 2.7 percent of all households receive remittances, and total quintile income only increases by 0.77 percent. The income of households that do receive remittances is increased by 81 percent for those in the lowest quintile, and by only 22.8 percent for those at the top quintile.

Janssen and Escobar[38] have also analyzed the opportunity cost of migration and related it to income inequality in Mexico. Their analysis estimates

Table 7.1. Remittances and Means of Transfer, 1995–2005, Percentages and Total (in billions of dollars)

Means of Transfer	1995	1996	1997	1998	1999	2000	2001	2002	2003	2004	2005
Money Orders	39.7	36.0	35.6	34.8	24.9	21.8	9.04	6.99	12.23	11.3	9.32
Electr.	51.5	52.6	54.2	56.2	67.1	70.6	87.5	89.64	85.8	87.3	89.3
Pocket	8.1	9.6	8.6	7.9	7.1	7.4	3.35	3.26	1.92	1.4	1.4
Other	0.7	1.8	1.6	1.1	0.9	0.2	0.11	0.1	0.04	0.0	0.0
TOTAL (U.S. bn) %	(3.67) 100	(4.22) 100	(4.86) 100	(5.62) 100	(5.91) 100	(6.28) 100	(8.89) 100	(9.81) 100	(13.26) 100	(16.61) 100	(20.03) 99.9

Estimates for 1995–2001: Mario López E., "Remesas de mexicanos en el exterior y su vinculación con el desarrollo económico, social y cultural de sus regiones de origen," *Estudios sobre migraciones Internacionales* 59 (Geneva: OIT /ILO, 2002); For 2002–2005: Banco de Mexico, *Informe Anual*, Mexico City, 2005/2006.

migrants' stay-at-home income on the basis of the 2000 Mexican Census. It shows that remittances reduce income inequality, but if migrants had stayed in their municipality and worked there inequality would be even lower.

The above is confirmed by analyses of the Mexican Census showing that while the *propensity to receive remittances* is greater than average among poor households, the determinants of the amount received disproportionately favor non-poor households. The largest available databases of poor households (the evaluation database for the *Oportunidades* program) show these migrants remit less frequently, and they send lower average amounts, than non-poor migrants. A large ethnographic study[39] of poor migrant households suggests that this should not be interpreted as an outcome of migrant intentions or weak family attachment, but rather of three factors: (1) the relative weakness of their social networks (the fact that they have fewer, poorer, and less well-connected network contacts in the U.S.), (2) their lower-than-average human capital, and (3) the fact that their decision to migrate is often driven by family needs and emergencies, rather than the availability of good *coyotes* and employment opportunities for them in the United States. As a consequence of all the above, poor migrants tend to spend more on their border crossing, to fail to cross more often than others, to undergo longer periods of unemployment in the United States, and to perform worse-than-average jobs. In that ethnographic study of thirty-two households in eight contrasting poor communities, only one in three individual migration cycles (measured from the outset to return) produced a net income for the household in excess of the migrant's average income prior to migration.

A different outcome is found, however, when regional change is analyzed. In this case, highly marginal regions receiving more remittances show more rapid improvements in their human development and economic variables than others.[40] While it cannot be concluded that the poorest households benefit the most, and the poorest municipalities do not, as a rule, receive higher remittances, there would seem to be an impact that should benefit them at least indirectly.

Analyses such as these have prompted a number of actors to promote specific policies aimed at remittances. Although international banks and the Mexico-U.S. agreement of 2002 that sparked the use of the Automated Clearing House (ACH) mechanism for money transfers have contributed significantly to the lower cost of transfers,[41] the Mexican government did play a role in 2001–2002 to pressure banks and other transfer companies to reduce commissions and exchange margins. This was also fostered from Mexico by the relative liberalization of the transfer market. Today, there are more companies, and the costs are lower. The promotion of the *matrícula consular* (see below) also helped, since it allowed undocumented migrant workers to open bank accounts and thus lower their transfer fees. In addition, Mexican consulates have often provided information on transfer costs and cheaper and efficient transfer schemes. To a certain extent, therefore, cost reductions have been the outcome of a policy decision at the beginning of the Fox administration. Nothing guarantees, however, that costs will continue to fall or stay low. The costs to banks of the ACH are much lower than what they charge to their clients today, and there is therefore much room for cost reductions. The Mexican government could still negotiate, or foster, further reductions.

The other policy aspect of remittances is the one discussed above. Remittances are only relatively progressive, in the sense that dependence is highest among the poor, but the absolute amounts received by poor households are very low. The main reasons, of course, are the lower migration rates and the lower incomes of poorer migrants. But dis-economies are important also. Relative costs for $100 dollar transfers are much higher than for $200–$300 transfers. While transaction costs are fixed, and Money Transfer Corporations (MTCs) therefore have a valid argument for higher relative costs at the lowest end of the market, analysts have suggested they could charge considerably less and still profit from the operation.

Other policies that could improve remittance levels among the poor have to do with the efficient regulation of migration. In order to achieve higher remittance levels among poor households, it would be necessary to manage migration to avoid wage depression at the lower levels of the U.S. labor market, and to use legal channels. Reducing supply would diminish the total number of households receiving remittances, but would make individual remittances higher. This would be a significant reason for Mexico-U.S. collaboration, if mechanisms such as those discussed above (for temporary migrant workers) were put into place.

Other Programs

The "3 × 1 Citizen's Initiative"[42] matches migrant Home-Town Associations' (HTA) community development funds. It started as a citizen initiative in Zacatecas but now operates nationwide. For every dollar contributed by the HTA, each level of Mexican government (municipal, state, and federal) provides another. It funds public works and community improvements. It was substantially strengthened during the Fox administration (to four times its 2000 budget), and new mechanisms are in place to facilitate approval of migrant initiatives and to oversee project completion. It is widely considered to be a best practice of migration management. Nevertheless, external evaluations and observers have criticized two aspects, namely (1) that it tends to flow mostly to nonmarginal (and less poor) communities, and (2) that a significant part of the projects are not productive.[43] Since the first criticism was put forward, a "quota" of marginal communities must be fulfilled, and this is one reason for the slow growth of the program in 2006. Since 2002, on the other hand, the government has tried to insist on productive investment, but this has not been successful (most productive ventures are private, so this would entail placing a collective investment in private hands). It still, however, represents a drop in the ocean of remittances. Its federal budget for 2006 was 10 million dollars, for a total of 40 million, assuming all other parties paid their parts in full.[44] Its administration must be strengthened, and state planning boards must have an incentive to coordinate their work with migrant groups. Most Home-Town Associations still act on their own, with no incentives from their local governments or else on the basis of local agreements that bypass the program. A recent evaluation of the *Programa Paisano* (see below) revealed that 14 percent of migrants visiting Mexico for the holiday season reported having contributed to hometown improvements.

Mexico has other migration-specific programs: The *Grupo Beta* was created almost twenty years ago to protect migrants along the Mexico-U.S. border from criminals and corrupt authorities. The groups were expanded to the southern border in the mid-1990s. They were staffed mostly from the army, and they have remained free from the problems associated with Mexican police. They are also a good example of cooperation among the three levels of government. At the end of 2004, *Beta* groups along the northern border included 105 persons, of which two-thirds were employed by the federal government, and the rest by municipalities and states, but they work together. The *Beta* groups along the southern border were comprised of forty-one individuals, with a relatively greater participation of municipal employees. Group leaders were, almost without exception, medical professionals. From 2002 and until 2006, the number of migrants rescued by these groups more than doubled, the number of migrants receiving medical attention roughly doubled, and most indicators show a marked rise, except that in 2006 a number of them fall, in accordance with an apparent fall in the number of migrants attempting to cross the border at the places where the groups operate.[45] They participate in approximately 500 to 600 bilateral collaborative operations per year. Nevertheless, *Beta* groups are still few and dispersed, insufficiently equipped and dependent on municipal support, although they seem to be better trained and prepared than in the past. They cannot easily deploy to new illegal border crossing points unless they receive support from poorer municipalities along the border. Also, the recent dispersion of undocumented migrants and coyotes away from the Sásabe-Altar corridor, which had become the focal crossing point in 1999–2000, has meant that the groups may have become less effective, since they have tended to be deployed along the most frequented border crossings, and these account for an increasingly smaller share of total border crossings.

Programa Paisano is launched every year before the Christmas holidays. At this time, millions of Mexicans residing in the U.S. return to Mexico to spend time with their families. Extortion of these temporarily returning migrants by Mexican authorities was quite common. The program provides leaflets and other information to incoming migrants on their rights, their customs allowances, and the procedures necessary to intern and return their U.S. vehicles. Through an 800 number, it is also open to complaints against anybody abusing the migrants, and passes these complaints on to the corresponding authorities. In the winter of 2004, the program call center was poorly staffed, but it handled 3,000 calls from migrants per month. Most of the calls, according to the head of the program, had to do with complaints caused by lack of information on the part of the migrants before they departed their U.S. homes: mostly, they were bringing too much merchandise, gifts, or forbidden articles, which were confiscated. Another source of complications lay in the paperwork and the cost involved in the internment of U.S. vehicles. But the portion of calls reporting true abuses has diminished consistently over the years. This is an inexpensive program employing few staff and including volunteer workers. Over two-thirds of all returning migrants know about the program. Most first learned about it from special (Hispanic) T.V. advertisements, or from the leaflets distributed at consulates and at the border. The vast majority consider that the information provided by the program is useful, and, when they have resorted to complaints or requests for specific information, they are satisfied with it. A very clear problem, however, lies in the 75 percent of labor migrants, on average over the past five years, declaring that they were not familiar with the complex procedure involved in bringing a U.S. car into Mexico.[46]

A small program was started by the National Finance Agency (NAFIN) and the Revenue and Expenditure Secretariat. It intends to co-finance return migrants' entrepreneurial initiatives. To this day, it cannot be considered more than a pilot. It would need to be implemented on a serious scale.

The Health Secretariat has just replaced its "Go healthy, return healthy" program (which was unknown to migrants and analysts alike) by a program providing health coverage to both migrants and their nonmigrant family. It is far too early to diagnose this program, which was announced in late September 2005. If it succeeds, it would provide an answer to one of the two most frequent demands posed by migrants, and significantly enhance the positive impact of remittances. Today, some of the largest financial inflows to poor families from their relatives abroad are devoted to the payment of catastrophic illnesses, accidents, and deaths. These flows are not only meaningless from the point of view of the receivers' acquisition of significant lifetime assets. They also drain migrants' incomes and projects in the United States. President Calderón has just started a program intended to provide universal medical care for children from birth. This program could lower catastrophic expenses considerably, but it must be remembered that the older population typically face higher health expenses, and this calls for a strengthening of the *Seguro Popular*. So far, capacity to provide services in this program has trailed far behind membership.

Other laws could provide the basis for further Mexican regulation of migration. The 2000 bylaws of the National Population and Migration Law clearly state[47] that Interior Secretariat officials are in charge of ensuring that all entries *and exits* from Mexico are carried out according to existing legal provisions. This contradicts the popular notion that the Mexican government is legally interdicted from intervening in emigration. These bylaws, however, remain unenforced. The cost of enforcement would be high, politically and financially. But a substantial U.S. immigration reform could call for Mexican enforcement, provided new legal avenues are open to migrant workers. Such an agreement would not require legal changes, but congressional approval of a specific budget would be necessary.

Pension Totalization

Although totalization is a bilateral policy, it is necessary to stress Mexican participation in it. In June 2004, the Mexican and U.S. executive branches concluded a pension totalization agreement which has not gone into effect. It would enable workers to accumulate their pension contributions in both Mexico and the United States to arrive at retirement faster and receive larger pensions. The agreement concerns only those funds that have already been paid into the system by interested workers, and it does not therefore affect the contributions made by other workers. It does not involve payment from one government to another either. Unauthorized workers with legitimate Social Security numbers in the United States (a minority) would be eligible to accumulate their contributions, but only before January 2004. It was then that the U.S. Congress passed a bill excluding unauthorized workers from pension benefits. Views forwarded in some U.S. media stating that a Social Security agreement would subsidize the Mexican government or the Mexican pension system are mistaken.

The Mexican government, and Mexicans in the United States, should insist on totalization. It is, first of all, a system allowing workers to recover their own contributions from both systems. Workers who have divided their time between Mexico and the United States run the risk of always contributing but never having the ability to retire. Second, it would allow workers to retire with less than a lifetime's contribution to either system. They would not receive full pensions, but adding U.S. and Mexico contributions would be very likely to allow them to retire in Mexico, at a lower cost, than in the United States. This would trigger some return migration. But the agreement is also likely to increase the pensions of Mexicans wishing to stay in the United States. This would lessen poverty levels of elderly Mexicans in that country. Easier retirement, on the other hand, is likely to create vacancies in the Mexican employment structure, which would be very beneficial for younger workers. One reason why the young are not being absorbed rapidly enough in Mexico is that older workers cannot retire. The agreement, finally, could also have a positive impact on the nature of migration. Since unauthorized workers are no longer eligible to benefit from their contributions to pension funds, totalization would provide an incentive to regular labor migration. Lack of an agreement on the contrary provides today equal treatment to authorized and unauthorized workers not qualifying on the sole basis of their U.S. contributions.

Voluntary Repatriation to the Mexican Interior: A Bilateral Pilot Experience

Starting in 2003, both governments have worked together to promote the return of apprehended undocumented Mexican immigrants from the U.S. side of the border to the interior of Mexico, and not simply to the closest Mexican city along the border. It was aimed at both diminishing repeat attempts to cross the border as well as at lowering the risk of death along the border during periods of extreme weather. It was concentrated on the Sonora–Arizona border, where undocumented flows had been growing and the risk of death in the desert is highest. Apprehended immigrants were asked whether they wanted to be returned to that closest Mexican city or whether they would accept a plane-and-bus ticket to the closest city to their hometowns. It involved the U.S. DHS, the Mexican Ministry of Foreign Affairs, and the Mexican Migration Institute. The term "voluntary repatriation" was initially derided by some Mexican media and congressmen, because apprehended migrants were repatriated regardless of their answer. The migrants' choice was to be returned to the border or to the interior city closest to their hometown. The legal grounds for the program lay in the MOU signed by the above-mentioned institutions, through which both governments agree to promote the return of Mexican migrants from high-risk border areas and during periods of extreme weather conditions. The first MOU on this subject dates from the immediate post-NAFTA period (1995) marked by intense dialogue and a number of positive bilateral agreements.

The program peaked in 2005.[48] Fifty-six thousand individuals were interviewed during the 113 days in which the program operated during the summer of 2005. Twenty thousand accepted the terms of voluntary repatriation to the closest city to their hometowns. Six hundred received medical assistance in the U.S., and a further 200 when they landed in Mexico City. During the program's first four weeks, the premises did not guarantee confidentiality, but this was corrected. Candidates for the program were selected by the U.S. Border Patrol, on the basis of their interest in the program or if the Border Patrol classified them as someone "at risk." This includes the elderly, minors, pregnant women, and wounded or ill persons. Transport was wholly financed by the U.S. government, at a cost of roughly $1,060 dollars per person. The Mexican government covers the cost of its dedicated personnel in the United States, some meals, and support staff. NGOs and Mexican officials interviewed candidates for the program, and complaints were turned over to the appropriate authorities in each government.

Since there were 1,070,000 apprehensions of Mexicans along the southern border of the United States in 2005, the program interviewed approximately 5.5 percent of all apprehended and transported approximately 2 percent. Program staff insist that the program significantly reduced the risk of death through dehydration. The risk of death through dehydration fell, roughly, from 1 per 2,000 apprehensions to 1 per 3,500 apprehensions. The program has only been implemented during the summer, on humanitarian grounds. During 2006 the program was scaled down somewhat. It transported 15,000 persons to the Mexican interior.

The Mexican government participated because the program was seen as primarily humanitarian, and migrants had a choice. Some in Arizona, however, called for the program to be implemented on a larger scale, and to make repatriation to the interior mandatory. Since the number of attempts to cross the border has been rising steadily, it would seem the program could diminish successful undocumented crossings, as well as deaths. In the event of a U.S. immigration reform effectively increasing regular migration opportunities, this program could be implemented on a much larger scale, in other risky areas and times of the year, with stepped-up cooperation from the Mexican government.

Mexican Policies toward the Diaspora

Although the origins of the Mexican diaspora have to do with the processes of national formation in both countries and the loss of Mexican territory after the U.S.-Mexican war of 1847, the political history of the Mexican diaspora can more clearly be traced to two internal conflicts: the Mexican Revolution and the "Cristiada," the civil war that pitted religious, anti-agrarian forces against the Mexican post-revolutionary government. Both led to the creation of a large population of political and economic exiles. Mexican policy, during the 1920s and 1930s, basically intended national reconciliation and the return of exiled and other Mexicans in the United States. In the context of the agrarian reform, for example, the government created several agrarian colonies intended to motivate Mexicans to return home. One early reason for the estrangement of the diaspora and the government lay in the cooperation of the Mexican and U.S. governments in fostering the often forced return of Mexicans and Mexican-Americans, in the wake of the U.S. depression. Mexican cooperation with the Bracero program, intended to move Mexican workers only temporarily to the United States, can also be understood within the larger national policy of allowing temporary legal migration, while promoting the return of Mexicans abroad. In 1954, for example, the Mexican government demanded that undocumented farmworkers be returned to Mexico, and their employers punished.[49] During this fairly long period extending from the Mexican Revolution to the 1960s, therefore, the Mexican government viewed the diaspora as an antigovernmental group created by internal conflicts, and its policy towards it consisted in inviting it to return to Mexico. When the Bracero program ended in 1964, Mexico migration policy was notable only for its nonexistence until 1990. This was partly due to mistrust in the United States, but also, and probably mostly, to a marked distance between the government and the diaspora.

In order to develop a policy toward the diaspora, the government needed to assimilate the fact that a new, permanent Mexican and Mexican-American population had formed in the United States as a result of many decades of labor, not political, movements, and that they needed to be approached as something other than potential return migrants.[50] Mexico's first major step came in 1990, when the Program for Mexican Communities Abroad was created in the Foreign Affairs Ministry, the consulate network in the United States was substantially expanded to forty-seven offices, and they began to contact existing organizations and to develop systematic exchanges. The creation of this program, and this period of increasing closeness to the diaspora, can't be understood, however, unless account is taken of the widespread support received from the Mexican diaspora by the opposition presidential candidate, Cuauhtémoc Cárdenas, in 1988. The diaspora clearly proved at that time that it had become an influential force in Mexican politics. It is also no coincidence that the program for communities abroad was created in 1990, as President Salinas began to lobby for NAFTA. By 1995, the consulates had a list of 400 clubs and other organizations in the U.S. cities with the largest Mexican populations (Los Angeles, Chicago, San Antonio, Houston, and many others). They developed a contact and organization strategy: a local club of a few dozen could not be treated in the same way as a panethnic federation of Oaxaca migrants, even if the consul discovered that "panethnic" was something of a misnomer. Consulates viewed elections and the increasing diversification of the clubs' activities as a positive sign. Some consuls intervened openly in the organization of elections, to such an extent that a few were accused of orchestrating elections to favor government sympathizers.

The clubs were mostly sporting and cultural, organizing football (soccer) matches and various celebrations. Some were ethnic; most were of a local character. Consulates provided citizenship services for these Mexicans, as well as the *matrícula consular* ID card. However, many organizations already had concerns that went beyond birth certificates, passports, or a consular presence at a Cinco de Mayo celebration. The Mexican government sought their support in its attempts to improve the bilateral relationship. For their part, the Mexican clubs and organizations wanted the Mexican government both to recognize their rights as Mexicans and to help them become better organized in the United States in order to acquire rights there.

Most of the time, however, most Mexicans in the United States were not aware of the existence of these organizations, nor did they have time to participate in their activities. As Navarro[51] and Zamudio[52] showed, for most Mexican migrant workers the overwhelming concern was making ends meet and obtaining a legal work permit and the right to stay in the U.S. In this sense, the bulk of the diaspora was very much cut off from Mexico.

Provision of Identity and the Right to Vote

From the early 1980s, the Mexican government started to provide a voter's card to all Mexicans aged eighteen and over. By the mid-1990s, this had become the official identity document in Mexico and was required in all government, banking, and higher education institutions. The only agency entitled to provide it, however, was the Federal Electoral Institute (IFE), an autonomous agency that played a significant part in the creation of a democratic election system. Mexican embassies and consulates were not allowed to issue the cards. By 1992, however, it was clear that many Mexicans who had left Mexico without it did not have an identity document. Consulates were allowed to issue passports on the basis of an ever-growing list of documentary proof of birth, military service, citizenship, and residence (birth certificates, previous passports, military service identity cards, etc.), which many migrants could not provide. However, the need for identification was growing, particularly among the undocumented Mexican population in the United States. The Mexican Ministry of Foreign Affairs responded by renewing the *matrícula consular*, a form of identification stating, in both English and Spanish, that the Mexican government recognized the individual's identity as a Mexican citizen and his/her address abroad.[53] The *matrícula* gained recognition in private and governmental U.S. institutions. This was a "silent process" that enabled Mexican citizens to open banking accounts,[54] enroll in educational institutions, obtain driver licenses, provide one official means of identification when accessing a new job and, sometimes most importantly, return to Mexico voluntarily without being deported by U.S. authorities or suffering various forms of extortion at the hands of local or federal police and other authorities in Mexico.[55] Once the mostly undocumented migrants used the *matrícula* to obtain a driver's license or register with local and state authorities in the United States, they gained access to some of the benefits provided by the welfare, education, and health systems. The *matrícula* was initially granted on the spot, with few if any background checks: the IFE card, a local birth certificate (whose reliability varied greatly), and even documents which had been accepted as proof of identity in Mexico in the early 1980s but had been phased out because of their unreliability were all accepted as proof of identity. *Matrícula* requirements soon became tougher, however, and today it is a document backed by reliable official documents and is very difficult to forge. It is called "High-Security *Matrícula.*" It also has an expiration date. The *matrícula* is proof of identity for the Mexican government in the United States and for many U.S. government agencies and private institutions, but its usefulness to migrants is threatened by new federal and state legislation in the United States, such as the Real ID Act and others.

The *matrícula* was not a basis for establishing legal residence in the U.S., nor did it allow expatriate Mexicans the right to vote in Mexican elections. In theory, they could vote, but only if they possessed the voting card, traveled to a special voting booth in Mexico during the elections, and if those booths had a sufficient extra number of ballots to allow nonresidents to vote.[56] Often, Mexicans traveled from Los Angeles, San Diego, San Antonio, and other places to vote in Mexican cities just south of the border, only to find local officials either denied them the right to vote or said they did not have extra ballots.

In 1997, the Mexican constitution was modified to give expatriate Mexicans an explicit right to vote; a universal right to vote was already enshrined in the constitution[57] but had not been explicitly extended to expatriates because it remained unregulated. During 1998 and 1999, a special commission set up by the IFE, the Mexican Congress, and the Executive deliberated on whether and how to implement this right in the federal (presidential and legislative) elections of 2000. The number of Mexican adults living in the United States was estimated to reach 5.2 million by 2000, but this was the absolute ceiling for which a procedure could be implemented. There were estimated to be far fewer Mexicans—approximately 2 million—in possession of an IFE card (which does not expire) and a survey of their voting intentions found that most were not interested. On the other hand, a comprehensive voting procedure, one that would make it possible for 90 percent of these Mexicans to vote if they had a voting card, would cost more than the total budget of several social programs. And in any case time was rapidly running out to put in place a new procedure allowing the IFE to issue voting cards to those who did not have them. However, it was reckoned that installing voting booths in all Mexican consulates and in certain areas where Mexicans had recently settled could offer 70 percent of the target population an opportunity to vote without having to travel long distances.[58] By this time, however, it was impossible to register new voters, so the percentage able to vote would be much smaller. The commission concluded that it was too costly (and too late) to implement a full-scale voting procedure, and that a smaller-scale operation was not worthwhile. Consequently, expatriate Mexicans were unable to vote in the 2000 election.

Although implementation of the right to vote for expatriates would have required substantial resources in order to deal with a very large, dispersed population, the reason why it was not implemented may lie elsewhere. Voting preferences among potential diaspora voters were surveyed, and it was clear that most of those wanting to vote intended to do so for the opposition, mostly for the left. According to some analysts, it was partisan interests that blocked the initiative.

However, the issue resurfaced in time for the federal elections in 2006. This time, the debate received considerable public attention. Pressure from the diaspora was much stronger and much better organized, thanks partly to the intervention of the Institute for Mexicans Abroad (IME: *see below*) as well as to the increasing political activism of other organizations, such as the World Association of Mexicans Abroad (AMME). The crucial stumbling block was the division within the major congressional party (the PRI). However, one day before the deadline, Congress finally passed a resolution that, for the first time, gave Mexican expatriates anywhere in the world the right to a postal vote. The procedure that was finally accepted was complex and demanded considerable attention from potential voters: they had to mail, months in advance, a copy of their voter's card. Then they received a ballot, and they had to vote using certified mail. The experience was disappointing: only 32,621 votes were tallied, of which 19,000 went to the National Action Party (conservative), 11,000 to the PRD-Trabajo-Convergencia coalition (center-left), and the rest to other parties. In retrospect, the reluctance of the PRI to ease the procedure seems to have been politically accurate. This party received only 4 percent of the vote of Mexicans abroad, far below its share of votes in Mexico.[59] It is safe to assume that those actually voting were literate, had access to the internet, and a particular interest in Mexican politics. The vast majority of Mexicans abroad did not vote. Nevertheless, it is significant that a procedure was implemented for the first time.

Building a Legitimate Organization for Mexicans Abroad

The government elected in 2000 decided to nominate Juan Hernández, a charismatic man, as the "expatriates' tsar." His status was akin to that of a minister, but he was attached to the president's office. He clashed with the ministries that had traditionally dealt with expatriates (Ministry of the Interior and Ministry of Foreign Affairs), and he lost his position. He was not replaced, and instead the government created an "Institute for Mexicans Abroad" (IME), to be located institutionally at the same office where the first program for the diaspora had operated. This time it was careful. Consulates organized caucuses in the United States, and out of these caucuses a board of over one hundred representatives was elected. They in turn elected a president. The Institute also has an executive director and it is part of the Ministry of Foreign Affairs, although other ministries are instructed to respond to its requests. It thus possesses both administrative and representative structures within the Mexican government. The aim, however, is not simply to provide a legitimate structure for the representation of the diaspora in Mexico. An additional gain could be that, through this new form of representation, Mexicans in the United States might strengthen their representation and lobbying power within that country. The IME is the core of a three-part system, including the CNCME, or National Commission for Mexican Communities Abroad, which is a cabinet-level group meeting to receive and discuss migration issues; the Institute itself; and the Advisory Council, or CCIME.

The Advisory Council was first elected in 2003, and renewed and reorganized in 2006. In addition to electing 105 representatives through five different authorized procedures, the 2006–2008 Council elected ten additional members in a new category called "Merit and Trajectory," basically representing large Mexican, Mexican-American and Latino organizations, ten special advisors, and one representative from each state government and the Federal District. This move increases its legitimacy, improves relations with state governments and legislatures, and improves its technical skills. The new council also includes representatives of Mexicans in Canada. One of its first tasks was to review requests for the cancellation of elections in a few jurisdictions. Two were cancelled.

The Advisory Council is divided into six working commissions: Education; Health; Political Affairs; Legal Affairs; Border Issues; Economic and Business Affairs; and Communications and Outreach. Each commission meets separately, sometimes even at a subcommission level. Each commission includes one official from the executive branch who is responsible for transmitting requests and for advising the commission on the institutionally and procedurally correct forms that are most likely to trigger positive responses from the various branches of government. The new council has insisted on a number of the themes pushed by the first, and has added new demands and concerns. A few among them include:

In the studies exploring the opinions of Mexicans and Mexican-Americans, education has figured most prominently. They view educational advancement as the area in which most assistance is needed. These issues have consequently received special attention. They include: an evaluation of the operation of *plazas comunitarias*.[60] They are basically booths that allow distance learning and provide Mexican certification to students approving each grade or level. Council members became acquainted with *Enciclomedia*, a combination computer-internet-blackboard technology introduced in Mexican elementary schools, and its piloting in the United States, in order to assess its incorporation in Spanish-language education in the United States; the promotion of cultural exchange; ensuring there always is a representative of the Ministry of Education in the meetings of the education commission, together with the creation of a special office at the Ministry of Education devoted to migrants; the training and hiring of specialized bilingual educational staff specializing in K–12 teaching, career counseling, special education, and curricular development;[61] mechanisms that ease the international transfer and recognition of studies from Mexico to the United States and vice versa; and the "IME Scholarships," a fund consisting initially of one million dollars. This fund has grown modestly as a result of a private fund-raising effort. The scholarship program specializes in adult education in the United States, although it also stimulates younger students to complete their high school education. On the basis of an open competition, it transfers funds to educational institutions, which then provide scholarships. The fund is based at the University of California.

Since the major political parties agreed in 2006 to nominate a migrant to Congress in a must-elect position, the CCIME asked to meet with the new migrant congressmen, and it later asked Congress to coordinate the nominations in the future with the CCIME, to guarantee these migrant congressmen represent migrant groups and organizations. As an alternative, they proposed the creation of migrant (or foreign) jurisdictions in Congress.

On the aftermath of the poor results of the vote abroad, several commissions coincided in setting up a direct link to Congress to ensure that the federal election law is modified. Their requests include easing the conditions for obtaining the voter's card and facilitating the postal voting procedure. The federal election law has not changed, but some state election bodies have been far more sensitive. For the elections in Michoacán, for example, the state electoral body issued copy-enabled voter registration formats, allowed migrants the use of ordinary (not certified) mail for the forms and for the votes, started a "double" address list, which includes the migrant's address abroad and in Michoacán, and stopped requiring proof of address abroad, which used to be a problem for migrants.

The Legal Affairs commission demanded that lawmakers be invited to become cosponsors of the legislation proposed by the CCIME. This has until now been a stumbling block for initiatives.

Political demands include: transforming IME into a ministry; increasing the budget for embassies and consulates; the revision of NAFTA; the collaboration of the Mexican and U.S. governments in immigration reform; and the incorporation of migrants in the presidential team.

Foreign (or bilateral) Affairs demands have included asking the Mexican government to demand from the U.S. government that the widows and the children of returned migrants who are banned from the United States but have outstanding Social Security claims receive visas, in order to arrange payment of those claims. They also demand that the Mexican government provide Social Security to migrants' widows. They have reported discriminatory treatment when applying for TN or NAFTA visas, and asked the Mexican government to complain.[62]

The Mexican government justifies the operation of the IME, and of the CCIME particularly, on two grounds.[63] First, it sees an imminent risk of what Portes calls "downward assimilation" of Mexicans in the U.S. second-generation immigrants who are, according to a number of studies, joining the underclass, not experiencing upward social mobility. Programs and policies that may revert that tendency are seen as an obligation. Secondly, it feels the need to train Mexican and Mexican-American leaders in the United States in general, but specifically in the nature, intentions, and capabilities of the Mexican government. Insofar as these leaders learn to draw effective resources and synergies from work with the Mexican government that may effectively support their advancement in the United States, the Mexican government will be seen as an ally. But even in a number of subjects on which council members either oppose the Mexican government or else they are divided as a council (the potential nature of immigration reform in the United States or the likelihood or convenience of a U.S.-Mexico migration agreement, for example), the assessment is that there will be a net gain from their inclusion as advisors on Mexican policy-making. The previous period of estrangement proved very negative for Mexico, when it tried to approach U.S. institutions and these organizations were by no means allies. On the other hand, some analysts see the IME as a fundamental platform for the political organization of Mexicans and Mexican-Americans in the United States. According to Ayón,[64] the CCIME created a network of leaders who interact much more intensely and effectively as a result of their inclusion in the council, and this helps explain the effectiveness of countrywide demonstrations in the United States in 2006.

The operation of the Institute has so far been successful, and a number of its requests have been heeded, although no major new programs have been specially developed on the basis of its recommendations. The first council achieved one major success, namely the right to vote for expatriates. A scheme the council demanded forcefully, namely a binational health scheme, went into partial operation, but has not drawn significant attention from migrants themselves.[65] But the bulk of its more than 200 demands either could not be implemented or were not suited to Mexican institutional and political arrangements. The transition from the first to the second councils was successful politically, and if anything its legitimacy has increased. However, it is apparent from the minutes of the meetings that the new generation of members joined the CCIME with the same lack of familiarity with Mexico as the first one. While this may be rephrased to say the first council ended its mandate on an altogether new level of expertise on Mexican issues, the executive branch of the IME will need to develop its training skills to reduce the amount of time which is spent on issues that can't be resolved, while maintaining a respectful distance from the substance of the council's recommendations. The new council is however starting at a somewhat higher point. It immediately demanded to work with the Mexican Congress, and it has very specific positions on the vote abroad and other issues. The second council also seems to be more cautious, in the sense that it has asked for evaluations and pilot studies for new programs. This may reflect the interaction of the experts with the elected members. It is possible that this second council, thanks to the changes introduced, will produce fewer demands and recommendations, but try to make them work more effectively.

FINAL REMARKS AND RECOMMENDATIONS

Mexico has recently come to realize that it is a country of emigration.[66] With 18 percent of its workforce abroad, and 50 percent of its annual labor force growth absorbed by emigration, it necessitates effective policies assuring that emigration benefits it, and to take proactive steps to regulate migration to ensure it meets national interests. If this transnational labor movement is a market, it has become a buyer's market, for two reasons. First, the illegal condition of millions of migrant workers renders them increasingly vulnerable and powerless. Second, Mexican policies have had no perceptible impact on market conditions. Mexican emigration policies must significantly impact market conditions in order to improve the conditions of migrants abroad.

Three objectives should guide the further development of Mexican migration-related policies and programs:

One is to provide real incentives to returns. Although the schooling level of the average migrant is quite low, there is a growing consensus in the sense that migrants are more entrepreneurial, healthier, and more prone to risk-taking than average. They can make a significant contribution to growth in Mexico. Economic policy, by creating jobs, would create the main magnet. But other specific policies (such as those outlined previously in this chapter for *Oportunidades*) can be important. *Oportunidades* only promotes schooling up to high school level. Large scholarship programs and incentives for higher education are needed, but they must be coupled with demand for these higher-educated workers. Mexico's "first job" program, aimed at these young workers and pioneered in 2007, was substantially under-subscribed and must be redesigned and launched nationwide with much more significant government support. Similarly, support for the employment of returning migrants is a priority. One possible avenue is to create "one-window shops" for returning migrants, in order to ease their access to Mexican social programs. This scheme could be developed through cooperation by the National Migration Institute and the Social Development Secretariat.

Secondly, easing Mexicans' access to lifetime and economic assets in Mexico would also eliminate incentives to initiate migration. This can be done on the basis of *household-level* (in addition to community level) fund-matching schemes, or by the provision of lower-cost credit and finance to poor families. The recent experience of *Elektra*, a large corporation providing finance to poor families, proves that lending to the poor can be financially sound. Interest rates charged by this corporation, however, are prohibitive and often counterproductive. Many families end up poorer as a result of *Elektra* loans. Whether through the massive use of microfinance mechanisms, or of banking and savings and loan institutions, effective provision of finance to the poor and the lower middle class is urgently needed. Savings and loans and popular savings cooperatives went bankrupt in the late 1990s and more recently as a result of poor management, money laundering, and legislative lobbying against them by major banks. Currently, their operating standards have been improved and they are under stricter government supervision. This low-end financial sector must be developed rapidly. The last component of a significant asset-development policy is pensions. The Mexican pension system is operating at a significant loss, thanks to an ill-managed rescue of Mexican banks in 1995–1997, and the aging of the Mexican population. New pension schemes are necessary, particularly for low-income Mexicans. The labor market will not provide massive access to the young as long as older workers feel that they need to stay in work to survive.

Finally, to provide policy instruments commensurate to the task: converting millions of migrants into agents for the development of their towns and regions will not be done on the basis of good but token programs, such as the 3 X 1 initiative. But for the Mexican government to commit large resources to this task, it must have (1) fiscal resources and (2) a positive outlook on Mexico's future, based itself partly on the positive role of remittances but mostly on an economic policy succeeding in providing growth. A comprehensive policy for migration purposes cannot be developed unless it is, simultaneously, a development policy. Schemes and programs that contribute both to migration objectives (returns, legal migration, and investment by migrants) and social and economic development need funding. There are two very large funds devoted to social and economic development that need to be realigned in the short-term in order to promote both objectives: *Ramo 33*, the collection of funds benefiting from expenditure decentralization since 1998, and the agricultural development funds in the Ministry of Agriculture. Both are very significant, and both are underachievers. They must be reformed

A comprehensive policy cannot be developed unless the various Mexican secretariats possess a mechanism that can (1) facilitate coordination and (2) guarantee the execution of their migrant-related agreements. Today, most secretariats develop their own policies, and coordination is carried out at a personal level between the secretariats and vice-secretariats. While all of the migrant-related agencies come together in the cabinet-level CNCME and the Institute for Mexicans Abroad (IME), within the Foreign Affairs Secretariat, the new, positive, institutional arrangement still lacks decision and implementation power.

Bilateral cooperation is necessary. As long as the U.S. job market remains open to undocumented workers and there are no legal avenues to take the place of illegal ones, Mexican efforts to regulate migration and to increase the developmental impact of emigration will have a limited impact.

A national intersecretariat coordination for migrant affairs with true decision and implementation powers is also absolutely necessary if a Mexico-U.S. comprehensive framework for administration and regulation of migration flows is ever to be developed. U.S. officials and representatives have complained of the lack of decision and implementation powers of their Mexican counterparts. Both countries must also realize that there are a number of new actors in this field. State governments in both countries have become significant players in migration policy, and both congresses must play a role. In Mexico, Congress must participate in this coordination or commission not only through representatives of the population and migration commission of both houses, but also through a representative of the hacienda commission.

NOTES

1. The author is grateful to Mexican authorities in the Social Development Secretariat, the Foreign Affairs Secretariat, the Mexican Embassy in Washington, the National Migration Institute, the Mexican Social Security Institute, the Institute for Mexicans Abroad, and several other public agencies for the information provided for this chapter. All mistakes and opinions, however, are the author's sole responsibility.

2. Santiago Levy, personal communication.

3. Kurt Unger, "Regional economic development and Mexican out-migration," NBER Working Paper no. 11432, 2005, http://www.nber.org/papers/w11432.

4. Approximately one-half of the women of working age, and children and the elderly, do not work. But the age distribution is strongly biased to persons of working age (see chapter 1).

5. Agustín Escobar and Eric Janssen, "Migration, The Diaspora and Development. The case of Mexico," IILS (ILO) Discussion Paper 167, (Geneva, 2006).

6. An average of 740,000 formal registered jobs, or about three-fourths of estimated growth of job demand.

7. León Bendesky, Enrique de la Garza, Javier Melgoza, and Carlos Salas, *La industria maquiladora de exportación: mitos y realidades* (Mexico City: Instituto de Estudios Laborales, 2003).

8. China Statistical Yearbook, 2005, http://www.stats.gov.cn/tjsj/ndsj/2005/html/R1804E.HTM, and INEGI, "Banco de Información Económica," 2006, http://dgcnesyp.inegi.gob.mx/.

9. The construction and sale of low- and medium-income housing increased rapidly since 2000, but it did so by opening the funds already available to the federal government and to the workers' housing trust fund, and through developing new financial schemes. Banks have so far risked very little capital in this effort.

10. Some wealthy Mexicans have also left during the last ten years. Their major complaint is insecurity. A number of them, or close members of their families, have been kidnapped.

11. Miguel Szekely, *Hacia una nueva generación de política social* (Mexico City: Sedesol, 2002).

12. Agustín Escobar Latapí and Bryan Roberts, "Urban stratification, the middle classes and economic change in Mexico," in *Social Responses to Mexico's Economic Crisis*, ed. Mercedes González de la Rocha and Agustín Escobar (La Jolla: Center for U.S.-Mexican Studies, U. of California San Diego, 1991), 91–113; Agustín Escobar Latapí and Bryan Roberts, "Mexican Social and Economic Policy and Emigration," in *At the crossroads: Mexico and U.S. Immigration Policy*, ed. Frank D. Bean, Rodolfo de la Garza, Bryan Roberts, and Sidney Weintraub (Boston: Rowman and Littlefield, 1997), 47–78.

13. Lynnette Neufeld, Daniela Sotres A., Paul Gertler, Lizbeth Tolentino M., Jorge Jiménez R., Lia Fernald, Salvador Villalpando, Teresa Shamah, and Juan Rivera Dommarco, "Impacto de Oportunidades en el crecimiento y estado nutricional de niños en zonas rurales," chapter I, in *Evaluación externa de impacto del Programa Oportunidades 2004, Vol. III Alimentación*, ed. Bernardo Hernández Prado and Mauricio Hernández Ávila (Mexico City: Instituto Nacional de Salud Pública, 2005), 15–50.

14. Jesús Reyes Heroles, *Política macroeconómica y bienestar en México* (Mexico City: Fondo de Cultura Económica, 1983).

15. *Solidaridad* undertook the construction of public works such as dams and roads, the provision of electricity and water, the construction and staffing of schools and clinics, scholarships, as well as investment in "social" enterprises, women's cooperatives, and other actions.

16. "Crédito a la palabra."

17. PROCAMPO distributed approximately 1.2 billion dollars to farmers in 2005.

18. These two programs have recently been joined by another, specifically aimed at subsidizing farmers in the case of falling prices. Its budget is approximately 800 million dollars.

19. Thanks to *Oportunidades*, PAL, and others, nutrition efforts are today much better targeted to the rural poor, although LICONSA still serves a mostly urban population.

20. The reason why this is the planned growth target for the program is that this figure coincides with the total estimated number of households under the "capacidades" poverty line (those not able to pay for all basic needs including education and health), although there is a certain mismatch between the actual households in the program and those under that poverty line, due to differences in the estimation of poverty and program eligibility.

21. Enrique Martínez C., "Emigrar por desesperación: Progresa y la migración interna e internacional," in "Logros y retos: una evaluación cualitativa de Progresa en México," ed. Agustín Escobar and Mercedes González de la Rocha, in *Progresa: Más oportunidades para las Familias Pobres. Evaluación de Resultados del programa de Educación, Salud y Alimentación. Impacto a nivel comunitario* (Mexico City: Secretaría de Desarrollo Social, 2000), 95–116.

22. Manuela Angelucci, "Aid and Migration: An Analysis of the Impact of *Progresa* on the Timing and Size of Labour Migration," IZA Discussion Paper no. 1187, (Bonn: Institut for the Study of Labor, 2004).

23. Guy Stecklov, Paul Winters, Marco Stampini, and Benjamin Davis, "Do Conditional Transfers Influence Migration? A Study Using Experimental Data from the Mexican Progresa Program," *Demography* 42, no. 4 (2005): 769–90.

24. Celia Badillo Bautista, "Evaluating the Direct and Indirect Effects of a Conditional Cash Transfer Program: The case of *Progresa*" (Ph.D. Dissertation, University of Essex, forthcoming).

25. Agustín Escobar Latapí, "Pobreza y migración internacional: propuestas conceptuales, primeros hallazgos," in *Los rostros de la pobreza. El debate, Volume IV*, ed. Mónica Gendreau (Puebla: Universidad Iberoamericana, 2005), 97–128.

26. CONEVAL tabulations show that, among the rural poor, income grew 24.2 percent in real terms from 1992 to 2006. The main source of this change is wages. The second is government transfers. Remittances account for 20 percent of the increased income. At the same time, other sources are falling in importance: household production for subsistence, other income, and gifts.

27. Unger, "Regional economic development."

28. And the Mexican Institute of Social Security in some areas.

29. Isolated instances of corruption include: mayors sticking political party labels on food supplements, or stating that people receive benefits in their communities as a result of their efforts; a few beneficiary representatives charging for their services; one mayor reputedly charged a commission for the delivery of transfers to faraway communities. Escobar and González have carried out six evaluations of the program (see http://evaluacion.oportunidades.gob.mx:8010/en/index.php). The only instance of corruption we verified corresponded to a beneficiary representative charging for her services as beneficiaries received their transfers. She was not aware of her wrongdoing. The vast majority of beneficiaries state that payments arrive in full and no one demands or charges any commissions on that amount.

30. Agustín Escobar L., "Propuestas para la legalización del mercado de trabajo agrícola binacional," in *Migración México—Estados Unidos. Opciones de política*, ed. Rodolfo Tuirán (Mexico City: CONAPO, 2000), 45–61.

31. Schemes aimed at refunding temporary migrants failed in the past.

32. We interviewed the first families participating in both *Oportunidades* and the *Seguro Popular* in 2003. They complained that the additional services and medicines had not been available to them. Since then, however, the Health Secretariat has improved its services to both the insured and the uninsured population.

33. H-2A recruiters were studied by Serrano in the state of Veracruz. Veracruz has increased its emigration rate much more rapidly than average during the past fifteen years. Javier Serrano, "El sueño mexicano: El retorno imaginado en las migraciones internacionales de Tapalpa y Tlacotalpan" (Ph.D. diss. CIESAS, Guadalajara, 2006).

34. Author's estimates on the basis of the U.S. Census bureau's population estimates by country of birth, IADB remittance estimates to individual Latin American countries for 2003, and World Bank GDP per capita reports for 2004.

35. Agustín Escobar L. and Eric Janssen, "Migration, the Diaspora and Development. The case of Mexico."

36. Analyses ranking Mexican households according to their total income (Mexican and U.S.-based), on the contrary, finds that remittances consist of a relatively flat portion (3-4 percent) of the income of each decile. Alejandro I. Canales, "Remesas, desarrollo y pobreza en México. Una visión crítica" (Guadalajara: Centro de Estudios de Población/Universidad de Guadalajara, forthcoming).

37. Escobar and Janssen, "Migration, the Diaspora and Development."

38. Agustín Escobar Latapí and Eric Janssen, "Remesas y costo de oportunidad: el caso mexicano," in *Pobreza y migración internacional*, ed. Agustín Escobar Latapí (Mexico City: CIESAS—PREM, 2008), 353-73.

39. Escobar, *Pobreza y migración internacional*.

40. Rodolfo Tuirán, "Migración, remesas y desarrollo," in *La situación demográfica de México 2002* (Mexico City: Consejo Nacional de Población, 2002), 77–87; Kurt Unger, "El desarrollo de las regiones y la migración mexicana: origen, evolución y política pública," in *Migración México-Estados Unidos, implicaciones y retos para ambos países*, ed. Elena Zúñiga H. et al. (Mexico City: CONAPO/UDG/CIESAS/Casa Juan Pablos/COLMEX, 2006), 247–68.

41. Manuel Orozco, "Hometown associations and their present and future partnerships: New development opportunities?" Report Commissioned by the U.S. Agency for International Development (Washington, DC: Inter-American Dialogue, 2003).

42. SEDESOL (Secretaría de Desarrollo Social), "Iniciativa Ciudadana 3 × 1. Cumplimiento de objetivos y metas," 2004, http://www.sedesol.gob.mx/cuentas/reporte_cuarto_trimestre_2003/06IniciativaCiudadana.pdf; "Iniciativa Ciudadana 3 × 1. Cumplimiento de objetivos y metas," 2005, http://www.sedesol.gob.mx/cuentas/reporte_ tercer_trimestre_2004/05IniciativaCiudadana.pdf.

43. UN/PNUD, *Informe sobre Desarrollo Humano Mexico 2006* (México City: Programa de Naciones Unidas para el Desarrollo, 2007).

44. In other words, total investment in 3 × 1 is equivalent to 0.2 percent of total remittances.

45. The number of mutilations was not recorded in 2002; by the end of 2006, however, they hovered at about 100 annually; also, the number of deaths recorded by the *Beta* groups on the Mexican side of the northern and southern borders is greater in the latter. Instituto Nacional de Migración, "Estadísticas Migratorias,

2004," Secretaría de Gobernación, http://www.inm.gob.mx/paginas/estadisticas/ 2004.htm; "Estadísticas Migratorias, 2006," Secretaría de Gobernación, http://www .inm.gob.mx/paginas/estadisticas/2006.htm.

46. http://www.paisano.gob.mx/evaluacion.php?.

47. Reglamento de la Ley General de Población, Article 91.B.a, *Diario Oficial de la Federación*, 14 de abril, Mexico City, 2000, www.diputados.gob.mx/LeyesBiblio/regley/ Reg_LGP.doc.

48. SRE (Secretaría de Relaciones Exteriores), "Evaluación del Programa de Repatriaciones al Interior México-Estados Unidos 2005," report (Mexico City: SRE, 2006), http://www.sre.gob.mx/servicios/documentos/ eval_final05.doc. While in 2006 the program did not grow, it seemed set to surpass all previous levels by mid-July 2007.

49. See David R. Ayón, "La política mexicana y la movilización de los migrantes mexicanos en Estados Unidos," (paper delivered at the meeting of the Latin American Studies Association, San Juan, Puerto Rico, March 15–18, 2006). The author provides a thorough review of his own and other work on the political history of Mexican organizations abroad.

50. Ayón, "La política mexicana y la movilización de los migrantes."

51. Alejandra Navarro S., "Mirando el sol: hacia una configuración del proceso migratorio hacia los Estados Unidos" (B.A. diss., ITESO, 1998).

52. Patricia Zamudio, "Huejuquillense Immigrants in Chicago: Culture, gender, and community in the shaping of consciousness" (PhD diss., Northwestern University, 1999).

53. The *matrícula* had been issued before. The decision was to convert an old practice into a widely available means of identification.

54. By 2005, the *matrícula* was accepted at more than seventy banks. Wells Fargo alone reported that it had accepted it to open 400,000 accounts from the end of 2001 to mid-2004: Carlos González Gutiérrez, "Del acercamiento a la inclusión institucional: La experiencia del Instituto de los Mexicanos en el exterior" in, *Relaciones Estado—Diáspora. Perspectivas de América Latina y el Caribe*, ed. Carlos González Gutiérrez (Mexico City: Miguel Angel Porrúa, 2006), 181–220.

55. Sometimes, undocumented Mexican citizens were deported to Central American countries, on the grounds that they could not prove they were Mexican citizens.

56. Up to and including the presidential elections of 1988, the number of ballot papers in any given voting booth was somewhat discretionary; there were often insufficient numbers of papers in opposition districts, while extra ballot papers were normally made available in pro-government districts (and votes for the government increased accordingly).

57. Mexican adults who were not allowed to vote included members of the clergy of any church, the mentally handicapped or ill and persons, with specific kinds of a criminal record. In practice, however, most of them could vote, because the procedure for granting the voter's card did not check for these conditions.

58. Jorge Durand, personal communication.

59. IFE, "Informe de los resultados de la votación emitida por los mexicanos residentes en el extranjero," report (México City: Instituto Federal Electoral, 2006).

60. Through these schemes, in 2005 10,000 persons were enrolled in adult education, 2,000 in senior high school (bachillerato), and there were close to 700 lo-

cations at which the courses were provided with the support of the Mexican government.

61. Mexicans in the United States have complained, for a number of years, that career counselors and advisors at the high-school level tend to point Mexicans in the direction of "easy" subjects that allow them to graduate from high school, but do not provide the correct credits when applying to a university. They therefore insist that they need counselors who understand them and will provide the right advice.

62. IME (Instituto de los Mexicanos en el Exterior), "Recomendaciones de la I reunión ordinaria del CCIME," 2003, http://portal.sre.gob.mx/ime/index.php?option =displaypage &Itemid; "Recomendaciones de la II reunión ordinaria del CCIME," 2003, http://portal.sre.gob.mx/ime/index.php?option=displaypage&Itemid; "Recomendación del CC-IME.13/econ/sedesol 'revisar reglas de operación del programa de atención a migrantes 3 X 1 y describir las principales razones por las cuales se rechazan los proyectos'," 2003, http://portal.sre.gob.mx/ime/recomendaciones/ cc_ime_i _13-con-sedesol.thm; "Recomendación del CC-IME 1.95/com/SSA 'crear un seguro de salud binacional para mexicanos documentados e indocumentados'," 2003, http://portal.sre.gob.mx/ime/ recomendaciones/cc_ime_i_95_com_ssa.htm. http://www.ime.gob.mx/ccime/comisiones/asuntos_economicos.htm.

63. González Gutiérrez, "Del acercamiento a la inclusión institucional."

64. Ayón, "La política mexicana."

65. Through consular offices, migrants are able to register their families in Mexico for subsidized health care in the Mexican Social Security Institute, one significant tier above the basic services provided by the Ministry of Health.

66. Agustín Escobar Latapí, "Migración y seguridad en la política exterior mexicana," *Revista Mexicana de Política Exterior*, no. 70 (February 2004): 85–98.

8

Lessons from the Mexican Seasonal Agricultural Worker Program in Canada

An Opportunity at Risk

Gustavo Verduzco Igartúa, El Colegio de México

INTRODUCTION

This chapter summarizes a study done in 2003 on the Mexican Seasonal Agricultural Worker Program in Canada and the workers that yearly travel to Canada.[1] This chapter illustrates key issues of the program, and highlights those that have allowed the continuation of the program. It is based on a survey carried out in the homes of Mexicans affiliated with the program. The data obtained allowed us to identify workers' perceptions regarding the operation of the program, and key aspects such as: income, living conditions, legal framework of their work, and conditions in the Canadian farms. The survey helped recognize the socioeconomic characteristics of the workers, their working experience, and to evaluate the impact of the program. The chapter intends to illustrate aspects of the program that should be taken into account by policy makers intending to reform U.S. temporary workers programs. Some could be adopted in new U.S. (or Mexican) policy. In other instances, however, this chapter finds aspects that are not replicable, or that should be avoided.

This program has operated continually since it was implemented in 1974. It is one of the few temporary worker programs that has been active for this time period between two countries, and throughout all these years it has not developed a parallel flow of unauthorized workers to Canada. It is important to stress this issue, since this is an unusual aspect for most temporary worker programs around the world. Also surprising is the permanence of the program, considering there is the competition of the American labor market where Mexican workers could seek better opportunities with higher wages. The limits of the study did not allow us to explore why the workers had a preference for either country, but we did find out that some have worked in agriculture in the United States under H-2A visas or illegally, and that they prefer the Mexico-Canada program.

The Mexican Ministry of Labor and its Canadian peer, Human Resources and Social Development Canada (HRSDC), as well as the Mexican Consulates, particularly the one in Toronto, have given the Seasonal Agricultural Worker Program a strong presence and framework for the workers involved. Also the advantages of benefits, such as life and health insurance, and its legal support have played an important role. Thanks to bilateral mechanisms, it also helps balance supply and demand in the labor market, offers a sense of security to seasonal workers, and consequently, promotes an encouraging relation between both countries. This study also illustrates that the program has been favorable for workers, although some of the benefits are a result of the workers' efforts, sacrifice, and long absences from their families.

The previous view does not explain why some workers prefer Canada vs. the United States, but does suggest that legality, selected program characteristics, and the presence of both governments have given the program an advantage in the minds of the temporary workers over the higher wages in the United States.

The study relied on two information sources: Firstly, interviews with government officials responsible for the program in Mexico were conducted. These officials also provided information from their files and experience. Second, a random survey of workers from the Mexico City database was undertaken. The survey dealt in detail with their experience in Canada, their perceptions, and benefits obtained. Socioeconomic data of the family and labor background was added to complement this work.

RESEARCH METHODOLOGY

We obtained our sample from the database of the program office in Mexico City. They have over 23,000 records of workers that have labored in Canada from one to several seasons between 1993 and 2006.

The Mexican workers registered under the program come from different states and a wide range of communities. To choose the places for our fieldwork we selected two characteristics: First, sites that had a large number of participants from the first years of the program, and second, states where we could find rural communities with a high concentration of workers to simplify the survey, due to budget constraints.

We decided not to work in states that had recently joined the program, to avoid losing workers that had more time under the program. One of the objectives of the study is to explore the possible impacts of the program in the workers' homes, therefore the importance of only including workers with several seasons in Canada. The second characteristic was the profile of the workers who live in rural communities. By choosing only rural communities we seek a larger homogeneity regarding the social origins of workers (i.e., the chances of having experience in agriculture are higher). This allowed us to have a base point, so that the data of the workers had a larger number of convergent tendencies in several characteristics, except in the number of years of work experience in Canada.

For the survey we selected the State of Mexico, Tlaxcala, and Morelos. The first and second have the largest numbers of workers in the seasonal program, followed by Guanajuato, Puebla, and Morelos. We did not include Guanajuato and Puebla because a considerable number of workers live in urban areas and a few live in scattered rural communities that could not be covered by the budget. Besides, including urban workers added a heterogeneous element in our sample, which we could not control due to the small number of questionnaires in the survey.

We therefore decided to include Morelos, which is the fifth state in importance for the program and has rural communities with a significant number of seasonal workers.

In the choice of municipalities for the fieldwork, we analyzed the socioeconomic information of each area of study. We then selected two municipalities from State of Mexico and Morelos and three from Tlaxcala. For each municipality we assigned a similar number of questionnaires in the workers' homes. Although each municipality is singular, our hypothesis stated that we would encounter a common socioeconomic profile among seasonal workers who go to Canada. The results confirm this hypothesis. Our sample consisted in 358 randomly selected cases.

THE CANADA-MEXICO PROGRAM

According to documents from the program office, there was a modest promotion of the program in its early stages, and it was limited to states close to Mexico City. By 1994, 80 percent of workers came from six states from the center of the country: Puebla, Tlaxcala, State of Mexico, Morelos, Hidalgo, and Guanajuato. Although the program has incorporated workers from all over the country, currently 70 percent of workers come from the center of Mexico, in spite of an increasing demand for workers and simplification in paperwork requirements.

Since the beginning of the program in 1974, the number of participants has increased annually by 18 percent, to 11,720 in 2005. This growth is determined by demand from Canadian employers. The largest increments happened between 1985–1989, and 1996 to 2000. The percentage of workers requested by name by an employer represents between 48 and 68 percent of the total number of Mexican seasonal workers that go to Canada. These workers have previous experience with that employer.

Women were first requested by Canadian employers in 1989. Today they only represent 3 percent. Although they are few, they continue to be requested, and their participation has doubled in a few years.

Operation

The operation of the Program has experienced several changes. An important one was the implementation of a system with an "all in one" processing office in Mexico. This has given swiftness to the process by having a dedicated office. In the past, workers had to visit several government offices in different places. In 1993, information was stored in electronic files, and in 2001 a system was implemented to further simplify the process and improve worker information.

Another upgrade has been the opening of Local Labor Service Offices (LLSO), under the supervision of the Ministry of Labor. There are 139 offices around Mexico. They promote the program, hand out information to workers interested in the program, and support the central office of the program by getting in touch with the workers requested by Canadian employers. Decentralization of other functions has been difficult, due to the lack of funds to provide skills for LLSO personnel.

Centralization is a constant in spite of the program's growth. This represents a cost for workers, since they have to travel on average six times to Mexico City to complete paperwork requirements for each season. In May 2002, the Mexican government subsidized trips to Mexico City, by handing $3,000 pesos to first-time applicants. During this time, the office evaluated the program and revealed that 88.3 percent of new workers received this aid.

Of the 358 cases of the study sample, three fourths answered that previous to their departure to Canada they received information from the program office. They mentioned they were informed about the work requirements in Canada, rules of behavior in the farms, and the legal rights for seasonal workers. Only nine specifically pointed out their labor rights, while the majority only cited being informed about the kind of work to be done.

When asked explicitly about their labor rights, 31 percent responded they did not know them or did not remember them. Even those that did reply positively could not recall which rights they had or how they could enforce them. There were also fifteen responses about obligations and prohibitions for workers. It is clear that the answers regarding this issue suppose a vague idea of their legal rights, although two thirds did mention at least one labor right.

The growth in the number of workers has surpassed the administrative capacity of the Mexican consulates in Canada, above all the one in Toronto, which covers the largest area where seasonal workers stay. The workers interviewed are aware that the consulates' role is to represent and aid them while in Canada. They also have an 800 number so workers can contact them.

Only 80 workers (22.3 percent of the sample) mentioned having required a service while being in Canada, and only 61 made use of the service. The 800 number is of great help, but due to the fact that workers are widely dispersed throughout Ontario—where traveling from farms to Toronto can take from two to seven hours—it complicates any assistance. Thirty percent of workers mentioned having needed services from the consulate; this translates to nearly 3,000 workers that each season would call for consular representation. This is an enormous demand versus the human and space capacity of Mexican consulates. In practice its personnel can only process a limited number of those requests.

This correlates to the fact that less than one fourth of the workers interviewed considered they received proper service from the consulate. According to 44.4 percent, the consulate does not represent them properly, and 21 percent answered they could not reply since they have not required their services.

The Mexican consulate in Toronto is considering establishing an administrative fund for the program, similar to the one already in existence for Caribbean workers. This fund is financed with 5 percent of the workers' income. The Mexican consulate believes it could be a viable option only if wages increased; otherwise it would be a burden on the workers.

Workers gave a favorable score to certain aspects of the program. Of the respondants, 36.6 percent answered they liked "everything" about the program; 28.2 percent answered the fact they have an employment opportunity; 7.5 percent made reference to wages and benefits; 5.9 percent highlighted the personal and work experience of participating in the Program; 5 percent mentioned its operation, and 4.2 percent liked the attitude from their employers. Only 8 workers (2.2 percent of the total) expressed a general negative opinion.

Regarding the question of what they dislike about the program, only half answered. The rest did not point out any disadvantages or did not specify any issues. Those complaining stressed problems regarding the operation of the program, the trips to Mexico City, the medical exam, and several incidents due to the deficiencies in the organization. Twenty-six workers (14 percent who answered the question) reproached the attention provided in the offices in Mexico and consulates. Twenty-one workers (11 percent) mentioned the unfavorable aspects of the program, referring to issues like being far from their families, living conditions in the farms, and climate among others. For eighteen workers (9.8 percent) a major disadvantage of the program is the behavior of Canadian employers. A small percentage of the workers interviewed (7 percent) had negative remarks regarding their working conditions, low wages, or discounts made to their salaries.

This study was not meant to evaluate the cost/benefit of the program; however, it did provide information regarding this issue. Throughout the years the Mexican government has accepted several conditions that have become a burden and increased costs both for the Mexican government and for seasonal workers.

Clear examples are the changes made to the memorandum of understanding (MOU) with which the program initiated. The first MOU established that the office of HRSDC, the counterpart for the Ministry of Labor in Mexico, must inform forty-five days in advance how many and which Mexican workers are required for the season. This period has been decreased to twenty days under the last MOU. Regardless of this change, it is common for the program office to receive this information with only ten days' notice. This causes difficulties and increases the cost of the program's operation.

During the first years of the program, the Mexican government was required to have a backup of 100 workers to respond to any urgent labor need. Today, it has been increased to 10 percent of the total demand. This translates to having to process over 1,000 backup workers each season. In 2002, 10,681 Mexicans went to work in Canada, but 11,659 cases were filed including medical exams.

Medical exams are another example of the costs and work incurred by the Mexican government. In the early stages of the program workers were examined by a doctor from the Canadian embassy in Mexico City. Later workers were also examined by Mexican Government Health centers that subsidized the cost of the exams, and since 2001 each worker must pay 70 pesos (or about 6.50 U.S. dollars) per exam. In 2003, workers were asked to pay 175 pesos for an HIV test, although this is no longer required.

It was not until 2002 that the cost of the Program was included in the National Budget in Mexico. The Ministry of Labor registered the Program for Agricultural Migrant Mexican Workers for Canada, with a budget of 23,396,454 pesos. The administrative costs of the Program for 2002 were close to 2,190 pesos (under 200 U.S. dollars) per worker. This budget does not include the aid of 3,000 pesos that new participants receive. In 2002, 2,341 workers received this aid adding 7,023,000 pesos to the cost of the program. Therefore, the average cost per worker was 2,848 pesos, or under 270 U.S. dollars.

Profile of Workers

The study presents the following results regarding workers' profiles. The average schooling is 7.7 years, close to the national standard from the national census for 2000.

Ninety-five percent of workers interviewed were family heads, most of them married and only a few divorced or separated. As mentioned previously the number of women is very small, just over 3 percent. In our random sample there were nine cases or 3.7 percent.

The age requirement in the program is between twenty-two and forty-five years of age for men, and twenty-three and forty years for women. For this study the average was thirty-eight years of age, reflecting the inclusion in the sample of workers who participated in the early stages of the program, but were no longer traveling to Canada.

Most of the workers (44 percent) mentioned having worked as day laborers in Mexican agriculture. Twenty-nine percent declared working in production areas. Few worked as masons and only a handful in service activities. Workers have similar profiles, although they come from different states and communities. Having experience in agricultural labor is one of the requirements.

Seasonal workers have very limited access to agricultural land in Mexico. Only 21.5 percent (seventy-seven workers) mentioned they have land, and most of their fields lack irrigation and are small (one to two hectares). The main product is corn for personal consumption and few plant any commercial products. For most workers farming is only a way to supplement other income. The study found that during the last season 16 percent of those that have access to land were not able to harvest, 32 percent mentioned that production was not enough for self-consumption, and only 13 percent made a profit. These numbers clearly indicate the precarious conditions of agricultural workers in Mexico. They also reflect the challenging problems they face due to deficient irrigation systems.

Almost half of the workers mentioned they have a close relative (brother or sister) that has participated in the program. It is clear that work in Canada is moderately related to family ties more than community networks. Another source of enrollment for the program has been the activities undertaken by the program office. These actions differ with seasonal workers that go to the United States where community networks play a mayor role.

Insecurity of an income and lack of a stable job in Mexico are the major causes that push seasonal workers to join the program. From the sample 58 percent mentioned that although they had an income in Mexico, it was not constant or enough to meet their needs. Another 14 percent joined the program because they lacked a job. Most workers, while in Mexico, hold occasional jobs and earn an average 544 pesos per week (close to 50 U.S. dollars).

Working Conditions in Canada

The sample included workers that have worked in Canada one or more seasons since 1977. Almost 73 percent of the workers were still active during the last season. We believe that the continuity of the workers in the program is a sign of their satisfaction and of steadiness of the program.

According to the evaluation of the program office for the 2002 season, 70 percent of the workers went to Ontario, 24.6 percent to Quebec, and the rest to Manitoba and Alberta. The largest sector that requires seasonal work is horticulture (41.6 percent) and greenhouses (18 percent).

On average, workers spend 4.9 months each season and do not have the opportunity to decide the length of their contract. Workers requested by their name must comply with the terms of the employer; the rest are subject to demand, working profile, physical condition, and the date the candidate starts the paperwork.

For the 2002 season, over 60 percent of the workers returned to Mexico before their contracts expired, since there was no more work in the farms. Several mentioned that while in the farms, they sometimes end the day early since there was no more work to be done. Some employers may try to transfer them to other farms. If that is not possible the worker must return to Mexico, with fewer earnings than expected. Workers complain that it is common for employers to send them back early, and they feel resentful since they have made a major commitment by leaving their families and traveling to another country.

Mexican workers are mainly hired for the harvest. In our sample only two workers carried out activities that require technical knowledge.

Employers provide housing, usually the old farmhouse. Others have built units, and a few employers use mobile homes. Housing facilities overall include all the necessary services. Almost half of the workers answered that the facilities and the services were better than what they have in Mexico. Only 18 percent mentioned that they had better conditions back home, and 27 percent said their level was similar.

Regarding working conditions in Canada, most expressed that it was as easy as or easier than what they did in Mexico; only 25 percent mentioned harder farming duties. One fifth said they were asked at least in one occasion to work more. They replied that it is frequent to have a harder working rhythm, and working days can surpass twelve hours.

During the survey we registered some complaints about treatment in the farms; the report for the 2002 season in the program office in Mexico illustrates this situation. According to this source one fifth responded being treated in a bad or regular manner, the latter being the most common answer.

During our fieldwork we found out that many of the workers interviewed said they suffered some kind of abuse by employers or supervisors. They mentioned they preferred not to report the case to the program authorities in Canada for fear that employers would not hire them the following season. It is possible that the application by name system, although it provides workers with certain security of continuity, may well work as a control mechanism.

With regards to the use of agrochemicals, 24 percent answered using them, 34 percent said they entered recently sprayed fields, and 43 percent said they had protective equipment while applying agrochemicals.

Although many of the tasks seasonal workers carry out are simple tasks, they receive hardly any training. Only 45 percent responded having received instructions. They made reference to information received while working in the fields by a supervisor or working companions. Only six said they have received a broader training.

Responses about accidents and health are generally with a positive view. Workers mentioned they receive adequate attention. Although, if a sickness becomes present after the contract is over, workers must cover the cost or find a public hospital in Mexico.

Wages and Tax Deductions

It was difficult to obtain information about wages and taxes. Records in the program office in Mexico and the data of the survey have omissions. The best information would come from employers records, which we could not access.

It is clear that wages for seasonal workers are much higher than what they receive in Mexico, even if they had the opportunity to work year round. This validates the workers' opinion that income is the reason they apply for the program.

For 2002, workers earned an average 8,573 Canadian dollars, equivalent to 57,440 pesos (for 4.9 month's work on average). The minimum wage in Mexico at that time was 40 pesos per day; the maximum amount a worker could earn in one year at the minimum wage was the equivalent to 2,065 Canadian dollars.[2]

Therefore, workers expressed no inconvenience in working extra hours. Some complained that those hours are not paid at higher rates, which is not required under Canadian law. It is also common for employees to work on Sundays and holidays. Some mentioned working shifts of seventeen hours, although in the survey the average was 9.3 hours per day.

Regarding taxes, deductions, and tax returns there is a general confusion of how the process is done. Workers perceive too much is deducted from their wages and believe it is unfair. From some of the answers obtained from workers, the difference between gross and net income is close to 20 percent.

Workers have no knowledge of how the social security and pension systems work. They are certainly interested in having additional information, considering that some have worked for a number of years and are close to the age limit allowed by the program. The retirement fund is determined by the number of weeks worked; therefore the seasonal conditions of the work limit the amount a worker could receive. The two workers that receive a monthly payment both expressed skepticism about the low sum of their checks.

Relations between Seasonal Workers and Canadian Communities

Integration with Canadian communities is not an easy task for seasonal workers. The biggest challenges are language and that workers in farms are isolated.

Ninety-six percent of workers labor in farms outside any village or community. It is frequent to find farms that are 20 kilometers (40 miles) away, and do not have an accessible transportation system. Over 70 percent mentioned that their employers took them to town, and they depend on them or someone else to buy their supplies, make telephone calls, and go to the bank. These conditions limit their ability to decide how to use their free time.

Some employers supply some forms of entertainment in the farms (TV, table games, and fields to play in). Some workers have been involved in sports tournaments and visit tourist places, but such activities have been very limited.

Few workers have had contact with volunteer groups and nonprofit organizations involved in supporting seasonal workers. The responses obtained make it clear that their work has been important for this workforce.

Program Impacts

Regarding the impacts of the program we can conclude the following:

- The greatest impacts are on the family and individual worker.
- This is due to the additional income.
- Positive impacts become evident only after several seasons of working in the program.

Almost all the workers interviewed mentioned that their family's well being has improved. This response was higher among workers that have been participating longer in the program. They mentioned that their families dress and eat better, improve their access to health services, and most importantly, their children are able to continue their studies and complete more years of school.

All of the indicators of housing conditions show that the more seasons workers are involved in the program, the better these conditions become.

Workers use the income of their first seasons for basic family needs, including general household expenses, health, education, or debts. Only after several seasons can they save and build or remodel their homes. However, the study shows that income is still not enough to buy other goods; for example few workers own a car or truck. The positive impact of the program varies according to the number and frequency of trips to Canada. It is therefore convenient to allow the same workers to travel for several seasons, maybe ten or more.

In a similar way productive investment is nonexistent. One reason is the limited amount of agricultural resources and another the characteristics of the origin communities that lack economic activity. Although this survey is not the proper tool to obtain this information, during the fieldwork we perceived that workers would limit the amount of information provided, fearing it could influence their involvement in the program.

Regarding their children's schooling, most said that the program allowed them to continue their studies. Although in Mexico overall children are completing higher grades, the program has also contributed, since the more seasons a worker has been in the program, the higher the schooling of their children.

It was also evident that schooling levels had an impact on their children's job opportunities. The study shows a tendency for children to work in non-agricultural activities. Fifteen children had university degrees, and most of them were from fathers that have been the longest in the program.

We have classified the impact of the program's indirect effects in the communities. We present three categories in accordance to the number of seasons that each worker has participated.

Group A consists of workers that have been to Canada from one to four seasons. It comprises 165 workers, 3 of which are women. Since 1986, these workers have gone to Canada. In 2002, 23 were still participating in the program.

Group B includes 81 workers; 3 are also women. This group has traveled to Canada at least five times and less than eight. Most of them went to Canada between 1989 and 1999.

Table 8.1.   Workers' Group According to the Number of Seasons in Canada

Group	Number of Workers	Percent
Group A. 1 to 4 seasons	165	46.1
Group B. 5 to 8 seasons	81	22.6
Group C. 9 and more seasons	112	31.3
Total Workers	358	100

Note: The source for all tables in this chapter, except Table 8.4, is the author's survey.

Group C are workers that have been nine or more seasons in the Program. They are 112. Most of them began the program in 1977. The last were included in 1994.

To analyze this information we selected those workers whose children were no longer in school and who were already in the labor force. Two hundred cases were produced (Table 8.2). The results underline what workers express in their answers: thanks to the program their children have been able to complete more years of school. When looking at the results according to the number of years that workers participated in the program, clear differences show the influence of it. In Group C (longest exposure to the program), 42.6 percent of the total of the children have been at school for ten years or more. This percentage is 28 percent for Group B, and 15 percent for Group A, the latter being the group with workers with the fewest number of trips. Let us recall that the years of school for the parents averaged 7.7.

Because family cycles can influence the differences in schooling, we repeated the exercise by only selecting workers from different age groups, but

Table 8.2. Education of Children That No Longer Attend School

Schooling	Group A	Group B	Group C	Total
Average years of Education	*8.7*	*9.9*	*10.5*	*9.8*
1 to 3 years	2			2
Group %	3%			1%
% of total	1%			1%
4 to 6 years	16	1	21	38
Group %	23.9%	4%	19.4%	19%
% of total	8%	.5%	10.5%	19%
7 to 9 years	39	17	41	97
Group %	58.2%	68%	38%	48.5%
% of total	19.5%	8.5%	20.5%	48.5%
10 to 12 years	7	6	29	42
Group %	10.4%	24.0%	26.9%	21%
% of total	3.5%	3%	14.5%	21%
More than 12 years	3	1	17	21
Group %	4.5%	4.0%	15.7%	10.5%
% of total	1.5%	.5%	8.5%	10.5%
TOTAL	67	25	108	200
	33.5%	12.5%	54.0%	100%

with the same time exposure to the program. This way we could measure two possible effects: one the welfare effect from the normal family cycle, measured through the variable worker's age, and second the welfare derived from a longer exposure to the program. We therefore grouped workers in two age clusters: one from twenty to thrity-five years of age, and another from thirty-six to fifty years of age; each one represented a different stage of the family cycle. We also ranked the years of education of their children according to their parents' number of trips to Canada and then compared results.

Firstly, we observed that children whose parents have gone to Canada more than nine times, independently of the age group to which they belong, average 9.9 years of schooling, versus the general average of 8.0, that is to say almost two years longer. For workers in the younger age cluster, 62 percent of their children achieved 7 or more years of school; for the second cluster this percentage rose to 87 percent. This way we observed both effects and confirm how both variables interact. We also examined that for the youngest workers their children had obtained fewer years of schooling, for example 10 or more years in only 8.1 percent of the cases, while in the second age cluster 35 percent had achieved the same level.

The Occupations of Program Workers and Other Family Members

The length of experience in the program is also reflected in the university schooling of their children (see Table 8.3). Thirteen of the fifteen children that have university degrees belong to families with workers from Group C. We also found that seven people from the interviewed homes that work in the United States also belong to families of Group C. It is likely that some of the savings from workers have allowed their children to search for work in the United States, but migration to the United States is an established phenomenon in these states. They may be going to the United States for other reasons. Within this group we found the highest proportion of children over eighteen years still studying, and those that work do so in commerce or service areas. Likewise, Group C has the fewest number of children working in agriculture.

This information allows us to state—with certain limits—that the longer a worker participates in the program, their children not only have more years of education, but find work in fields other than agriculture.

Family Welfare

The seasonal working program has brought clear advantages to the workers involved. According to 93.1 percent, their welfare and family has improved. All of the workers from Group C answered in a positive way. For

Table 8.3. Occupation of Children over 18 Years of Age, by Worker Group

	Group A	Group B	Group C	Total
Home duties	27	29	52	108
Group %	30%	43.9%	27%	31%
Student	6	13	42	61
Group %	6.6%	19.7%	21.8%	17.5%
Worker in the U.S.			7	7
Group %			1.6%	2%
Commerce and services	13	6	30	49
Group %	14.4%	9%	27%	14%
Manual labor or craft	2	0	3	5
Group %	2.2%		1.5%	1.4%
Laborer	3	3	1	7
Group %	3.3%	4.5%	0.5%	2%
Professionals[a]	2	0	13	15
Group %	2.2%		6.7%	4.3%
Construction-mason	6	1	4	11
Group %	6.6%	1.5%		3.1%
Agriculture	31	13	36	80
Group %	34.4%	19.7%	18.7%	22.9%
No data			4	4
Total	90	66	192	348

[a]Meaning they have finished undergraduate studies.

Groups B and A the percentages are 96.2 and 86.8 percent, respectively. Only 24 workers mentioned their conditions have not improved; 21 are from Group A and only 3 from Group B. It is possible that their short exposure to the program has not given them enough resources.

RECOMMENDATIONS

The following recommendations come from the opinions that workers expressed throughout the survey. We believe they are important, not only because of the value of their opinions and perceptions, but also because they are a sample of issues that need improvement and adjustment.

1. It necessary to revise the legal situation of seasonal workers. Although they work year after year with the same employer, Canadian laws consider them as part-time workers with reduced legal benefits.

2. HRSDC must identify which nonprofit organizations are working with seasonal workers, and promote their activities. It is important that HRSDC works with these organizations and the Mexican consulates to analyze the needs of seasonal workers. Cooperation agreements should be established to coordinate efforts. We suggest offering aid services in: (a) accounting, to request welfare benefits and tax reimbursements, (b) conversation classes in English and French, (c) recreation, (d) make workers acquainted with local stores, churches, banks and other institutions.

3. It is important to regulate and reinforce farm inspections, and make sure workers have access to information, and that documents and any relevant warning and information signs are in Spanish.

4. It is necessary to review the tax framework and consider avoiding retaining any wage tax to workers earning less than $14,000 a year. This is the legal limit. This would avoid reimbursement paperwork for 77 percent of workers.

5. It is important to review the cost incurred by the Mexican government for each worker and the sum they need to disburse in the process, which amounts to a considerable subsidy to Canadian farms. They should have knowledge of these costs and therefore a proper evaluation can be done.

6. Any new program promoting the temporary employment of Mexicans in Canada should be based on a bilateral arrangement similar to the one in the agricultural program. Otherwise it runs the risk of corruption and illegal practices in the process of enrollment or labor.

FUTURE OF THE PROGRAM: MEXICO'S PERSPECTIVE

Two issues must be addressed regarding the future of the program. The first is the situation in Mexico's agriculture and the second is the socioeconomic context of the country.

The excessive fragmentation of rural property, which is understandable from a historic viewpoint, has been a factor that has obstructed the expansion of an efficient economy in this field.

As mentioned in the study, small owners with land without irrigation that usually farm corn are the ones that have the least possibilities of success.

The survey revealed that the few that have land are *ejido* owners,[3] with small lots, and therefore have no incentive to either invest in their own

properties or buy more land. We must consider that the majority of seasonal workers are agricultural laborers in Mexico which is one of the worst-
paid occupations. As mentioned, workers in the program have used their income to improve their homes and provide education for their children. This
is a very important impact for workers who believe, correctly, that a better
education will provide their family with improved economic and social
standing. Sociological literature regarding farmwork reminds us that even
though farmers are usually poor and ignorant, they are very pragmatic regarding their wealth. This situation is also confirmed with Mexican workers
that seasonally go to Canada. Their involvement in the program has allowed them to improve their life. Another evidence for this is that close to
20 percent of the workers have left their rural communities and moved to
Mexico City or Puebla, surely because they know they can improve their income and work experience. Unfortunately we were not able to research this
issue, and focused only on rural communities. This should be studied in the
future.

In conclusion, in spite of its flaws, the program clearly has offered personal and family benefits for seasonal workers. It would be prudent to consider expanding the program to other Canadian farms or even other economic areas whose labor needs are similar. The research allowed us to
detect some problems that can easily be overcome with a small increase in
funding and some strategic planning.

It is important to highlight that demand for seasonal workers in Canada
has not been obstructed or limited through the years by the strong demand
for the same kind of workers in the United States. We must remember that
since the 1970s there has been strong demand for low-skill workers in the
United States. Our research shows most workers prefer the legal and other
conditions of the Canada-Mexico program. The second situation is that a
number of the seasonal workers that have been to Canada have traveled to
the United States where they receive better pay for the same type of work.
Why do some decide to go to the United States or Canada? A hypothesis is
that the Canadian program offers a legal framework and labor security
which workers see as an added value. We believe this has been essential for
the stability of the program.

It is important that any new Mexico-Canada program retain the current
design of the Seasonal Agricultural Worker Program with the involvement
of the Mexican Ministry of Foreign Relations and the Ministry of Labor, by
implementing agreements between the two countries with similar administrative controls, with the warranty that Mexican workers currently have and
seeking to reduce costs for workers and the Mexican government.

As mentioned earlier, currently both governments are incurring some
costs, which translates into a subsidy to Canadian farmers. Looking into the
future and possible broadening of the program, it is important to think

about the key issues that could allow new sources of funding and prevent increasing costs for both governments, which could limit the number of workers. It is vital that costs should not be a burden for seasonal workers, who already pay a heavy toll by leaving their families behind for long periods and have to live in a foreign environment.

This study also shows that throughout the history of the program the number of Mexicans that have established their residence in Canada is very limited, and they have followed legal channels. This surely has a positive impact for the government of Canada and the policies it may implement in this area.

There are two important aspects to consider for the short-term future: first, there is a growing number of women applicants. Canadian farms are starting to realize their importance, and in the near future their numbers will likely increase; second, because of the possible increase of requests of retirement funds from seasonal workers, it is important that the firm managing worker contracts, HRSDC, and the Mexican Ministry of Foreign Relations and the Ministry of Labor are prepared. The Ministry of Foreign Relations reported that currently 357 workers have requested this benefit, although they lack information on how to process these requests.

We estimate the possible future increase of retirement fund applications. We looked into the database of the program office, which has over 23,900 registered workers. We used the date of birth of workers already enrolled in 1993, workers that enrolled since that year and were active until 2002. We did not include workers prior to 1993 or that dropped off the program in 2002.

Average age was 37.6 years (similar to our sample which was 38 years of age). Table 8.4 shows the total number of workers enrolled in the program

Table 8.4.   Worker Age Groups, from Program Records. Data from 1993 to 2002

Age group	Frequency	Percent
40 years or less	14,716	61.5
41 to 44 years	4,415	18.5
45 to 49 years	2,457	10.3
50 to 54 years	1,234	5.2
55 to 59 years	711	3.0
Over 60 years	367	1.5
Total	23,900	100

Source: Database from workers enrolled in the Program, Ministry of Labor, 2002.

by age group: 367 are over 60 years of age, 711 are between 55 and 59 years, and 1,234 are between 50 and 54 years. These data allow us to appreciate that requests for social security will rise over threefold over the next years. It is therefore important to design a process that will expedite the benefit for the workers.

EPILOGUE

In summary, the bilateral Canada-Mexico temporary farmworker program can claim several significant achievements: in the long term, the quality of life of workers and their families in Mexico has improved markedly; their children's level of education has increased very significantly; and no undocumented flows have been created.[4] These successes can be explained in terms of the transparency of the recruitment practices, the falling administrative costs for workers after their first year, the absence of illegal or informal recruitment fees, the satisfaction of Canadian employers manifest in their propensity to stay in the program and recruit the same workers year after year, and the fairly high—though imperfect—level of compliance with Canadian pay, labor, and other standards. The administrative costs to Mexico are significant, but not overwhelming. The Mexican government, in my opinion, would be willing to incur similar costs in a similar program with the United States, if the outcomes promised to be equivalent.[5] In many respects, this program illustrates the virtues of government intervention. The question is whether this arrangement can work in other settings and at a much larger scale without the creation of a massive administration.

On the other hand, it seems Canada is moving away from this model. Recently, the policy regarding work in Canada for seasonal workers from Mexico and other countries has expanded to new areas that have a high demand for labor. This has happened in ecotourism, waste collection and disposal, and construction. The novelty with these processes is that contracting between workers and employers is much more thinly regulated. A similar case happens between the U.S. and Mexico with the H-2A and H-2B programs. The private enterprise Mexi-Can in Saltillo, state of Coahuila, is responsible for recruiting workers to work in Canada, especially in areas of high demand. This happens with a minimum involvement of the Canadian government, which limits itself to determine if there is real need for seasonal workers. Also the Mexican government has only intervened to reaffirm these new practices, without any control or supervision. It may well seem that the experience throughout the last thirty-two years has not been enough to caution both governments about the ease with which certain minimum rights can be threatened by private enterprises seeking to increase their profits. For the case of seasonal agricultural workers, their situation seems acceptable, although leaning to lower limits. As the study shows, not all workers are able to achieve benefits, and this happens only after many seasons of hard work involving long costly absences from their families. In addition, both governments seem oblivious to the fact that less-regulated programs generate a parallel flow of undocumented workers. This flow, in turn, creates discontent in the host country. Even with the close supervision of both governments, there are issues that are not addressed while the farmworkers stay in Canada. What would happen with seasonal workers and employers if the current framework was absent? We are referring to the MOU and the practice of collaboration by the two countries. Government officials from both countries are aware of the many problems faced by Mexican workers, not only because of their low education level and the challenges posed by a different culture, but also the abuses they sometimes endure without the aid of any authority.

Unfortunately, there are no studies for market-driven cases like H-2A and H-2B workers in the United States that can tell us about their experiences and this new context of minimum protection of labor rights. A study of these cases would generate information regarding the positive and negative aspects of this new practice. However this new framework that Canadians are replicating from their southern neighbors does not predict positive results for Mexican workers who are willing to try this new labor path. Some news reports are an indicator of this. For example Kyle G. Brown of the *Toronto Star* wrote (November 6, 2006), stressing how workers were disappointed with their earnings in Calgary, due to their bad and expensive housing conditions. They could not send money to their families and had dire living conditions. They also complained that the Canadian company that hired them had retained their passports. It is a fact that when the free market is allowed to determine working conditions, abuses easily occur.

The Mexican and Canadian governments must not renounce their obligations, since the labor relation could be affected, and threaten the farms and the work opportunities that support seasonal workers.

The Mexican Seasonal Agricultural Worker Program in Canada has also helped expand and improve fruit and vegetable production. In recent years this sector has become highly competitive, as the North-South Institute in Ottawa has recently reported in its Web page.

It would be positive to supervise the new employer-based programs in a manner similar to the case of the Mexican Seasonal Agricultural Worker Program in Canada. In the case of Mexico-U.S. migration, this author is of the opinion that current or future programs should resemble the Mexico-Canada Seasonal Farm Worker Program in terms of government regulation.

NOTES

1. This study was sponsored by the North-South Institute of Ottawa, Canada, with finance from the Rockefeller Foundation. To request a copy of the full report, please contact the author at: gverduz@colmex.mx. The author thanks the Institute for permission to use some material from the report.

2. Actual agricultural wages are higher than the minimum, but employment is not year-round.

3. Land ownership similar to common land.

4. The World Bank estimates an overstay rate of 1.5 percent. Tanya Basok, "Canada's Temporary Migration Program: A Model Despite Flaws," *Migration Information Source*, November 2007, http://www.migrationinformation.org/Feature/display.cfm?id=650.

5. The concluding chapter deals with detailed policy lessons based on the comparative study of this and the H-2A programs.

Conclusion[1]

Susan Martin and Agustín Escobar Latapí

INTRODUCTION

We view increasing Mexican emigration as driven mostly by the economic disparities which have persisted, and in some respects broadened, since Mexico suffered a series of economic shocks, and later joined GATT (now the WTO) and NAFTA. While in the recent short-term past demand has played a dominant role in changing migration levels, it is those disparities that explain the medium-term behavior of the flow. Successful policy interventions to regulate Mexico-U.S. migration should, in this context, be based both on *economic* policies targeting these disparities, mostly through economic, employment, and income growth in Mexico, and through specific *migration* policies. Both, in our view, imply deepened bilateral collaboration. Mexican employment and income growth offers far more possibilities in terms of reinforcing prosperity in the North American community than similar growth levels in Europe or Asia. The Mexican economy is much more closely tied to the United States than others. On the other hand, Mexican employment and income growth is likely to have a scant effect on the flows, in the short-term at least, if both countries do not collaborate to regulate migration.

This final chapter focuses on migration policies that will tend to (1) improve the manageability of Mexican migration in both countries, (2) enhance its development potential, and (3) reduce its undesirable impacts on both societies. But it must be remembered that these policies should work together with wider and more ambitious reforms that should promote Mexican development and reduce U.S. reliance on cheap imported labor.

At present U.S. employers and Mexican workers appear to be mutually dependent on migration. In the near future, conditions in both countries are likely to maintain the flow at close to its current levels, with ups and downs defined, in the short term, by U.S. employment growth and policies. Over the longer term Mexican development holds the best likelihood of reducing the number of migrants. Demographic changes will contribute to lessen emigration pressures. Concerning Mexican employment, while the prognosis is sometimes disappointing, there is reason to believe that formal sector employment may regain its momentum of the late 1990s. But there is little room for complacency. Some critics reasonably point out that today's migration momentum may carry on indefinitely and, as long as today's institutions for (mis-)managing migration remain unchanged, they could well be right.

The prospects for wide-ranging collaboration on migration issues have suffered remarkable ups and downs since 2000. And yet, collaboration is essential to improving the management of migration and deriving positive impacts in both countries, and today both governments could attempt to renew their efforts to regulate migration. A high level of cooperation and institutionalization already exists in the fields of trade and investment. It has been useful to both countries, and these two models can serve to further cooperation in migration affairs. And cooperation has also risen to new highs in other fields, such as security, although it is less institutionalized.

We are proposing an arrangement in which renewed dialogue, improved national migration policy coordination in Mexico and the United States, and a binational administrative body gradually develop substantial levels of cooperation. Together with a series of confidence-building steps, they would create practical, day-to-day collaboration. A bilateral approach to the management of migration opens up avenues for the more secure, effective, and humanitarian control of the northward movement. Specifically, we are proposing a number of specific components to redirect movements from largely unauthorized migration to legal work programs. At the same time, we are suggesting elements that, if proactively targeted, can boost Mexican development. Finally, we believe the time has come for Mexico and the United States to cooperate more systematically in the enforcement of migration laws along the Mexico-U.S. border, provided that new legal avenues are opened to migrants and employers. Cooperating on the border, facilitating legal status, deterring unauthorized employment, providing legal alternatives for new migrant flows benefiting from new social and information infrastructure in both countries, leveraging remittances, encouraging return migration, and maintaining ongoing and close consultations on all aspects of the binational relationship will lead to a substantial improvement in the regulation of migration, and to a much more satisfying Mexico-

U.S. relationship. Acknowledgement of the responsibility shared in the current state of Mexico-U.S. migration should evolve into practical collaboration for its solution.

The economic context of Mexican migration changed fundamentally with the advent of the North American Free Trade Agreement (NAFTA) in 1994, but there has been no immediate impact on migration because of the greater integration of Mexico and the United States. Rather, the small but positive impact of low-skilled migrants on the U.S. economy, in tandem with the economic boom of the late 1990s, reinforced labor demand for Mexican workers. At the same time, although population growth diminished in Mexico, the working-age cohorts still expanded between 2.5 and 2 percent per annum until the year 2000, and economic conditions have not progressed rapidly enough to offset the pull of U.S. jobs and wages. Taken together, supply and demand factors outline a scenario in which a major reduction in emigration is unlikely in the near future.

Mexico-U.S. migration is a robust system, sustained by economic and social factors in both countries. In the United States, employment of immigrants not authorized to work has become common in mainstream industries and firms. While Mexican migrants were found predominantly in agriculture in the 1960s, today it is estimated than only 3 percent of unauthorized migrants living in the U.S. work in agriculture, while 33 percent work in service jobs. Irregular migrant workers are employed by households, small family enterprises, and multinational corporations. Most of these firms have never been inspected for violating work authorization requirements. Of the few that have, a very small proportion has been prosecuted: only three employers in 2005 although there has since been an increase.

As employment of undocumented Mexicans and other foreigners becomes highly diversified, a part of the mainstream economy, and of the standard business model, employer attitudes have also tended to vary: they range from overcompliance, which may include rejection of seemingly false (but sometimes legitimate) documentation, and the requirement of documents they are not entitled to demand (which can lead to lawsuits by the workers), to the active and knowing recruitment of undocumented workers, and the "coaching" of supervisors and lower managers in what they need to help workers get some kind of documentation.

Enterprises have come to depend on unauthorized workers to varying degrees. Some profit from the lower pay, hire and fire flexibility, and lower taxes and benefits accepted by irregular workers, but most employers argue that U.S. workers are unavailable or unwilling to apply for these positions. At any rate, most undocumented Mexican workers are typically found in jobs and industries requiring few skills where employers seek to keep their labor costs down in order to make their products cost competitive, in a context of falling domestic and international prices for a large number of goods.

In February 2004, the Bureau of Labor Statistics (BLS) issued projections for 21 million more workers for the decade 2002 to 2012 and a remarkably strong demand for workers with few formal skills. Among the occupations with the fastest projected growth are registered nurses and university teachers; however, seven of the ten occupations with the fastest growth are in low-wage services that require little education: retail salesperson, customer service representative, food-service worker, cashier, janitor, waiter, and nursing aide and hospital orderly. These latter jobs tend to employ significant numbers of immigrants. At the same time, fifteen of the thirty occupations projected to have the "largest numerical" growth require only short on-the-job training, and these jobs are projected to account for 24 percent of total labor force growth. Here too Mexicans make up a substantial share of the occupational workforce: 20 percent of all landscape and groundskeepers; 14 percent of all food preparation workers; 11 percent of all janitors; 10 percent of all heavy and 5 percent of light truck drivers; and 8 percent of all waitress and waiters' assistants. These BLS projections therefore support the idea that there will be continuing demand for low-skill foreign workers, from Mexico or elsewhere. In effect, it is not simply the projection of expansion of certain occupations that underlies the current and potentially future robustness of the flow, but the growth of a business model which relies on a certain kind of labor, in construction, meatpacking and food processing, catering, janitorial services, hotels and resorts, farming, and other industries.

U.S. enforcement practices have, since the mid-1990s, had little or no effect on migration flows. While trends in apprehensions on the border do not correspond directly to changes in the volume of actual migration, they nevertheless mirror underlying trends. Apprehensions increased in a mostly linear pattern from 1989 through 1999, when they reached approximately 1.7 million (and the Mexican government reported 1.2 million returns of apprehended migrants). They fell sharply in 2000, as the rate of job creation in the U.S. declined, and during the last three years have stood at lower levels similar to those during the immediate aftermath of IRCA or the early 1980s.

Notably, apprehensions (and, as mentioned earlier, flows) increased from 1994 to May 2000,[2] although this was also a period of enhanced enforcement when the U.S. put in place a new border enforcement strategy including new barriers, rapidly increasing numbers of border patrol agents, technological aids, and new apprehension strategies. Some observers believe new border enforcement strategies have led to vastly increased smuggler fees. Although border enforcement seems to be a factor in this rise, smuggler fees have increased much less than border patrol personnel, and they have remained largely stable since the late 1990s. Some observers also believe the new enforcement strategy is responsible for an increase in the number of deaths of border crossers. We believe border enforcement can be directly related to the type of deaths observed (dehydration and exhaustion), but it is difficult to ascertain the alternative or counterfactual number and type of deaths, had the new strategy not been put in place. Yet, it can clearly be observed that irregular border crossings are more dangerous and risky today than in the past, and relatively stable numbers of deaths in relation to falling apprehensions point at rising death *rates* after the year 2000.[3] Further, analyses of Mexican communities suggest that the expansion of barriers along the border had a "rush to the border" effect on some of them, as migrants tried to cross the border before it became impassable.

Most of all, border enforcement does not seem to have affected the overall, medium-term propensity of Mexicans to migrate to the United States. Before U.S. job growth fell in 2000, migration and apprehensions continued to rise, even as the new strategy was implemented.

In 1996, the United States adopted policies that significantly reduced the access of immigrants and their families to a range of social benefits, including programs designed for the working poor (such as food stamps and some forms of medical assistance). The legislation also increased the number of deportable offences and reduced due process protections for people in removal proceedings. In the aftermath of the September 11 attacks, still further restrictions have been placed on the legal rights of foreigners in the country. To a large extent, these legal changes have focused on removal of persons who have committed crimes in the United States. There is no evidence, however, that these restrictive policies have deterred new flows of undocumented Mexican migrants or that they resulted in any reduction in the number of unauthorized migrants residing in the United States. The lesson from these restrictive measures is that similar initiatives are not likely to be very effective in the future.

Large backlogs and long waiting times for family reunification are also problematic, contributing to unauthorized migration. Unknown but significant portions of the unauthorized population in the United States are close family members of legal permanent residents (LPRs). At present, there is more than a five-year wait for spouses and minor children of Mexican LPRs to obtain legal status. Not surprisingly, many Mexicans circumvent U.S. immigration law in order to live with their immediate families. U.S. immigration policy holds out the promise of family reunification but offers an unrealistic route to this most basic of family values.

In Mexico, evidence from the Household Income and Expenditure Survey shows that the number of Mexican families depending on remittances, and the share of total household income derived from them, has grown continually since the early 1990s, as can also be gathered from the sheer growth in total remittances, averaging over 15 percent annually since the year 2000. In 2006, remittances accounted for more than 3.5 percent of Mexican GDP. Those households that depend most on remittances are found in the lowest income brackets, although those at the top of the income structure receive absolutely larger amounts. As the social networks that used to link Mexicans to Mexican jobs become thinner and more competitive, those opening channels and opportunities to travel to the U.S. have tended to become the norm. Whether to acquire basic assets, escape poverty, or meet emergencies, migration to the United States is today a far more prominent option than it was even in the mid-1990s. Mexican non-farm jobs are not growing at the rate required to absorb the population displaced from agriculture. The option for many farmers and would-be farmworkers has clearly changed to be viewed mostly as the United States, although a portion of this outflow still finds its way to Mexican cities, especially in the North.

Conditions in Mexico therefore undoubtedly sustain this migration system. Some factors in Mexico that may contribute to change migration dynamics include:

- Fertility rates, which have continued to decline.
- Mexican labor participation levels. They have stabilized in general, and young Mexicans are delaying their entry into the job market and studying longer, thus lowering pressure on the job market.
- The growth of the population of working age is diminishing steadily, although it will remain positive until 2020.
- Formal job growth has resumed, although it remains significantly below levels reached in the late 1990s.
- Wage levels in the formal urban economy and in the rural sector especially have increased slightly over the past five years.
- Rural poverty rates, in particular, which have fallen clearly and significantly from 2000 to 2006.[4]

While these forces should work to reduce emigration, there are reasons to be less than sanguine, at least in the short to medium term. Of primary concern is the fifteen-year decline in Mexican agricultural employment. It currently provides one-sixth of all employment in Mexico, but its falling share of employment means it generates migration to other sectors of the Mexican economy and to the United States. Some evidence indicates that the most painful phase of rural restructuring has passed, and that social policy programs are finally reaching the most marginal communities and families, but rural Mexico is still losing population rapidly. At present, however, the cumulative forces of past migration reinforce the choice to migrate northward, as does the dependence on remittances that may take a long time to change.

However, our analysis of the importance of formal sector employment in reducing migration, coupled with a prognosis for ongoing economic liberalization, leads us to forecast economic conditions favorable for the possibility of a long-term decline in northward migration.

This view is supported by most long-run migration projections. They agree that, in the medium-to-long term, Mexico to U.S. migration will slow, although there is disagreement on the timing and size of the reduction. These forecasts are only as accurate as the correctness of their underlying assumptions for the future. At least one of them (by CONAPO), however, is based on sophisticated regressions that incorporate the interplay of the various factors that influence the flow. While always highly fallible, most current forecasts reflect a widespread presumption that, however powerful the forces that will continue to push short-to-medium term migration, the long-term prognosis is for reduction in emigration pressures.

NAFTA has loomed large in appraisals of changing migration dynamics. The treaty went into effect in 1994 and was expected to create jobs in Mexico, raise wages, and eventually decrease unauthorized Mexico-U.S. migration. But an appraisal of NAFTA and its relationship to evolving migration flows should proceed with caution. NAFTA was not the first, and is probably not the main, factor underlying the liberalization of Mexican agriculture, or of the changes and reforms affecting the Mexican economy in general. A number of key changes had taken place long before Mexico and the United States started the negotiations leading to NAFTA, and others followed.

Of course, NAFTA has produced a number of changes. During its first ten years, trade grew at rates three to four times higher than the Mexican GDP. Foreign direct investment (FDI) has also grown rapidly. It has tended to flow to the service sector, but manufacturing has also received consistently increasing amounts of FDI, and these flows are less variable. And there are clear indications that trade and investment are significantly transforming the Mexican economy.

It is valuable to restate the reasons for economic analysis to suggest a short-to-medium term increase in migration with reductions occurring only in the long term. Primarily, the difference in the short-to-medium with long-term expectations is best explained with the migration hump that is an interim increase in migration that precedes slowing migration. A migration hump in response to economic integration between labor-sending and -receiving countries leads to a paradox: the same economic policies that can reduce migration in the long run can increase it in the short run.

Thus, it should not be too surprising that the first decade of NAFTA did not reduce migration and that the other factors mentioned here reinforced that phenomenon, e.g., the strong and diversifying demand of the U.S. economy for low-skilled workers, and the low and variable rates of formal-sector employment growth in Mexico. While economic integration between the two countries, as well as parallel economic liberalization within Mexico, should speed up job growth, they also are forces of "creative destruction" that restructure the economy, streamline private and public employment, moving jobs from one industry to another, and temporarily speed up emigration. At some point, the generation of formal sector jobs in the Mexican economy (see below) should progressively apply the brakes to future migration flows. It is difficult to say when exactly these downward pressures will occur, but once wage differences narrow to four to one or less, and formal-sector job growth offers opportunities at home, the "hope factor" can deter especially irregular migration—most people prefer to stay near family and friends rather than cross national borders.

Although convergence did not occur, NAFTA did strengthen North American integration in practice and, to some extent, in notion. As closer economic integration became a reality, it fostered increasing and deepening dialogue on a number of subjects, including migration. NAFTA may therefore underlie the progress made in the late 1990s, when the two governments signed and implemented a number of administrative agreements for the improvement of migration management, and the negotiations of 2001, which included an ambitious vision for migration and regional development. The fact that these two societies accepted to follow a path of increasing integration should stimulate governments to engage more systematically in other bilateral policy areas, including migration. NAFTA's foremost lesson is that an agreement brought order and regulation to a controversial issue deeply affecting the national economies of North America. When the U.S. Congress approves new legal avenues for migration, we believe Mexico should seek various partial agreements that also bring order to the migration relationship. A unilateral reform is unlikely to succeed, without Mexican cooperation.

POLICY RECOMMENDATIONS

The hope for increased bilateral cooperation was dealt a harsh blow with the tragic events of September 11, 2001, which derailed Mexico-U.S. migration talks. These terrorist attacks led the United States to emphasize its own security, and also shifted its focus of interest from Mexico and Latin America to other regions.

Today, U.S.-Mexico relations show visible strains. Mexico-U.S. unauthorized migration is the most salient source of these strains. U.S. foreign policy has centered on the Middle East and other areas posing considerable risk, but this has hurt the prospects of a better regional future through co-operation. In addition, the repeated failures to achieve consensus on comprehensive reform in the U.S. Congress have created scepticism in both countries about the political will to tackle migration problems.

We propose a way forward for Mexico-U.S. migration management. This way forward is based on the fact of increased North American economic integration, much enhanced cooperation in security matters, and an incremental approach that sets out achievable policies. Integration and cooperation have relied on the establishment of institutions and procedures that, in spite of appearances, have improved binational understanding at various levels. The vast majority of Mexico-U.S. trade and investment transactions now takes place smoothly, and there are working trilateral institutions that allow citizens and firms to solve their differences.

Mexico-U.S. cooperation works in regard to economic integration. This has proved that cooperation is good not only as an abstract principle in country-to-country relations. It has furthered each nation's policy goals and objectives. Cooperation, we believe, will also be key to successful immigration reform in the United States and to improvements in the developmental impact of migration in Mexico.

NAFTA was a significant step forward in North American integration and cooperation. Nevertheless, it alone did not lead to Mexican economic and social convergence with its North American partners. Mexican development remains an unfulfilled Mexican responsibility. Cooperation for the regulation of migration movements must be set in the context of Mexican development policy.

We are proposing that, for the first time, Mexico and the U.S. effectively cooperate in the enforcement of the two countries' migration laws. Unilateral approaches, which understandably arise from each country's priorities and felt needs, must be articulated with bilateral actions ensuring their success. Nevertheless, it is necessary to place this altogether new form of cooperation within a framework that fosters Mexican development that will truly lead to diminished pressures for unauthorized migration in the future. Demographic dynamics, although a positive influence, will not suffice to eliminate this pressure. This framework should include increased and innovative avenues for legal migration, cooperation in border enforcement, new and effective means for workplace enforcement, and a series of welfare-enhancing mechanisms in Mexico. Naturally, the sooner Mexico is able to generate a continuous supply of formal jobs and means of access to welfare for its citizens, the sooner this pressure will ease. We believe there is a growing awareness in Mexican society that the creation of more and better jobs and a more productive rural sector are urgent national priorities. This is so because there is consensus that development, not the export of labor, is Mexico's overriding goal.

Institutionalizing Bilateral Cooperation

Revitalizing the binational dialogue will help find mutually beneficial solutions to the migration challenge

Immigration and border issues have been handled in a working group that focuses specifically on ways that the two countries can cooperate to manage migration and border security. During the immediate post-NAFTA period, the work group[5] met frequently and regularly to ensure continued momentum in discussing areas of both agreement and disagreement. Its role was eclipsed in 2001 by the presidential-level negotiations and the visibility given to a potential broad agreement. It needs to be revitalized. More frequent meetings of the work group on the type of changes outlined in this report could help restart momentum toward a set of achievable agreements. In the medium term, the Binational Commission should include a binational migration mechanism with sufficient authority to agree on administration-wide migration measures, and to oversee their implementation. For the larger, longer-term issues requiring legislation at the federal or state levels, this binational management mechanism should be enlarged to include representatives of both congresses and state governments.

Strengthening and Deepening the Migration Dialogue in North and Central America Will also Provide an Environment Conducive to Beneficial Reforms

The Regional Conference on Migration or *Puebla* Process is and has been a positive forum for migration issues. It opened a very significant means of communication and cooperation and is useful to members. But it is insufficient. A migration subregion has come to comprise mostly the NAFTA partners, but also a number of Central American countries. Governments value *Puebla* as a positive forum for dialogue, nonbinding agreements, and administrative cooperation, but a number of them are eager to deepen their dialogue and their level of commitment. A commitment to a more humane and efficient but safer southern Mexican border calls for the inclusion of Central American countries. A number of Central American countries have deepened their collaboration and agreed on free transit schemes, although implementation has been slow. Countries arriving at this level of cooperation may benefit from an additional bilateral or multilateral mechanism for regulation of migration.

Policy Coordination and Management Must Be Improved at the National Levels to Foster Deeper Bilateral and Regional Collaboration

National-level coordination of migration affairs is necessary for binational cooperation to make any progress in the management of migration.

In Mexico, the secretariats dealing with migrants do come together in various instances. Most notably, the under-secretariat for North America, the under-secretariat for migration affairs, and the National Migration Institute have intensified mutual ad-hoc consultations, and they come together in the National Commission for Mexicans Abroad. However, these instances lack the structure and the authority to create binding agreements, plan their budgets accordingly, and to oversee execution. A national coordination body for migration affairs is urgently needed. In the United States, the Department of Homeland Security has become the principal focal point for immigration, although the departments of Justice, State, and Labor retain important roles in managing migration. Responsibility for immigration is primarily in three bureaus in the DHS: Immigration and Customs Enforcement and Customs and Border Protection share responsibility for enforcement, while Citizenship and Immigration Services has responsibility for immigration and naturalization services. Policy coordination within the DHS and between DHS and the other federal departments is essential to ensuring a coordinated, cohesive response to the challenges posed by migration. These various national instances must improve their level of coordination, and come together at the Binational Commission with an agenda that effectively leads to more relevant administrative decisions and their effective implementation.

Opening New Legal Avenues for Migration

Although a comprehensive change in migration will require policies that address the large unauthorized Mexican population already in the United States, cooperation in the management of temporary worker programs is necessary in the short term, as is a reform of current practices.

Targeted Temporary Worker Programs Will Be Needed to Manage Migration in the Short-to-Medium Terms

Current temporary unskilled migrant programs (H-2A and H-2B) are relatively large, but they have a mixed record in terms of migration management. Also, in spite of their size they fall short of the scale necessary to deal with supply and demand. Additionally, recruitment practices, albeit efficient, tend to trigger new migration flows, to increase total[6] costs and fees to the workers until they match those of undocumented migration—which leads legal temporary workers to overstay,[7]—and to supply workers only to those industries unable to locate willing *undocumented* workers already in the United States. Many workers start migrating under H-2, and then abscond from their jobs in the United States to search for other jobs or migrate again as undocumented workers. Employers face considerable red tape, and many have left the programs. Housing provisions, in particular, pose problems for many smaller companies. The housing boom of 2000–2005 hurt H-2A employers. Some of them resorted to lower-quality housing for the workers.

The Canadian temporary worker program with Mexico, the Caribbean, and most recently, Guatemala deserves to be analyzed closely. It has not triggered undocumented flows, employers and workers are satisfied, and it has had a positive impact on the level of living of the workers and their families in Mexico, helping them to keep their children in school. The "naming" provision means some employers treat their workers with a long-term perspective, as people who will not have to be trained the next year, and who acquire value to them as time goes by. Access to Canadian pensions after the requisite time in the program is also positive, although workers should receive much more advice on this issue from the Canadian authorities. Most workers consider the quality of the services provided by the employer as good. Canadian analysts have criticized it because workers remain unfree. It is virtually impossible for them to move employers if they feel abused. It has mostly been criticized in the United States by its high bureaucratic cost. Verduzco's chapter estimates that this cost is perfectly manageable, and that the Mexican government may therefore be willing to absorb a significant portion of the cost of recruitment provided that workers can be chosen on the basis of technical criteria that can benefit Mexico's poorest regions of emigration. It must be noted, however, that in the current U.S. context the Canadian program would not work. The program relies on the complete or virtually complete inexistence of undocumented agricultural workers. Canadian employers are not free to choose from documented and undocumented pools of workers. As long as U.S. employers have this choice, the Canadian and other models are not feasible options.

Temporary work programs can be successful only if both worker and employer have an incentive to pursue legally sanctioned employment. While many observers apparently believe that large scale temporary programs may effectively displace all unauthorized workers, without border and worksite enforcement it is hard to imagine why many employers would opt for a change from the status quo. Temporary work authorization that spans years and especially work in year-round jobs seems likely to deepen employer dependence on workers, to encourage workers to settle in the United States, and ultimately to foster large-scale permanent populations.

The challenge is to build a new model for temporary worker programs that effectively takes advantage of the lessons learned and the improvements in social, informational, and technological infrastructure that have been developed in the United States and Mexico. New and larger programs must make sure that the *total effective costs* of registering and migrating within the program are significantly lower than those of undocumented migration both for the workers and their employers.[8] They must also assure that jobs are attractive and labor rights are respected, to which end a portable visa is desirable. Portability allows workers to leave abusive work conditions and find jobs with employers who respect their rights, thus lessening the potential market-depressing impact of temporary labor migration. There must also be mechanisms to ensure that work and pay conditions match those offered to other prospective workers. Health costs need to be covered in such a way that employers do not discourage access to medical services or pass the costs on to public programs. In the event of abuse, there need to be appropriate penalties for recruiters and employers who fail to perform, including banishment from the program if the abuses are recurrent or particularly egregious. The penalties should include the local and informal networks of recruiters on which authorized recruiters normally rely, because they are the main actors driving up the cost of recruitment for the workers.

Temporary work programs also need to provide migrants with incentives for return to Mexico in the form of the reimbursement of fees, taxes, and other returnable contributions, to which specific financial incentives for the acquisition of housing and productive assets and the development of micro-enterprises could also be added. The pay should be sufficient that a family's needs and goals in terms of welfare and asset-building are fulfilled after a small number of work stays in the United States, and do not trigger permanent worker dependence on annual labor migration. On the receiving end, temporary work programs should target jobs that are seasonal or time-limited, to avoid having temporary migrants entering for permanent jobs that encourage them to stay.

In the United States, we believe a new, potentially larger temporary worker system should include:

1) Provisions guiding employers clearly and smoothly through the process.
2) Minimum effective earnings provisions. Currently, a minority of employers deducts a large number of goods and services supposedly provided to workers in such a way that effective earnings are extremely low. Labor lawyers have shown Escobar a number of weekly paychecks which, because of various deductions, amount to between $5 and $25 dollars. This is ethically unacceptable, and leads to overstays.
3) Workplace enforcement of immigration law, to avoid incentives to abandoning the program.
4) New provisions for worker health care, possibly of a binational nature.
5) New mechanisms to help reduce future dependence on foreign workers. In too many cases, access to cheap labor impedes investment in a

higher skilled workforce or mechanization that may improve productivity. Fees paid by employers who hire foreign workers could usefully be targeted at exploring alternatives. The residual demand for foreign workers is likely to be lower than current levels and could be handled by new programs.

But the most innovative aspects of management in such a new system lie in Mexico. The Mexican government is able to seriously and transparently improve temporary worker programs by:

1) Providing the analysis to target worker selection in communities where undocumented migration already exists, to avoid creating new flows.
2) Overseeing contracts and their fulfillment.
3) Operating transparent mechanisms for certification of returns, linked to the reimbursement of fees and applicable taxes and contributions. The infrastructure to do this is already available through Mexican social program payrolls linked to production (PROCAMPO)[9] and poverty levels, which are tied to education and health care (*Oportunidades*).[10]
4) Providing effective health coverage to migrant workers' families in Mexico. This can be done through a small fee deducted from the worker's payroll, or else through state-federal agreements (some are already in operation) which provide free access to extensive health care services. The provision of health care guarantees that remittances will not be used for catastrophic expenditures, but instead for the family's well-being and asset building. Mexico has created such a health scheme in the *Seguro Popular*. While its effectiveness must be improved by means of more health infrastructure and personnel, it is exactly the kind of program that can contribute to the well-being of poor and migrant families in general, and to increase the development impact of migration management.
5) Through family fund-matching schemes which increase a migrant's savings when they are devoted to asset building,[11] and eventually,
6) Excluding migrant workers who abandon legal programs from these benefits, as well as employers whose workers fail to return.

We are suggesting programs that are targeted in three senses. First, they would begin with specific economic sectors of the U.S. economy. Second, they would target high emigration Mexican towns and municipalities. Third, they would concentrate on means-tested low-income Mexicans enrolled in social programs.

It would be valuable to test the conditions under which temporary programs might be successful, particularly in industries with a need for truly temporary, seasonal, and "peak season" employment. Developing such programs in industries already highly dependent on undocumented workers would make most sense. As discussed in Susan Martin's chapter, three U.S. industries have repeatedly expressed an interest in participating in such targeted, pilot programs for temporary workers: the U.S. meatpacking industry, multinational hotels/services, and agriculture. Other sectors that are highly dependent on unauthorized workers could be considered as well. This means a successful temporary worker system would need to be tested, and to expand gradually, as these procedures are implemented. In order to maintain continuity in the workforce, unauthorized workers currently employed in these positions would be eligible to convert to a legal status without departing the country. Hence, the focus of the new temporary worker programs would be on the conversion of a largely unauthorized to a largely legal workforce.

Finally, if private recruitment is unable to reform its current undesirable impacts, the Mexican government would be able to develop efficient and transparent mechanisms for recruitment, on the basis of its social program payroll, which includes migration information and is based on household welfare. This would have the added benefit of targeting remittances to poor households. Increased government participation, however, would need to be carefully assessed, since it would quite likely involve subsidies and additional government employment and infrastructure.

The Long-Term Undocumented Mexican Population in the U.S.
Should Receive Authorization to Remain Indefinitely and, If
They Meet the Requirements, to Naturalize as U.S. Citizens

Regularization has been a highly controversial issue in the United States, but legalizing the large unauthorized population is essential to a reformed, legal system of mutually beneficial migration. For a very significant part of the Mexican born, the United States is already their home; they have been there for decades or even grown up there. Many do not speak Spanish fluently. A large proportion live in mixed-legal status families with perhaps only one spouse being undocumented, while one adult may be an LPR, and the couple's children are most often U.S. born. Clearly, it would be nearly impossible for such individuals to readily contemplate returning to Mexico, but a large underclass that is unknown to the government is not in the interest of either nation. Regularizing the status of the millions of unauthorized migrants in the country would bring them out of the shadows and allow them to more fully participate in society. A regularization program should also be inclusive not only of the migrant working in the United States but also his or her immediate family. Otherwise, regularization will lead to new and large backlogs for family reunification that will also encourage new illegal movements.

Phasing in regularization may be the only way to achieve these goals. As discussed below, clearance of the family backlog is an essential first step. Indeed, many Mexicans living illegally in the United States are simply awaiting approval of their applications for family reunification. In this sense they are not undocumented, although they still lack authorization to remain in the United States. When policies promise legal admissions for such close family members, but take years to fulfill, it is not surprising that some applicants resort to unlawful entry instead of waiting for their turn in the queue. One way to humanely address a portion of the undocumented problem would be for the United States to implement a rapid clearance of this backlog and adoption of sufficient admission numbers for spouses and minor children to allow all eligible applicants to receive their green cards within one year of application.

Allowing unauthorized workers to regularize through the recommended new temporary worker programs is a second step. These workers should be allowed to transition to permanent status, however, in recognition of the roots they have already established in the United States. The large, long-term undocumented population is there because job growth has provided them with permanent job opportunities. Temporary worker programs without a mechanism for adjustment to permanent status cannot deal with the growth in permanent jobs. This would entail moving millions of workers annually after a few years in operation. Depriving U.S. employers of this labor would have serious consequences for the U.S. economy. The U.S. economy must learn to moderate its demand for low-skill labor. But this must be a gradual process.

At the same time, incentives similar to those available to temporary workers, but designed carefully to avoid abuse, should be made available by both governments to Mexican undocumented residents of the United States. A portion of this undocumented population would willingly return to Mexico if such incentives are available. Moreover, regularization should be implemented in conjunction with the temporary worker program and new enforcement mechanisms recommended in this report in order to ensure that undocumented migration does not continue, to avoid future large legalizations.

Enforcement

Phase Down Irregular Migration through Cooperation in Border Enforcement

Border corps cannot perform an effective task if jobs are ready and waiting for undocumented migrants. Further massive construction of border barriers, without workplace enforcement, is only likely to create another "rush to migrate," such as the one seen during the early stages of Hold-the-Line, Gatekeeper, and Rio Grande operations. A comprehensive solution to the status quo will be the outcome of growing Mexico-U.S. understanding, and growing administrative cooperation, on migration issues. To the extent that realistic avenues for legal migration can be opened, the Mexican government should involve itself increasingly in the enforcement of emigration.

Up to this moment, the political difficulties involved in Mexican regulation of its population laws have been highlighted. The Mexican government cannot be perceived as blocking its citizens' initiatives to work hard and improve their lives, if jobs are scarce in Mexico, legal avenues for migration are few, and there are many U.S. employers who demand their labor. The Mexican army cannot currently, and probably never should, round up Mexicans simply because they approach the U.S. border. Mexicans living and working on the Mexican side of the border should not be threatened by the authorities. But under an improved migration scenario, the Mexican government should act to regulate emigration.

The *operational* difficulties involved in the enforcement of a 3,000 kilometer border comprising several significant cities are probably as daunting as those relating to politics and human and citizenship rights. But cooperation is viable and necessary.

Away from inspection areas and border cities, there are sufficient humanitarian grounds to intervene both in particularly dangerous areas and in the case of particularly vulnerable persons (pregnant women, minors, the elderly and the ill). The protection of the lives of Mexican nationals calls for this intervention. There should be no entry zones in dangerous areas or during extreme weather. Of course, thought needs to be given to such joint strategies and to the appropriate and incremental phasing in of such efforts.

In the medium term, *once new legal avenues have been implemented and mutual trust has increased*, the only sound operational solution for the extensive common border is to have far increased collaboration between Mexican and U.S. border authorities, with each performing specific tasks in specific areas, or by means of joint patrolling operations, as trust and communication improve. A double border protection corps would be unaffordable to Mexico and redundant: if the two enforcement agencies trust each other, it is unnecessary. If they don't, Mexican enforcement will be useless. A positive initiative in this regard is already underway in the voluntary repatriation program. This program has been criticized in Mexico and its transparency should be maintained and increased, but it has in general afforded vulnerable, ill, penniless, or exhausted migrants apprehended at the border a chance to return home rather than to the Mexican side of the border. Under a scenario of increased avenues for legal migration, Mexican intervention at the Mexican side of the border to help return migrants home on a fully voluntary basis (they have the right to live in border settlements) will be very positive, provided their human rights are fully respected and there are specific incentives to return home.

We are therefore recommending that, for the first time, Mexico engages in a systematic, costly, and politically difficult operation to ensure that, gradually, all emigration takes place legally. But this can only be done if two conditions are satisfied: (1) that there are significant new opportunities for legal labor migration and (2) that Mexico will not have to deal with the job demands of large amounts of deported migrant workers and their families. At the same time, however, a larger responsibility should be shouldered by Mexico with U.S. cooperation: that of providing more and better jobs for Mexican citizens in Mexico.

There Should Be Greater Cooperation at Legal Crossings along the Border

Cooperation at the official border crossings has improved markedly in recent years. More can and should be done to foster cooperation to ensure secure and efficient borders. Increased dedicated commuter lanes should serve the millions of persons who cross regularly to visit family, shop, and work in the other country to do so without undue delays. Increased cooperation between U.S. and Mexican police authorities would further reduce crime and violence along the border, make it more difficult for exploitive smugglers to operate, and encourage migrants to seek lawful mechanisms for admission to the United States. Some of these programs should be targeted at border regions where the economies are becoming more integrated.

Effectively Managing Undocumented Migration Requires Effective Workplace Enforcement

Unauthorized migration is primarily driven by the ability to secure a job in the United States. In a scenario of increased cooperation and increased avenues for legal migration, border enforcement should be complemented by effective mechanisms for workplace enforcement. Efforts to stem illegal migration or to redirect persons seeking work into legal channels are unlikely to succeed without effective mechanisms for workplace enforcement. Employers generally fall into two categories: those who hire unauthorized workers simply because other workers are not available, and those who knowingly target such persons in order to exploit their labor. Worksite enforcement to ensure labor standards and to bring criminal sanctions against traffickers and smugglers is essential not only to stop illegal hiring but also to protect highly vulnerable workers. The United States must institute a workable program of documentation based on secure means of establishing identity, accurate information on authorized status, and universal enforcement regime.

Observers in Mexico and elsewhere have been disappointed that the punishment for migration violations is extremely uneven for employers and workers. Undocumented workers are extremely vulnerable, while employers are practically immune to prosecution. Once new avenues for migration have been opened, and an employee verification system is in place, penalties for both employer and employee should be significant.

New Restrictions on Due Process in Removal Proceedings Should Not Be Adopted as They Are Neither Needed nor Desirable as a Form of Enforcement

Legislation introduced in earlier Congresses that would further erode the due process protections afforded to immigrants in the United States would do little to deter unauthorized migration and much to undermine the rights of foreigners in the United States. Failures to remove unauthorized migrants from the country have far less to do with their access to fair judicial hearings and much more with lack of resources and will to identify and take actions to effect their deportation. When persons ordered removed do not leave the country, it is a management issue, not an excess of due process that allows them to elude deportation.

Developmental Impact

A Twin Goal Is to Increase the Developmental Impact of Migration through Remittances and Returns

The Mexican 3 for 1 program is a best practice. For every dollar that migrant organizations contribute to a public works fund in their hometowns, municipal, state, and federal governments contribute another dollar each. It expanded fourfold from 2001 to 2005, and its procedures have been improved to allow more diaspora projects to be approved and improve supervision. It is still, however, a drop in the ocean. It comprises 0.05 percent of remittances, and its total budget is just over 0.2 percent of the total flow. More funds should be earmarked for 3 for 1 investment in local communities with ongoing outreach to U.S. migrants. It is also likely that government funding should be differentiated, along at least two axes: first, most marginal communities should probably receive larger proportional support than less marginal ones; second, improvements with direct impact on a community's well-being and its chances of development should also be prioritized. The program's rules have been modified to increase the share of investment in highly marginal communities, but developmental investment needs to be further promoted.

Migrants should also have access to matching-fund programs similar to the 3 for 1 initiative, but at a family or household level. Schemes matching migrant savings with a federal or state contribution toward housing, the purchase of productive assets, and retirement will draw back target migrants. Care must be taken, however, not to discriminate against workers who remain in Mexico. They should also have access to these schemes. Access to these migrant schemes should become generalized, on a scale similar to the *Oportunidades* program. The new universal health insurance program for children launched by President Calderón is a positive initiative, although the health expenses and risks faced by the elderly should not be forgotten.

Mexico should also institute procedures and incentives that allow every migrant to develop and carry out plans to bring U.S. earned savings and assets into Mexico, and financing, customs, and administrative mechanisms that render those efforts viable. We are suggesting that, together with regularization, the United States and Mexico offer them options and incentives to return to Mexico, such as the family fund-matching schemes already discussed. Since these long-term migrants tend to possess more experience and assets, their impact upon Mexican towns and villages is likely to be positive. But they should have access to these schemes in towns with greater development potential than their places of birth. A positive factor stimulating return to Mexico would lie in congressional approval of the Mexico-U.S. social security agreement. Mexican workers in the United States who are offered jobs in Mexico would be able to end their working careers in Mexico, and retire there at lower living costs.

We are suggesting that a major factor in emigration is poor access to financing for both "lifetime" assets (housing, pensions) and productive activities. And our work also shows that persons having productive assets in small businesses, whether formal or informal, migrate less. Large schemes that facilitate the acquisition of assets by poor Mexicans will reduce emigration.

Health and Education Cooperation Can and Should Be Increased

The two governments' health and education authorities have engaged in positive exchanges. Agreements have been signed which facilitate information on services available to workers and their families in the United States. A few Mexican primary education teachers travel every year to the United States to aid in the education of Mexican children there, but these programs have scant budgets, extremely small coverage, and little intragovernment clout. The Mexican secretariat of education, for example, is not eager to provide large numbers of teachers to the teacher exchange program in spite of stable or falling demand for them in Mexico due to the falling size of primary education student cohorts, because they feel these teachers are among the best, and often they are unwilling to return to Mexico. In a scenario of increasing regular, and decreasing irregular, migration, bilateral cooperation can help to (a) improve the Spanish skills of teachers in the U.S.; (b) teach English in Mexican schools; (c) further develop and implement binational health expenditure insurance schemes, including those providing effective care to migrant workers.

A Wider Regional Approach May Help to Successfully Implement Significant U.S. Immigration Reforms and Promote Regional Development

Although this study has focused on Mexico-U.S. migration, it is worth considering whether or not Mexico, together with its Central American neighbors, can help implement policies in the region that, together, will enhance the success of major U.S. immigration reforms. Implementation of a number of the above measures on a regional, rather than a national, scale, is likely to enhance the success of reforms, promote Central American development, and diminish the currently significant problems faced by undocumented Central American immigrants as they traverse Mexico toward its northern border.

NOTES

1. The authors thank B. Lindsay Lowell for his contributions to an earlier version of this chapter that appeared as the Executive Summary of the project report.
2. Nasdaq crashed in April 2000.
3. This cannot be stated with certainty. Falling apprehensions suggest, but do not establish, that the total flows are smaller.
4. Rural poverty rates increased unexpectedly from 2004 to 2005. This may reflect the impact of two major hurricanes, which drastically reduced crops and local employment prospects for many rural Mexicans. While this could be a short-term variation, it nevertheless highlights the vulnerability of poor Mexicans to major weather events and other changes, such as desertification.
5. The working group dealt with migration and consular affairs.
6. In addition to the fees officially charged by registered recruiters, workers pay a large number of other fees, which lead them to a total close to U.S. $2,000.
7. We have come across frequent evidence of H-2 worker overstays.
8. And consequently, that migrants will cover their expenses and be able to save money in a single season.
9. PROCAMPO provides cash transfers to farmers. There is a parallel system targeted at subsistence farmers, called *"Crédito a la palabra."*
10. *Oportunidades* has been in operation for nine years, and it is an extremely efficient and transparent program that has served as a model for cash transfer programs in more than ten countries. Today, it provides cash transfers and other

benefits to five million poor Mexican families, in the rural and urban sectors. In addition, it manages a seven million household database, which includes migration data. Each household's compliance to program rules is processed every two months. It requires that family members attend health talks and check-ups, which is useful in order to certify migrants' returns.

11. A new component of the *Oportunidades* program is precisely a scheme that promotes savings among poor families, by doubling the amount saved in a certain fund.

Bibliography

Airola, Jim, and Chinhui Juhn. "Wage inequality in post-reform Mexico." Working Paper 2005-01, Department of Economics, University of Houston, 2005.

Alba, Francisco. "El Tratado de Libre Comercio y la emigración de mexicanos a Estados Unidos." *Comercio Exterior* 43, no. 8, (August 1993): 743–49.

———. "Migración internacional: consolidación de los patrones emergentes." *DEMOS: Carta demográfica sobre México*, no. 13 (2000): 10–11.

——— . "El Tratado de Libre Comercio, la migración y las políticas migratorias." Pp. 215–42, in *Diez años del TLCAN en México. Una perspectiva analítica*, edited by Enrique R. Cásares and Horacio Sobarzo. México: Fondo de Cultura Económica, 2004.

Alba, Francisco, Sydney Weintraub, Rafael Fernández de Castro, and Manuel García y Griego. "Responses to Migration Issues." Pp. 437–509, in *Binational Study. Migration between Mexico and the United States Vol. I*. Austin: Commission for Immigration Reform—Foreign Affairs Secretariat, 1997.

Aleinikoff, Alexander. "No Illusions: Paradigm Shifting on Mexican Migration to the United States in the Post-9/11 World." *U.S. Mexico Policy Bulletin*, no. 5, Wilson Center (June 2005). http://www.wilsoncenter.org/topics/pubs/MexicoPolicyBulletin .Aleinikoff.Immig.May.pdf.

Angelucci, Manuela. "Aid and Migration: An Analysis of the Impact of *Progresa* on the Timing and Size of Labour Migration." IZA Discussion Paper no. 1187, 2004.

Ayón, David R., "La política mexicana y la movilización de los migrantes mexicanos en Estados Unidos," paper presented at the meeting of the Latin American Studies Association, San Juan, Puerto Rico, March 15–18, 2006.

Badillo Bautista, Celia. "Evaluating the Direct and Indirect Effects of a Conditional Cash Transfer Program: The case of Progresa." Ph.D. dis., University of Essex, forthcoming.

Banco de México. "Informe Anual." Banco de México, 2005–2006. http://www .banxico.org.mx/publicadorFileDownload/download?documentId={5AA1E2B9 -58FE-147D-C97B-6B9E7406630B}.

Banerjee, Biswajit. "The Role of the Informal Sector in the Migration Process: A Test of Probabilistic Migration Models and Labour Market Segmentation for India." *Oxford Economic Papers* 35 (1983): 399–422.

Basok, Tanya. "Canada's Temporary Migration Program: A Model Despite Flaws." *Migration Information Source*, November 2007. http://www.migrationinformation .org/Feature/display.cfm?id=650

Bean, Frank D., Roland Chanove, Robert G. Cushing, Rodolfo de la Garza, Gary P. Freeman, Charles W. Haynes, and David Spener. *Illegal Mexican Migration and the United States/Mexico Border: The Effect of Operation Hold the Line on El Paso/Juarez.* Population Research Center, University of Texas at Austin and U.S. Commission on Immigration Reform (U.S. Commission on Immigration Reform), 1994.

Bean, Frank D., Barry Edmonston, and Jeffrey S. Passel, eds. *Undocumented Migration to the United States: IRCA and the Experience of the 1980s.* Washington, D.C.: RAND and The Urban Institute, JRI-07, 1990.

Bean, Frank D., and B. Lindsay Lowell. "NAFTA and Mexican Migration to the United States." Pp. 263–84, in *NAFTA's Impact on North America*, edited by Sidney Weintraub. Washington, D.C.: Center for Strategic and International Studies, 2004.

Bean, Frank D., and Gillian Stevens. *America's Newcomers and the Dynamics of Diversity.* New York: Russell Sage, 2003.

Bendesky, León, Enrique de la Garza, Javier Melgoza, and Carlos Salas. *La industria maquiladora de exportación: mitos y realidades.* Mexico City: Instituto de Estudios Laborales, 2003.

Borjas, George J. "The Economics of Immigration." *Journal of Economic Literature* 32, no. 4 (December 1994): 1167–717.

———. "The Labor Demand Curve is Downward Sloping: Re-examining the Impact of Immigration on the Labor Market." *Quarterly Journal of Economics* 118, no. 4 (November 2003): 1335–374.

Broadway, Michael, and Terry Ward. "Recent Changes in the Structure and Location of the U.S. Meatpacking Industry." *Geography* 75, no. 1 (1990): 76–79.

Calvo, Guillermo. "Urban Unemployment and Wage Determination in LDC'S: Trade Unions in the Harris-Todaro Model." *International Economic Review* 19, no. 1 (1978): 65–81.

Canales, Alejandro I. "Remesas, desarrollo y pobreza en México. Una visión crítica." Guadalajara: Centro de Estudios de Población/Universidad de Guadalajara, Forthcoming.

CERC (Competitive Edge Research & Communication, Inc.). "Competitive Edge Research Immigration Poll—October, 2004." San Diego: CERC, 2004. http://www .cerc.net/.

Cerrutti, Marcela, and Douglas S. Massey. "On the Auspices of Female Migration From Mexico to the United States." *Demography* 38, no. 2 (2001): 187–200.

CIR/SRE (Commission for Immigration Reform, Secretaría de Relaciones Exteriores). *First Binational Study of México-US Migration.* Washington, D.C., Mexico City, 1997.

Cleveland, Lisa, John Gunnell, Salvatore Restifo, and Jason Russo. *Running for the Border: The Impact of Privatizing Essential Services in Mexico on Patterns of Mexican Migration.* Arizona State University West, 2001.

CLINIC (Catholic Legal Immigration Network, Inc.). "Chaos on the U.S.-Mexico Border: A Report on Migrant Crossing Deaths, Immigrant Families and Subsistence-Level Laborers." Report no. 5, 2004.

Colegio de la Frontera Norte, El. "Evaluación del Programa Paisano." 2005. http://www.paisano.gob.mx/evaluacion.php

Comité Técnico para la Medición de la Pobreza en México. *Medición de la pobreza 2002–2004*. Mexico City: Author 2005.

Commission for the Study of International Migration and Cooperative Economic Development. *Unauthorized Migration: An Economic Development Response*. Washington, D.C.: U.S. Government Printing Office, 1990.

Cornelius, Wayne A. "California Immigrants Today." In *California Immigrants in World Perspective: The Conference Papers*, Institute for Social Science Research, 1990. http://repositories.cdlib.org/issr/volume5/10.

Corona Vázquez, Rodolfo. "Magnitud de la migración mexicana en años recientes." Paper presented at the Congreso Nacional sobre Migración, Guadalajara, Mexico, November 21–23, 2002.

Coronado, Roberto, and Pia M. Orrenius. "The Impact of Illegal Immigration and Enforcement on Border Crime Rates." The Federal Reserve Bank of Dallas–El Paso Branch, Working paper 0303, 2003.

Costanzo, Joseph, Cynthia J. Davis, Caribert Irazi, Daniel M. Goodkind, and Roberto R. Ramirez. "Evaluating Components of International Migration: The Residual Foreign Born." Washington, D.C.: U.S. Census Bureau, 2002.

Cragg, Michael Ian, and Mario Epelbaum. "Why has wage dispersion grown in Mexico? Is it the incidence of reforms or the growing demand for skills?" *Journal of Development Economics* 51 (1996): 99–116.

Davis, Benjamin, Guy Stecklov, and Paul Winters. "Domestic and international migration from rural Mexico: Disaggregating the effects of network structure and composition." *Population Studies* 56, no.3 (November 2002): 291–309.

Deardorff, Kevin E., and Lisa M. Blumerman. "Evaluating Components of International Migration: Estimates of the Foreign-Born Population by Migrant Status in 2000." Washington, D.C.: U.S. Census Bureau, 2001.

Durand, Jorge. "From Traitors to Heroes: 100 Years of Mexican Migration Policies." *Migration Information Source*, March 2004. http://www.migrationinformation.org/Feature/display.cfm?ID=203

Durand, Jorge, Douglas S. Massey, and Fernando Charvet. "The Changing Geography of Mexican Immigration to the United States: 1910-1996." *Social Science Quarterly* 81, no. 1 (2000): 1–15.

Durand, Jorge, Douglas S. Massey, and René M. Zenteno. "Mexican Immigration to the United States: Continuities and Changes." *Latin American Research Review* 36, no. 1 (2001): 107–26.

The Economist. "Immigration. Opening the Door." *The Economist* 365, no. 8297 (November 2002): 11.

Escobar Latapí, Agustín. "Propuestas para la legalización del mercado de trabajo agrícola binacional." Pp. 45–61, in *Migración México-Estados Unidos. Opciones de política*, edited by Rodolfo Tuirán. Mexico City: CONAPO, 2000.

———. "Migración y seguridad en la política exterior mexicana." *Revista Mexicana de Política Exterior*, no. 70 (February 2004): 85–98.

262 Bibliography

———. "Pobreza y migración internacional: propuestas conceptuales, primeros hallazgos." Pp. 97–128, in *Los rostros de la pobreza. El debate, Volume IV*, edited by Mónica Gendreau. Puebla: Universidad Iberoamericana, 2005.

———. *Pobreza y migración internacional.* Mexico Ciaty: CIESAS-PREM, 2008.

Escobar Latapí, Agustín, and Eric Janssen. "Migration, the Diaspora and Development. The Case of Mexico." IILS (ILO) Discussion Paper 167, Geneva, 2006.

———. "Remesas y costo de oportunidad: el caso mexicano." Pp. 345–64, in *Pobreza y migración internacional*, edited by Agustín Escobar Latapí. Mexico City: CIESAS-PREM, 2008.

Eschbach, Karl, Jacqueline Hagan, and Nestor Rodríguez. "Deaths During Undocumented Migration: Trends and Policy Implications in the New Era of Homeland Security." *Defense of the Alien* 26 (2003): 37–52.

Escobar Latapí, Agustín, and Bryan Roberts. "Urban stratification, the middle classes and economic change in Mexico." Pp. 91–113, in *Social Responses to Mexico's Economic Crisis*, edited by Mercedes González de la Rocha and Agustín Escobar. La Jolla: Center for U.S.-Mexican Studies, University of California San Diego, 1991.

———. "Mexican Social and Economic Policy and Emigration." Pp. 47–78, in *At the Crossroads: Mexico and U.S. Immigration Policy*, edited by Frank D. Bean, Rodolfo de la Garza, Bryan Roberts, and Sidney Weintraub. Boston: Rowman & Littlefield, 1997.

Esquivel, Gerardo, and Miguel Messmacher. "Economic Integration and Sub-national Development: The Mexican Experience with NAFTA." Paper presented at the Conference *Spatial Inequality in Latin America*, Universidad de las Américas-Puebla/WIDER/Cornell/LSE, November 2002.

Fallon, Peter R., and Robert E. B. Lucas. "The Impact of Financial Crises on Labor Markets, Household Incomes, and Poverty: A Review of Evidence." *The World Bank Research Observer* 17, no. 1 (2002): 21–45.

Feenstra, Robert C., and Gordon Hanson. "Globalization, Outsourcing and Wage Inequality." NBER Working Paper No. 5424, Cambridge, MA: National Bureau of Economic Research, 1996.

Feliciano, Zadia M. "Workers and Trade Liberalization: The Impact of Trade Reforms in Mexico on Wages and Employment." Working Paper, Harvard University, 1994.

Fernández de Castro, Rafael, and Andrés Rozenthal. "El amor, la decepción y cómo aprovechar la realidad." Pp. 107–19, in *México en el Mundo: En la Frontera del Imperio*, edited by Rafael Fernández de Castro. Mexico City: Planeta, 2003.

García, Brígida. "Medición del empleo y el desempleo. Indicadores complementarios." *DEMOS: Carta demográfica sobre México*, no. 5 (2002): 5–6.

García y Griego, Manuel. "La emigración mexicana y el Tratado de Libre Comercio en América del Norte: dos argumentos." Pp. 291–304, in *Liberación económica y libre comercio en América del Norte*, edited by Gustavo Vega. Mexico City: El Colegio de México, 1993.

Gathmann, Christina. "The Effects of Enforcement on Illegal Markets: Evidence from Migrant Smuggling along the Southwestern Border." IZA Discussion Paper No. 1004, 2004.

González Gutiérrez, Carlos, "Del acercamiento a la inclusión institucional: la experiencia del Instituto de los Mexicanos en el exterior." Pp. 181–220, in *Relaciones*

Estado–Diáspora. Perspectivas de América Latina y el Caribe, edited by Carlos González Gutiérrez. Mexico City: Miguel Angel Porrúa, 2006.

Gozdziak, Elzbieta, and Susan F. Martin, eds. *New Immigrant Communities: Addressing Integration Challenges.* Lanham, Md.: Lexington Books, 2005.

Guzman, Mark G., Joseph H. Haslag, and Pia M. Orrenius. "Coyote Crossings: The Role of Smugglers in Illegal Immigration and Border Enforcement." The Federal Reserve Bank of Dallas, Working Paper 0201, 2002.

Hanson, Gordon. "What has happened to wages in Mexico since NAFTA? Implications for Hemispheric Free Trade." NBER Working Paper No. 9563. Cambridge, Mass.: National Bureau of Economic Research, 2003.

Hecker, Daniel. "Occupational Employment Projections to 2012." *Monthly Labor Review* 127, no 2 (February 2004): 80–105.

Hemming, Ethan, and N. Prabha Unnithan. "Determinants of Privatization Levels in Developing Countries." *Social Science Quarterly* 77, no. 2 (June 1996): 434–44.

Hernández Licona, Gonzalo. "Oferta laboral familiar y desempleo en Mexico: los efectos de la pobreza." *El Trimestre Económico* LXIV(4), no. 258 (1997): 531–68.

Hinojosa-Ojeda, Raúl, and Sherman Robinson. "Labor Issues in a North American Free Trade Area." Pp. 69–108, in *North American Free Trade: Assessing the Impact,* edited by Nora Lustig, Barry P. Bosworth, and Robert Z. Lawrence. Washington, D.C.: The Brookings Institution, 1992.

Hollmann, Frederick W., Tammany J. Mulder, and Jeffrey E. Kallan. "Methodology and Assumptions for the Population Projections of the United States: 1999 to 2100." *U.S. Bureau of the Census. Population Division Working Paper* no. 38, Januar, 2000.

Hufbauer, Gary, and Jeffrey Schott. *North American Free Trade: Issues and Recommendations.* Washington, D.C.: Institute for International Economics, 1992.

IFE (Instituto Federal Electoral). "Informe de los resultados de la votación emitida por los mexicanos residentes en el extranjero." Mexico City: IFE, 2006.

Huntington, Samuel. *Who Are We? The Challenges to America's National Identity.* New York: Simon & Schuster, 2004.

IME (Instituto de los mexicanos en el exterior). "Recomendaciones de la I reunión ordinaria del CCIME." 2003. http://portal.sre.gob.mx/ime/index.php?option =displaypage &Itemid

———. "Recomendaciones de la II reunión ordinaria del CCIME." 2003. http://portal .sre.gob.mx/ime/index.php?option=displaypage&Itemid.

———. "Recomendación del CC - IME.13/econ/sedesol "revisar reglas de operación del programa de atención a migrantes 3 X 1 y describir las principales razones por las cuales se rechazan los proyectos." 2003. http://portal.sre.gob.mx/ime/recomen daciones/cc_ime_i _13-con-sedesol.thm

———. "Recomendación del CC-IME 1.95/com/SSA, "crear un seguro de salud binacional para mexicanos documentados e indocumentados." 2003. http://portal.sre .gob.mx/ime/recomendaciones/cc_ime_i_95_com_ssa.htm

———. "¿Qué es el CCIME?" 2005. http://www.ime.gob.mx/ccime/ccime.htm

INEGI (Instituto Nacional de Estadística, Geografía e Informática). *Conteo de Población y Vivienda 1995. Resultados definitivos.* Mexico City: INEGI, 1996.

———. *Encuesta nacional de la dinámica demográfica 1997 (ENADID).* Mexico City: INEGI, 1997.

——. *XII Censo General de Población y Vivienda 2000.* Mexico City: INEGI, 2000.

——. *Encuesta Nacional de Empleo 2002 (ENE).* Mexico City: INEGI, 2002.

Jachimowicz, Maia. "Bush Proposes New Temporary Worker Program." *Migration Information Source,* February 1, 2004. http://www.migrationinformation.org/Feature/display.cfm?ID=202.

Justich, Robert, and Betty Ng. "The Underground Labor Force Is Rising to the Surface." Bear Stearns Asset Management, January 3, 2005.

Kanaiaupuni, Shawn M. "Reframing the migration question: an analysis of men, women and gender in Mexico." *Social Forces* 78, no. 4 (June 2000): 1311–348.

Lederman, Daniel, William Maloney, and Luis Servèn. *Lessons from NAFTA for Latin America and the Caribbean.* Washington, D.C.: The World Bank and Stanford University Press, 2005.

Leiken, Robert S. "Enchilada Lite: A Post-9/11 Mexican Migration Agreement." Report, Center for Immigration Studies, Washington, D.C., March 2002. http://www.cis.org/articles/2002/leiken.pdf.

Levy, Santiago, and Sweder van Wijnbergen. *Labor Markets, Migration and Welfare: Agriculture in the Mexico-USA Free Trade Agreement.* Washington, D.C.: World Bank, 1991.

——. "Mexican Agriculture in the Free Trade Agreement: Transition Problems in Economic Reform." OECD Development Centre Working Paper no. 63, Paris, 1992.

López E., Mario. "Remesas de mexicanos en el exterior y su vinculación con el desarrollo económico, social y cultural de sus regiones de origen." *Estudios sobre migraciones Internacionales* 59, OIT/ILO, 2002.

Lowell, B. Lindsay. "Circular Mobility, Migrant Communities, and Policy Restrictions: Unauthorized Flows from Mexico." Pp. 137–58, in *Migration, Population Structure, and Redistribution Policies,* edited by Calvin Goldsheider. Boulder: Westview Press, 1992.

Lowell, B. Lindsay, and Frank D. Bean. "Does the Wave Change? Reinvestigating Mexican Migration in the 1990s." Paper presented at the Meetings of the Population Association of America, Atlanta, May 2002.

Marcelli, Enrico, and Wayne A. Cornelius. "The Changing Profile of Mexican Migrants to the United States: New Evidence from California and Mexico." *Latin American Research Review* 36, no. 3 (fall 2001): 105–31.

Marcelli, Enrico A., and Paul M. Ong. "2000 Census Coverage of Foreign-born Mexicans Residing in Los Angeles County: Implications for Demographic Analysis." Paper presented at the Meetings of the Population Association of America, Atlanta, May 2002.

Martin, David A. "Twilight Statuses: A Closer Examination of the Unauthorized Population." Migration Policy Institute. 2006. http://www.migrationpolicy.org/ITFIAF/publications.php.

Martin, Philip. *Trade and Migration: NAFTA and Agriculture.* Washington, D.C.: Institute for International Economics, 1993.

——. "Good intentions gone awry: IRCA and U.S. agriculture." *The Annals of the Academy of Political and Social Science* 534 (July 1994): 44–57.

——. "Migration and Development: The Mexican Case." Pp. 181–198, in *La migración internacional y el desarrollo en las Américas,* edited by CEPAL, Santiago, Chili: CEPAL, 2001.

———. *Promise Unfulfilled: Unions, Immigration, and Farm Workers.* Ithaca: Cornell University Press, 2003.

———. "Economic Integration and Migration: The Mexico-U.S. Case." World Institute for Development Economics Research Discussion Paper no. 2003/35, United Nations University, 2003.

Martin, Philip, and Alan L. Olmstead. "The agricultural mechanization controversy." *Science* 227, no. 4687 (February 1985): 601–6.

Martin, Philip, and Michael S. Teitelbaum. "The Mirage of Mexican Guest Workers." *Foreign Affairs* 80, no. 6 (November/December 2001): 117–31.

Martin, Susan. "Politics and Policy Responses to Illegal Migration in the U.S." Paper presented at the Conference on Managing Migration in the 21st Century, Hamburg, Germany, June 21–23, 1998. Available at http://isim.georgetown.edu/ Publications/SusanPubs/SMartin_PoliticsAndPolicy.pdf.

———. "The Politics of U.S. Immigration Reform." Pp. 132–49, in *The Politics of Migration: Managing Opportunity, Conflict and Change,* edited by Sarah Spencer. Malden, Mass.: Blackwell Publishing, 2003.

Martínez C., Enrique. "Emigrar por desesperación: Progresa y la migración interna e internacional." Pp. 95–116, in "Logros y retos: una evaluación cualitativa de Progresa en México," edited by Agustín Escobar and Mercedes González de la Rocha, Pp. 1–131 in *Progresa: Más oportunidades para las Familias Pobres. Evaluación de Resultados del programa de Educación, Salud y Alimentación. Impacto a nivel comunitario.* Mexico City: Secretaría de Desarrollo Social, 2000.

Martínez Pellegrini, Sara, Carla Pederzini V., and Liliana Meza González. "Autoempleo como mecanismo de arraigo de la población en México: el caso de cuatro localidades." *Revista de Estudios Urbanos y Demográficos* 21, no. 3 (September–December 2006): 547–623.

Massey, Douglas S. "Backfire at the Border: Why Enforcement without Legalization Cannot Stop Illegal Immigration." Washington, D.C.: CATO Institute, 2005.

Massey, Douglas S., Joaquín Arango, Graeme Hugo, Ali Kouaouci, Adela Pellegrino, and J. Edward Taylor. "Theories of International Migration: A Review and Appraisal." *Population and Development Review* 19, no. 3 (1993): 431–66.

———. "An Evaluation of International Migration Theory: The North American Case." *Population and Development Review* 20, no. 4 (1994): 699–751.

Massey, Douglas S., Jorge Durand, and Nolan J. Malone. *Beyond Smoke and Mirrors: Mexican Immigration in an Era of Economic Integration.* New York: Russell Sage Foundation, 2003.

Massey, Douglas S., Kirstin E. Espinosa, and Jorge Durand. "Dinámica migratoria entre México y Estados Unidos." Pp. 49–67, in *Población, desarrollo y globalización,* edited by René Zenteno. Mexico City: Sociedad Mexicana de Demografía/El Colegio de la Frontera Norte, 1998.

Massey, Douglas S., and Rene Zenteno. "The Dynamics of Mass Migration." *Proceedings of the National Academy of Sciences* 96, no. 8 (1999): 5325–335.

Meissner, Doris. "Managing Migrations." *Foreign Policy,* no. 86 (Spring 1992): 66–83.

———. "U.S. Temporary Worker Programs: Lessons Learned." *Migration Information Source,* March 1, 2004. http://www.migrationinformation.org/Feature/display .cfm?ID=205.

Meza González, Liliana. "Cambios en la Estructura Salarial de México en el periodo 1988–1993 y el aumento en el rendimiento de la educación superior." *El Trimestre Económico* LXVI (2), no. 262 (April-June 1999): 189–226.

———. "Mercados laborales locales y desigualdad salarial en México." *El Trimestre Económico* LXXII, no. 285 (January–March 2005): 133–78.

MGT of America. "Medical Emergency: Costs of Uncompensated Care in Southwest Border Counties." Report. Washington, D.C.: United States/Mexico Border Counties Coalition, 2002.

Mundell, Robert A., "International Trade and Factor Mobility." *American Economic Review* 47, no. 1 (June 1957): 321–35.

Myers, Dowell. "The Impact of Ebbing Immigration in Los Angeles: New Insights from an Established Gateway." Paper presented at the Population Association of America, Philadelphia, April 2005.

Navarro S., Alejandra. "Mirando el sol: hacia una configuración del proceso migratorio hacia los Estados Unidos," B.A. diss., ITESO, 1998.

Neufeld, Lynnette, Daniela Sotres A., Paul Gertler, Lizbeth Tolentino M., Jorge Jiménez R., Lia Fernald, Salvador Villalpando, Teresa Shamah, and Juan Rivera Dommarco. "Impacto de Oportunidades en el crecimiento y estado nutricional de niños en zonas rurales," Chapter I, Pp. 15–50, in *Evaluación externa de impacto del Programa Oportunidades 2004, Vol. III Alimentación*, edited by Bernardo Hernández Prado and Mauricio Hernández Ávila, Mexico City: Instituto Nacional de Salud Pública (INSP), 2005.

Nevins, Joseph. "Thinking Out of Bounds: A Critical Analysis of Academic and Human Rights Writings on Migrant Deaths in the U.S.-Mexico Border Region." *Migraciones Internacionales* 2, no. 2 (2003): 171–90.

Orozco, Manuel. "Hometown associations and their present and future partnerships: new development opportunities?" Report Commissioned by the U.S. Agency for International Development. Inter-American Dialogue, Washington, D.C., 2003.

Orrenius, Pia M. "The Effect of U.S. Border Enforcement on the Crossing Behavior of Mexican Migrants." Pp. 281–290, in *Crossing the Border: Research from the Mexican Migration Project*, edited by Jorge Durand and Douglas S. Massey. New York: Russell Sage Foundation, 2004.

PAHO (Pan American Health Organization). "Leading Causes of Mortality on the United States–Mexico Border." *Epidemiological Bulletin* 20, no. 2, (June 1999): 1–5.

Passel, Jeffrey S. "Unauthorized Migrants: Numbers and Characteristics." Report. Washington, D.C.: Pew Hispanic Center, 2005. http://pewhispanic.org/files/reports/46.pdf

———. "The Size and Characteristics of the Unauthorized Population in the U.S." Report. Washington, D.C.: Pew Hispanic Center, March 2006. http://pewhispanic.org/files/reports/61.pdf

Passel, Jeffrey S., and Roberto Suro. "Rise, Peak, and Decline: Trends in U.S. Immigration 1992–2004." A Pew Hispanic Center Report, 2005. http://pewhispanic.org/files/reports/53.pdf

Passel, Jeffrey S., Jennifer Van Hook, and Frank D. Bean. "Estimates of Legal and Unauthorized Foreign Born Population for the United States and Selected States,

Based on Census 2000." Report to the Census Bureau. Washington, D.C.: Urban Institute, 2004. http://www.sabresys.com/i_whitepapers.asp

Passel, Jeffrey S., and Wendy Zimmerman. "Are Immigrants Leaving California? Settlement Patterns of Immigrants in the Late 1990s." Paper presented at the meetings of the Population Association of America, Los Angeles, 2000.

Portes, Alejandro, and Robert L. Bach. *Latin Journey: Cuban and Mexican Immigrants in the United States*. Berkeley: University of California Press, 1985.

Reyes, Belinda I. "U.S. Immigration Policy and the Duration of Undocumented Trips." Pp. 299–320, in *Crossing the Border: Research from the Mexican Migration Project*, edited by Jorge Durand and Douglas S. Massey. New York: Russell Sage Foundation, 2004.

Reyes, Belinda I., Hans P. Johnson, and Richard Van Swearingen. *Holding the Line? The Effect of Recent Border Build-up on Unauthorized Immigration*. San Francisco: Public Policy Institute of California, 2002.

Reyes Heroles, Jesús. *Política macroeconómica y bienestar en México*. Mexico City: Fondo de Cultura Económica, 1983.

Reynolds, Clark W. "Will a Free Trade Agreement Lead to Wage Convergence? Implications for Mexico and the United States." Pp. 477–86, in *U.S.-Mexico Relations: Labor Market Interdependence*, edited by Jorge Bustamante, Clark W. Reynolds, and Raúl Hinojosa-Ojeda. Stanford, CA.: Stanford University Press, 1992.

Reynolds, Clark W., and Robert K. McCleery. "Modeling U.S.-Mexico economic linkages." *The American Economic Review* 75, no. 2, Papers and Proceedings of the Ninety-Seventh Annual Meeting of the American Economic Association (May 1985): 217–22.

Richter, Susan M., Edward J. Taylor, and Antonio Yúñez-Naude. "Impacts of Policy Reforms on Labor Migration from Rural Mexico to the United States." NBER Working Paper no. W11428, 2005.

Riding, Alan. *Distant Neighbors: A Portrait of the Mexicans*. New York: Alfred A. Knopf, 1985.

Riosmena, Fernando. "Return versus Settlement among Undocumented Mexican Migrants." Pp. 265–80, in *Crossing the Border: Research from the Mexican Migration Project*, edited by Jorge Durand and Douglas S. Massey. New York: Russell Sage Foundation, 2004.

Robertson, Raymond. "Wage Shocks and North American Labor Market Integration." *American Economic Review* 90, no. 4 (September 2000): 742–64.

Salinas de Gortari, Carlos. "TLC ayer, hoy y mañana." *Enfoque, Reforma*, December 15, 2002.

Samora, Julián. *Los Mojados: The Wetback Story*. Notre Dame, Ind: University of Notre Dame Press, 1971.

SEDESOL (Secretaría de Desarrollo Social). "Iniciativa Ciudadana 3 X 1. Cumplimiento de objetivos y metas." 2004. www.sedesol.gob.mx/cuentas/reporte_cuarto _trimestre_2003/06IniciativaCiudadana.pdf.

———. "Iniciativa Ciudadana 3 X 1. Cumplimiento de objetivos y metas." 2005. www.sedesol.gob.mx/cuentas/reporte_ tercer_trimestre_2004/05IniciativaCiudadana.pdf

Serrano, Javier. "El sueño mexicano: El retorno imaginado en las migraciones internacionales de Tapalpa y Tlacotalpan." Ph.D. diss. CIESAS, Guadalajara, 2006.

Smith, James P., and Barry Edmonston, eds. *The Immigration Debate: Economic, Demographic and Fiscal Effects of Immigration.* Washington, D.C.: National Research Council, 1997.

Sohn, Jon, and Stephanie Hayes. "Making Privatization Work." Friends of the Earth Review, Unpublished Report, Washington, D.C., 1999.

SRE (Secretaría de Relaciones Exteriores). "Evaluación del Programa de Repatriaciones al Interior México-Estados Unidos 2005." Report, Mexico City: SRE, 2006. www.sre.gob.mx/servicios/documentos/ eval_final05.doc.

Stark, Oded. *Economic-Demographic Interactions in the Course of Agricultural Development: The Case of Rural-to-Urban Migration.* Rome: Food and Agriculture Organization of the United Nations, 1978.

Stark, Oded, Edward Taylor, and Shlomo Yitzhaki. "Remittances and inequality." *The Economic Journal* 96, no. 383 (September 1986): 722–40.

Stecklov, Guy, Paul Winters, Marco Stampini, and Benjamin Davis. "Do Conditional Transfers Influence Migration? A Study Using Experimental Data from the Mexican Progresa Program." *Demography* 42, no. 4 (2005): 769–90.

Stoops, Nicole. "Educational Attainment in the United States: 2003." *Annual Social and Economic Supplement,* U.S. Census Bureau (2004): 20–550.

Stull, Donald D., Michael J. Broadway, and David Griffith. *Any Way You Cut It: Meat Processing in Small-Town America.* Lawrence: University Press of Kansas, 1995.

Suro, Roberto, and B. Lindsay Lowell. "Highs to Lows: Latino Economic Losses in Today's Recession." Report, Washington, DC:, Pew Hispanic Center, 2002. http://pewhispanic.org/files/reports/1.pdf.

Szasz, Ivonne. "La perspectiva de genero en el Estudio de la Migración Femenina en Mexico." Pp. 167–210, in *Mujeres, Género, y Población en México,* edited by Brígida García. Mexico City: El Colegio de México/Sociedad Mexicana de Demografía, 1999.

Szekely, Miguel. *Hacia una nueva generación de política social.* Mexico City: Secretaría de Desarrollo Social, 2002.

Taylor, J. Edward. "Undocumented Mexico-U.S. migration and the returns to households in rural Mexico." *American Journal of Agricultural Economics* 69 (1987): 626–38.

Taylor, J. Edward, Phil L. Martin, and Michael Fix. *Poverty amid Prosperity: Immigration and the Changing Face of Rural California.* Washington, D.C.: The Urban Institute Press, 1997.

Thomas-Hope, Elizabeth. "Emigration Dynamics in the Anglophone Caribbean." Pp. 232–84, in *Emigration Dynamics in Developing Countries: Mexico, Central America and the Caribbean, Volume III,* edited by Reginald Appleyard. Aldershot, U.K.: Ashgate Publishing Ltd., 1999.

Tichenor, Daniel. *Dividing Lines: the Politics of Immigration Control in America.* Princeton University Press, 2002.

Trilateral Commission, *The (A Report to . . .). International Migration Challenges in a New Era.* New York: The Trilateral Commission, 1993.

Tuirán, Rodolfo. "Migración, remesas y desarrollo." Pp. 77–87, in *La situación demográfica de México 2002.* Mexico City: Consejo Nacional de Población, 2002.

Tuirán, Rodolfo, Virgilio Partida, and José Luis Ávila. "Las causas de la migración hacia Estados Unidos." Pp. 53–75, in *Migración México-Estados Unidos. Presente y fu-*

turo, edited by Rodolfo Tuirán. Mexico City: Consejo Nacional de Población, 2000.

United Nations. *World Population Prospects: The 2002 Revision, Volume II: The Sex and Age Distribution of Populations.* New York: UN, 2002.

Unger, Kurt. "Regional economic development and Mexican out-migration." NBER Working Paper no. 11432, 2005. http://www.nber.org/papers/w11432.

———. "El desarrollo de las regiones y la migración mexicana: origen, evolución y política pública." Pp. 247–268, in *Migración México-Estados Unidos, implicaciones y retos para ambos países*, edited by Elena Zúñiga H., Jesús Arroyo A., Agustín Escobar L., and Gustavo Verduzco I. Mexico City: CONAPO/UDG/CIESAS /Casa Juan Pablos/COLMEX, 2006.

USCIS (U.S. Citizenship and Immigration Services). "Backlog Elimination Plan: Fiscal Year 2004, 4th Quarter Update." Washington, D.C.: U.S. Citizenship and Immigration Services, 2005.

U.S. Commission for the Study of International Migration and Cooperative Economic Development. *Unauthorized Migration: An Economic Development Response.* Washington, D.C., 1990.

World Bank. *World Development Report,* various years.

Yúnez-Naude, Antonio. "Cambio estructural y emigración rural a Estados Unidos." *Comercio Exterior* 50, no. 4 (April 2000): 334–39.

Zamudio, Patricia. "Huejuquillense Immigrants in Chicago: Culture, gender, and community in the shaping of consciousness." Ph.D. diss., Northwestern University, 1999.

Zúñiga, Elena, and Paula Leite. "Estimaciones de CONAPO con base en INEGI, Encuesta Nacional de la Dinámica Demográfica (ENADID), 1992 y 1997 y Encuesta Nacional de Empleo (ENE) módulo sobre migración, 2002." Mexico City: Consejo Nacional de Población, 2004.

Index

About the Contributors

MEMBERS OF THE BINATIONAL TEAM

Francisco Alba is Professor and Researcher at *El Colegio de México*. He was director of the Center for Demographic and Urbanization Studies, at the same institution. An economist by training, he also graduated in philosophy, and has done postgraduate work in demography and other social sciences in Mexico, France, and the USA. Currently, Professor Alba is a member of the Advisory Board of Mexico's National Migration Institute, and of the UN Commission for the Protection of Migrants' Rights. Recently, he was a member of the Global Commission on International Migration (2004–2005). He was a member of the Mexico/United States Binational Study on Migration (1995–1997). He is a member of Mexico's National Researchers System, since 1985. Prof. Alba obtained the National Prize in Demography in 1991, and shared the Banamex National Award in Economics in 1971. His books and articles in many Mexican and international journals deal with international migration issues, Mexican and U.S. migration policy, issues on population and development, economic integration, and Mexico-U.S. relations, among other topics. He recently published "Change and Continuity in Government Responses to Mexican Migration," in *Population, City and Environment in Contemporary Mexico*, ed. by J. L. Lezama and J. B. Morelos (El Colegio de Mexico, 2006).

Agustín Escobar Latapí is a professor at CIESAS Occidente, where he was regional director from 2001 to 2003. He holds a Ph.D. in sociology from the University of Manchester. He is a member of the National System of Researchers (SNI, level III) and the winner of the National Award for Scientific

Research, of the Mexican Academy of Sciences, in 1994, together with Mercedes González de la Rocha. He is a member of the Academy since 1991. In February 2006 he was elected to the National Social Policy Evaluation Council. His main interests include international migration and Mexican social policy. He has directed the external qualitative evaluation of the *Progresa–Oportunidades* program, and his current interest in migration focuses on the migration of the poor, and the impact of migration on poverty and inequality in Mexico. He has advised the Mexican Social Development Ministry on the design of program evaluations. His latest book, *Pobreza y migración internacional*, was published by CIESAS in 2008.

Rafael Fernández de Castro is founder, director, and professor at the Department of Foreign Relations of the ITAM (Mexican Autonomous Technological Institute). He earned his B.A. from ITAM, his M.A. on public policy form the Lyndon B. Johnson School at the University of Texas at Austin, and his Ph.D. from Georgetown. Dr. Fernández de Castro is an expert on bilateral Mexico-U.S. relations and their various aspects, and on Mexican foreign policy generally. He has published books, chapters, and articles very widely on these and other issues, such as *¿Socios o adversarios? México y Estados Unidos hoy* with Jorge Domínguez (also in English); *El actor controvertido: El Congreso de Estados Unidos y América del Norte* with Robert Pastor (also in English); *México en el Mundo: Los desafíos para México en 2001* (2001); *Cambio y continuidad en la política exterior de México* (2002), *En la frontera del Imperio* (2003), and *La agenda internacional de México 2006–2012* (2006). He has participated in significant efforts such as the Binational Migration Panel, which led to the Binational Study of Mexico-U.S. Migration. Dr. Fernández de Castro is active in the media. He directs *Foreign Affairs en Español*, and writes weekly columns in *Proceso* and *Excélsior*, two of the most important press media in Mexico.

B. Lindsay Lowell is director of policy studies for the Institute for the Study of International Migration at Georgetown University. He was previously director of research at the congressionally appointed Commission on Immigration Reform where he was also assistant director for the Mexico/U.S. Binational Study on Migration. He has been research director at the Pew Hispanic Center of the University of Southern California, a labor analyst at the U.S. Department of Labor, and a teacher at Princeton University and the University of Texas at Austin. Dr. Lowell coedited *Sending Money Home: Hispanic Remittances and Community Development*, and he has published over a hundred articles and reports on his research interests in immigration policy, labor force, economic development, and the global mobility of the highly skilled. He received his Ph.D. in sociology as a demographer from Brown University.

Philip Martin earned a Ph.D. in economics from the University of Wisconsin–Madison. He is professor of agricultural and resource economics at the University of California-Davis. Martin worked on labor and immigration issues in Washington, D.C., and testifies before Congress frequently. His book on labor in California agriculture was the *Outstanding Book in Labor Economics and Industrial Relations* in 1996. Martin works on labor and migration issues for UN agencies around the world, including assessing the prospects for Turkish migration to the European Union and evaluating the effects of foreign workers on the economies of Thailand and Malaysia and on Austria, Germany, and Spain. He has studied the effects of NAFTA on Mexico-U.S. migration and the changing structure of the global wine industry.

Susan Martin holds the Donald G. Herzberg Chair in International Migration and serves as the director of the Institute for the Study of International Migration in the School of Foreign Service at Georgetown University. Previously Dr. Martin served as the executive director of the U.S. Commission on Immigration Reform, established by legislation to advise Congress and the President on U.S. immigration and refugee policy, and director of research and programs at the Refugee Policy Group. Her publications include *Refugee Women, The Uprooted: Improving Humanitarian Responses to Forced Migration; Beyond the Gateway: Immigrants in a Changing America* (ed.); *Managing Migration: The Promise of Cooperation; The World Migration Report: 2000* (ed.), and numerous monographs and articles on immigration and refugee policy. She is also the principal author of the *2004 World Survey on Women and Development: Women and Migration,* commissioned by the United Nations Division on the Advancement of Women. Dr. Martin earned her M.A. and Ph.D. in American studies from the University of Pennsylvania and her B.A. in history from Douglass College, Rutgers University. She is the president of the International Association for the Study of Forced Migration and serves on the U.S. Comptroller General's advisory board, the Academic Advisory Board of the International Organization for Migration, and the Board of the Advocacy Project.

Liliana Meza González is in charge of the technical secretariat of the social cabinet, at President Calderón's office. She is on leave from the Department of Economics at Universidad Iberoamericana, Mexico, where she coordinated a program on migration studies. She received her B.A. and M.Sc. degrees in economics from the Instituto Tecnológico Autónomo de México, and her M.A. and Ph.D. degrees in labor economics from the University of Houston. She holds a diploma in international business and trade, and her areas of research interest are inequality, migration, and the effects of economic integration on labor markets. She has received prizes for her research work and has published several articles in specialized journals. She has presented her papers in numerous conferences throughout the world, especially in Latin America. Dr. Meza has worked for the World Bank, she was a visiting professor at American University in Washington, D.C., and is part of the Mexican National System of Researchers.

Jeffrey S. Passel, a nationally known expert on immigration to the United States and the demography of racial and ethnic groups, joined the Pew Hispanic Center in January 2005. His research focuses on the demography of the Hispanic population. He previously worked at the Urban Institute where he concentrated on the impacts and integration of immigrants into American society, and the demography of immigration, particularly the measurement of undocumented immigration. Dr. Passel and his colleagues have been investigating the demography and purchasing power of the Hispanic population, the integration of immigrants and the second generation, welfare use by immigrants, and the fiscal impacts of immigrants, especially taxes paid. His interests also include measuring and defining racial/ethnic groups in the U.S. and census undercount. Prior to joining the Urban Institute in 1989, Dr. Passel directed the Census Bureau's program of population estimates and projections and its research on demographic methods for measuring census undercount. He has served on several committees of the Population Association of America and has been a member of National Academy of Sciences' Panels. Dr. Passel is a fellow of the American Statistical Association and of the American Association for the Advancement of Science. Passel earned his Ph.D. in Social Relations from The Johns Hopkins University, and M.A. in sociology from the University of Texas at Austin, and a B.S. in mathematics from M.I.T.

Carla Pederzini Villareal is a full-time professor at the Department of Economics at Universidad Iberoamericana. She holds a bachelors degree in economics from the Universidad Autónoma Metropolitana-Iztapalapa (UAM-I) and a Ph.D. in demographic studies from El Colegio de México. The title of her doctoral thesis is "Gender and Schooling in Mexican Families." From February 2002 to March 2004 she was coordinator of the bachelors degree program in economics at the Universidad Iberoamericana in Mexico City. She taught courses in demography and applied economics at her alma mater as well as at FLACSO, Colegio de México, UAM–I and CONAPO. Between 2000 and 2003 she was head of the Migration and Small Enterprise Research Program which was conducted between the Universidad Iberoamericana and the Colegio de la Frontera Norte. She currently is part of a team of researchers that work on immigration affairs at the Universidad Iberoamericana. Her research interests include migration, education, and gender studies.

INVITED AUTHORS

Roberta Clariond Rangel studied international relations with honors from Tecnológico de Monterrey (ITESM), Campus Monterrey; received a masters in Latin-American studies with honors from the University of California, Los Angeles; and a masters in international relations, at the University of Chicago. She has been research professor in the Department of International Relations, ITESM, Campus Monterrey, and at the Instituto Tecnológico Autónomo de México (ITAM). She has carried out fieldwork with migrant Mexican women in Los Angeles, and volunteered to develop alphabetizing Spanish courses for adults for Hispanic migrants in Chicago. Clariond has coordinated symposia and seminars on Mexico-U.S. relations, and is currently involved in a number of projects regarding immigration. She has published articles in various magazines like *Urbi et Orbi* from ITAM, and *Beyond Law and Society.*

Gustavo Verduzco Igartúa has a Ph.D. in sociology, obtained in 1980 at the University of Texas, Austin, with a major in demography. He served as director at the center for sociological studies of El Colegio de México in Mexico City (January 2000–January 2006). He has been a member of the Executive Committee of CLACSO (Latin American Council for the Social Sciences) for the period 2006–2009. Dr. Verduzco was a core member of the research team for the Binational Study on Migration Between Mexico and The United States (1995–1997). He is a Member of the Academia Mexicana de Ciencias since 1987 (Mexican Academy of Sciences). Among Dr. Verduzco's books are: *Organizaciones no lucrativas: visión de su trayectoria en México* (Nonprofit Organizations in Mexico: An Historical Approach), *The Binational Report on Migration Between Mexico and The United States* (coauthor as member of the Binational Team), and *Una ciudad agrícola: Zamora. Del Porfiriato a la agricultura de exportación (An Agricultural Center: Zamora. From the Porfiriato to Agribusiness).*